THE INTELLIGENT GUIDE
TO
STOCK MARKET INVESTMENT

Kevin Keasey
Robert Hudson
and Kevin Littler

JOHN WILEY & SONS

Chichester • New York • Weinheim • Brisbane • Singapore • Toronto

This publication is designed to provide accurate and authoritative information in regard to the
subject matter covered. It is sold with the understanding that neither the authors nor the publisher
are engaged in rendering legal, investing, or any other personal service.

The investments referred to in the text of this book are for illustrative purposes only and are not an
invitation to deal in them. This book was originally written in June 1998 but market conditions
change. Neither the authors nor the publisher accept any legal responsibility for the contents of the
work, which is not a substitute for detailed professional advice. Readers should conduct their own
investment activity through an appropriately authorized person.

Halifax plc is an Appointed Representative of Halifax Share Dealing Limited which is regulated by
The Securities and Futures Authority, a Member of the London Stock Exchange and a participant in
the Investors' Compensation Scheme. The value of shares and the income from them can go down as
well as up. If you are not sure what to do, please consult an independent financial adviser.

Other Wiley Editorial Offices

John Wiley & Sons, Inc., 605 Third Avenue,
New York, NY 10158-0012, USA

WILEY-VCH GmbH, Pappelallee 3,
D-69469 Weinheim, Germany

Jacaranda Wiley Ltd, 33 Park Road, Milton,
Queensland 4064, Australia

John Wiley & Sons (Asia) Pte Ltd, 2 Clementi Loop #02-01,
Jin Xing Distripark, Singapore 129809

John Wiley & Sons (Canada) Ltd, 22 Worcester Road,
Rexdale, Ontario M9W 1L1, Canada

British Library Cataloguing in Publication Data

A catalogue record for this book is available from the British Library

ISBN 0-471-98581-3

Typeset in 11/13pt Palatino.
Printed and bound in Great Britain by Biddles Ltd, Guildford
This book is printed on acid-free paper responsibly manufactured from sustainable forestry, in which
at least two trees are planted for each one used for paper production

CONTENTS

FOREWORD

At a time when we are all being encouraged to take greater personal responsibility for our financial futures, more and more people are increasingly aware of the important role direct share ownership can play as an integral part of their overall financial planning. However, this awareness is often still tempered by the perception that stock market investment is extremely complex and not for everyone. This book sets out to dispel that myth.

Written by independent experts in the field of financial education, the contents of this book strip away the traditional barriers and mystique. It provides, in plain English, incisive and impartial insight into both the theory and practice of share dealing as a means of creating wealth. In short, this book gives you the key tools you need to unlock and exploit the potential of stock market investment, no matter whether you are a beginner or a seasoned investor.

At the Halifax, we believe that the public dissemination of knowledge and expertise enables our customers to make better-informed decisions about their personal finances and, for this reason, we are delighted to sponsor this particular initiative.

Throughout its history, the Halifax has consistently applied its resources to serve both the individual needs and changing circumstances of its many millions of customers and by so doing, has developed from its humble origins 150 years ago, into one of the top four banks in the UK today. The original founders of the Halifax would probably find both the scale and scope of the current organisation incredible. To cite just one recent example, our conversion to plc status created over 7.6 million new shareholders through the largest-ever stock market flotation. And yet, the founders would doubtless recognise the endurance of their underlying aims which, translated into modern day language, can be summarised as providing ready access, equal opportunity and good value. This can be seen in both the new services offered by Halifax Share Dealing, as well as in the extensive range of products provided by other companies within the Halifax group. As we move into the 21st century, Halifax will continue to serve the diverse interests of all its customers in the field of financial services, by upholding and building on our traditions.

I wish you enjoyable and productive reading.

John R Miller
Chairman
Halifax Share Dealing Limited

Halifax, July 1998

ACKNOWLEDGEMENTS

Kevin Keasey

There are many colleagues and friends that I could and should pay thanks to. For the sake of brevity, I will try to keep the list as short as possible. Professor Robert Sugden of the University of East Anglia gave me a lasting interest in the behaviour of individuals when he suffered the task of teaching me a masters course in public choice theory at the University of Newcastle upon Tyne. Without his enthusiasm and his outstanding ability to structure academic argument, it is doubtful whether I would have pursued an academic career. I would also like to thank my two co-authors for making this book and the International Institute of Banking and Financial Services such enjoyable experiences. Of course, it needs to be recognised that neither this book nor the Institute would have been possible without the continued good-natured support of John Miller, a Director of Halifax plc. Finally, no acknowledgement would be complete without thanking my family - Adam, Alayne and Holly for acting as a counterpoint to the stresses and strains of modern academic life.

Robert Hudson

I would like to thank my two co-authors for all their hard work and good ideas, and for being so easy to work with. I would also like to thank my wife, Lesley, for her considerable tolerance and support and my parents and father-in-law, Doreen, Ray and Alan, for all their encouragement. Additionally, I would particularly like to remember my late mother-in-law, Sheila, who worked selflessly to help us.

Kevin Littler

It is with a deep sense of gratitude that I wish to acknowledge the enduring acceptance and patient support of my family, friends and colleagues who have - whether knowingly or otherwise - provided me with the conviction, continuity and sense of community which underpins all my creative efforts. Particular thanks go to my co-authors, Kevin and Robert, for their trust, encouragement and inspiration.

Finally, we would like to thank Sue Concannon (Managing Director, Halifax Share Dealing Limited), Louise Allardice (consultant to the project) and Sally Smith (John Wiley) for their patience, skill and support in the construction of this book.

INTRODUCTION

The information technology revolution presents modern day investors with a paradox - ever more information to guide their investment decisions but seemingly less and less time to use it. One general consequence of this paradox is that the demand for executive summaries - 'the 10 minute finance MBA', '3 easy steps to being the next George Soros' etc. - has never been greater. Now, at this juncture, let us make the point that there are no quick and easy answers to making a million on the stock market! Prices in the stock market summarise a whole set of real and perceived events and it takes time, skill and perseverance to appreciate the potential returns. Having said this, stock market investment can be both rewarding and fun so long as sufficient time is given to appreciate its many facets and characteristics.

THE PURPOSE OF THIS BOOK

We have written this book because we believe that stock market investment is a good way to protect and increase wealth, whilst also providing a further interest in many people's lives. We still enjoy opening the morning business pages, with a cup of coffee, and seeing if our expectations have turned out to be correct. Equally, it is part of the morning ritual to scan the rest of the papers to see if there have been any market events that we should start thinking about. For example, at the start of 1998, banking sector

NUTSHELL

Optimistic investors who think the stock market and share prices will rise are described as **bulls**. Pessimistic investors who believe prices will fall are known as **bears**.

shares were looking, in general, very bullish (on the rise) and a lot of this was down to take-over bid speculation. At the same time, there was the crisis in the Far East with all its banking and financial sector problems. How should we account for this Asian crisis when considering our own holdings of British bank shares - was it time to sell and take the profits? We find that these kind of thoughts add an interesting aspect to our lives as we go about our more mundane duties. Such thoughts form a sanity-maintaining counterpoint when dealing with an awkward supplier, sitting through another interminable meeting or trying to remember the shopping list.

To protect and increase your wealth, and enjoy the experience at the same time, however, needs an understanding of the basic building blocks of stock market behaviour and an appreciation of some of its finer detail. Now let's be honest, you are not going to achieve this by reading a single book or even a set of books. As for all arts, the art of stock market investment can only be gained by actually doing it. For example, the art of landscape painting is only progressed by considering a landscape, by applying the paint and then assessing the end result. By such practice you will learn what works for you, how you can mix the paints, capture light, counterpose detail with impression, and so on. Learning through practice can, however, be speeded up. You can be given guidance on how to read a landscape, the essentials of colour and how they can be mixed, and the means of capturing light within pictures. In other words, books can help you develop your appreciation, understanding and knowledge of an art. But at the end of the day, nothing can replace the learning and sheer understanding that comes from the actual practice of the art. All books can do is help speed up your learning process and, as we've already said, with time in ever shorter supply, the faster the learning the better.

So this is not a 'get rich quick in 10 easy steps' book. Although time is increasingly short, it is impossible to speed up the learning process by the statement of 10 simple rules. Rather, you have to take the time initially to try to understand some of the detail of the subject and reflect on what others have achieved.

The aim of this book is to be different from the many stock market investment books that currently fill the book shop shelves. As we've already said, this is not one of the 'get rich quick' types of book which seem to do so well at airports. Many of these books will leave the reader with nothing of substance; which is, of course, not a bad strategy if you want to sell your second and third blockbuster on stock market investment. Yet it seems curious why anybody with the secrets to 'investor heaven' would be willing to share them with the rest of the investment public for the measly sum of £15 to £30. Also, if they have made so much money, why are they going to all the bother of writing books on the subject? In general, the advice of such books is impractical for the average investor and/or not based on any reliable evidence. It is in the nature of such books to preach a few simple rules from the promoted investment approach, without giving any consideration to its drawbacks or how it complements other approaches. Furthermore, all contradictory evidence seems to be conveniently forgotten when evaluating the worth of the chosen investment method. What is particularly annoying is that a number (if not the majority) of these 'get rich quick, practical investment' books give no indication of the likely risks involved with the investment strategy. Returns are often quoted without any statement that they have been achieved over a particular period and the results could have been markedly different if a few events had gone the other way.

One view of such books is that they merely give the reader a narrow perspective on stock market investment. A less charitable interpretation is that they are positively misleading in their simplistic approaches. In fact, a few of this genre (and we won't mention any names) seem to make a marketing virtue of the naiveté of the investment approach being pushed. It is no exaggeration to note that we have come across advice of the form 'buy low and sell high' in more than a couple of these types of text.

A further approach to writing investment books is to review, in reasonable depth, the approach of a given investment guru. Some of these are very good and are aimed at the lay reader, albeit readers with a strong and often informed interest in investment. The primary weakness of most of these types of book is that they are often uncritical of the guru being reviewed and they rarely put the investment method to the test over different time periods and portfolios of companies. None the less, a critical review of a number of the investment gurus can provide useful insights.

A third broad literature on stock market investment is provided by academics. This literature is definitely not aimed at the lay reader but it does contain some important lessons for the investing public. Sadly, the way in which the academic literature on stock market investment has developed makes it difficult for even the keenest of lay investors to extract the pertinent lessons. Academic articles and texts are often written in fairly obscure, theoretical language and the results of rigorous, in-depth empirical analysis are presented in statistical terms that are not part of everyday language. However, behind all this terminology, there are insights to be gained - it is just a matter of having the appropriate amount of time, background and perseverance to dig out the nuggets.

It is the intention of this book, therefore, to provide the interested investor, who wants to gain an in-depth understanding and a keen appreciation of the way in which the stock market works, with a synthesis of the insights from a range of investment authors, investment gurus and the academic finance literature. In addition, the key elements of the synthesis are summarised as points of practical advice. In these respects this book is unique. The rationale is to overcome the weaknesses of the individual approaches described previously. A balanced appreciation of the various approaches will give you a head start in understanding how you might approach investing in shares as a means of creating wealth and as an additional enjoyable aspect of your everyday life.

It is now time to offer a brief summary of what you can expect from the rest of the book. In this introduction, we will provide you with general summaries of the broad parts. This approach should offer sufficient detail to keep you interested without being bored. Let's wait and see . . . .

THE MYTHS AND REALITIES OF STOCK MARKET INVESTMENT

The first part offers an insight into the historical facts concerning key stock markets across time. It will illustrate that, in general, the possible returns achieved from shares during the past decades have been attractive compared to other investments, such as cash deposits and property. However, there is a slight catch in the phrase 'in general'. Individual shares have fallen drastically in value and the overall market has had its bad periods - the '87 crash being just one example. Therefore, while past long-term statistics indicate that good average returns could have been made from shares, there is always the possibility, for a given period, that an individual share bought by an investor will fall or indeed the market itself may take a tumble.

Given such risks, it is easy to see why many people forgo the potential long term gains that can be achieved. Such risk aversion is, however, overdone. Let's be clear. The stock market needs to be treated with a healthy caution but, with a firm handle on financial commitments and the characteristics of the adopted investment model, there is little reason why financial losses should be realised. In essence, the first part of the book starts to put the expected returns and risks from stock market investment into better perspective.

THE BASIC FACTS

Having considered the general history of the movement of stock markets in Part One, the second part of the book looks at the detail of stock markets. The stock market activities of raising capital and secondary trading are analysed, as are a whole range of market events - such as dividend policies, rights issues, mergers and acquisitions, and company failures. If you are investing in a company, either when the shares are being issued or in the secondary market, you need to ask yourself two simple questions:

> **NUTSHELL**
>
> Markets that deal in the issue of new shares are called **primary markets**. When existing shares are bought and sold, they are said to be traded in a **secondary market**.

Does the business appear to have a convincing plan for the future, __and__ how are the funds going to be used?

Taking the first point, it is quite possible that a business is taken to the equity markets to allow the owner(s) to liquidate part of their interest in the business; it may have nothing to do with needing funds to grow the business. At times, the markets are 'hungry' for new investment opportunities and the owners can often achieve a far better deal by listing the company on the stock market than by trying to achieve a private sale. We are not saying that this is always, or even often, the case but it is a factor to bear in mind.

NUTSHELL

Rights issues are one way for a company to raise further finance by giving shareholders the option to buy new shares in proportion to their current holdings.

In addition to considering the potential reasons for a company seeking a listing or a rights issue, there are other events you need to consider. While it is to be hoped that a fair amount of the share price performance reflects the underlying performance of the company (allowing for market and investor sentiment - more of which later), it is clear that expected market events have an impact. For example, the slightest rumour of a bid tends to send prices upward. Thus, this second part also considers the general movement of share prices leading up to and following different market events. This type of analysis should allow you to start to consider how far share prices reflect the fundamentals of the business(es) as compared to market sentiment and speculation.

After having reviewed the nature of stock markets and ordinary shares (the primary emphasis of this book), the second part moves on to consider alternative investments such as preference shares, convertibles, warrants, options, bonds and gilts. These alternatives are analysed because there are times when they make far more sense than ordinary shares. In addition, they can add balance to a portfolio.

The final chapter in this part looks at the financial analysis of companies. In trying to make sense of the actions of firms and whether they might be a good investment, it is clearly important that you have at least a basic understanding of company accounts. We show that company accounts are not too difficult to understand.

ACADEMIC PERSPECTIVES ON MARKET BEHAVIOUR

Having introduced you to the broad historical trends (what can be expected from shares prices in the longer term) and the detail of events (what can be expected in the shorter term) that occur within stock markets, the third part turns to the academic theory and evidence on the way investors should behave. It is not the purpose of this part to trawl through what can only be described as a lot of tedious academic detail, but rather to make you aware of the practical conclusions to be drawn from the scientific analysis of stock markets.

Essentially, the academic literature on stock markets lets the following types of conclusion be drawn:

! A large proportion of share price changes are random movements. No method can predict future changes with any substantial degree of certainty; any system has its limitations.

! Statistical properties of share prices are such, however, that reasonable estimates of the lower and upper bounds on expected returns can be made. In other words, investors can form some useful rules of thumb.

! There is increasing evidence that shares 'mean revert'; that is, shares are likely to come down after a good period and go up after a bad period.

! Even allowing for mean reversion, the riskier the share, the higher the expected return.

! One means of minimising risk is to hold a portfolio of 'independent' shares; for example, in consumer electronics and water utilities.

NUTSHELL

The terms '**equities**' and '**shares**' mean the same thing and are used interchangeably throughout this book. You will also come across '**securities**'. Strictly speaking, this term encompasses all types of tradeable financial instruments.

Whilst this is not a complete list of what can be concluded from the academic literature, it does indicate the potential lessons to be drawn from this source.

CLASSICAL APPROACHES TO INVESTMENT

Part Four covers the essential ideas of the classical approaches to stock market investment. All of these approaches are based on the notion that the careful study of 'one aspect' of the investment situation can lead to superior investment decisions. For example, the technical analysts (also known as chartists) believe that the careful study of the behaviour of a price of a share is sufficient to make a good investment decision. There is no need to understand the company, its sector or the economy because all the relevant information is impounded in the price of the share. In this regard, the technical analysts are similar to a lot of the academic finance researchers; except the technical analysts believe that share prices display predictable patterns, whereas the academics do not.

The aim of Part Four is to give you an introduction to the range of investment techniques and models developed and used by investment gurus and practitioners. It assesses how effective the techniques have been in the past and how effective they may be in the future. It also assesses whether individuals can realistically benefit from using the various methods. Some of the methods may be too risky, require too much individual flair or even a particular type of personality to be practical for most readers. This part of the book will help you to make a balanced and informed assessment of the different investment techniques.

The first approach to be analysed is out-and-out **'Trading'**. There are many different approaches to trading, ranging from highly disciplined quantitative methods to the intuitive approach of some individuals who, rather like poker players, have a feel for the strength or weakness of the hand. In addition to a variety of trading approaches, there are also a range of time-scales that could be the focus of attention. For amateur investors with other commitments, it is doubtful whether their trading periods will be as short as those of the minute or hourly horizons of some professional investors. More likely, they will trade across a number of days or even weeks. After having reviewed trading approaches to investment, the discussion then proceeds to a consideration of the **'Technical Analysis'** approach to investment. As indicated above, technical analysis is the use of past patterns in share prices to predict the future movement in share prices. Not surprisingly, the art of technical analysis has developed a range of share patterns that should prompt action on the part of the investor.

CLOSE-UP

In **Technical Analysis**, for example, if a rising share price chart displays a pattern that looks like a person's head and shoulders, technical analysts would contest that the share price will go into a downward trend.

Part Four then discusses the **'Top Down'** approach to investment. This section also mentions the **'Bottom Up'** approach. Top down investors look for large social, economic and political trends, and then invest accordingly. For example, in the not too distant past, investors may have decided that the Far Eastern economies were a good investment because of their high economic growth rates. Similarly, the oil industry may have been seen as a good bet because its shares, in general, look undervalued compared to its economic prospects. This type of investment is based on a broad assessment of economies and industries. With this approach, the detailed analysis of particular companies is of secondary importance. In contrast, bottom up investors work from the premise that the best approach to investment is to identify successful companies. They take the view that if the individual investments are right, the whole portfolio will look after itself.

The idea of bottom up investment is developed further in the **'Fundamental Analysis'** approach to investment. Fundamental analysis is the careful study of the underlying business of the company in which the investor is considering investing. In this type of study, the stock market behaviour of the company's shares takes a secondary role. The emphasis is on the need to understand the underlying company and not concentrate on the share price in isolation. Many advocates of fundamental analysis would argue that companies are much more predictable than their share prices. If the investor picks a good company at the right price, eventually the market will agree with him or her.

INVESTMENT GURUS AND AUTHORS

This part aims to provide some insights into how investment gurus and authors have harnessed the basic approaches described in Part Four to develop their own investment styles. As will become clear, few of the well known investment specialists use a single investment method; rather they blend and mix the individual investment approaches to suit their own needs. Part Five follows the basic structure of Part Four, with specialists who emphasise trading and technical analysis being considered first. This is then followed by reviews of specialists emphasising top down and fundamental analysis approaches to investment. For each set of approaches, a range of investment gurus and authors will be considered.

INVESTMENT GUIDELINES

The first five parts of the book have given you the basic building blocks needed to appreciate how you should approach investing in equities. This remaining part takes you through the day-to-day practicalities of being a successful investor.

You need to make stock market investment decisions in the light of your own personal circumstances and characteristics. Chapter 14 will prompt you to ask questions about your financial and time commitments. Thinking about personal financial planning issues will help you make an informed choice about how much to invest in the stock market. You will also need to think about how much time and effort you will be able to spend on following the market. Furthermore, you will also need to develop an understanding of your (and your family's) attitude towards risk. Understanding risk will help select the most suitable and enjoyable investment approach.

Chapter 15 gives you advice as to how you should undertake your investment in equities. You will need to decide whether to invest directly or to use a collective investment. In terms of the latter, unit trusts, investment trusts and OEICs (the latest replacement for unit trusts) will all be discussed. The purpose of this section is to allow you to compare and contrast the potential benefits of building and controlling your own portfolio with the situation of investing in a single or number of collective investments.

Building on the content of Chapters 14 and 15, Chapter 16 aims to set out the information you need to know about the way the market works and how stockbrokers act for investors. This covers such things as the CREST electronic settlement system, share certificates, nominee accounts and sponsored membership. The advantages and disadvantages of the various ways of managing your investments are analysed. Similarly, the choice of stockbroker (discretionary, advisory or execution-only) and the questions you need to ask are also considered.

We have almost reached the end of this introduction and our summary of what comes next. The concluding chapter offers a guide to further reading. As each of the individual chapters ends with a 'lessons to be learnt' section, we have decided not to draw a second set of conclusions.

Anyway, enough of this, it is time to move on to the main chapters. Good reading and remember that stock market investment can be one of the few exceptions to the following words of R. E. Drennan:

"All the things I really like to do are either illegal, immoral or fattening."

PART ONE

THE MYTHS AND REALITIES
OF
STOCK MARKET INVESTMENT

CHAPTER 1

The Attractions of Equity Investment

It is very easy to demonstrate why individuals should be interested in stock market investment. Quite simply, over long time spans, shares have generally outperformed other investments by an **enormous** margin. For example, imagine your grandfather had invested £100 into a family trust at the end of 1929 and you were now entitled to the proceeds. If he had put the money into a portfolio of UK equities, by the end of 1996 it would have grown to £197,578.[1] If he had taken a more cautious approach and invested in fixed interest securities issued by the UK government (gilts), which are considered to be the benchmark for secure investments, £100 would have grown to a mere £6,089.

Over this period, the difference between investing in equities and investing in gilts would have meant the difference between buying a very nice house or a second hand car. It is quite entertaining to dream that one's grandfather had really managed to invest say £1,000. In this case the proceeds would be nearly £2 million and a life of luxury would be within reach.

Pleasant daydreams aside, it is clear that investing in equities would have been outstandingly successful over these years. The more cynical reader is probably starting to suspect that the figures are too good to be true and that this particular period was chosen to make equity investment look distortedly attractive. This is **not** the case.

NUTSHELL

As their name suggests, **fixed interest securities** pay a fixed income each year. Vast quantities of such investments are issued by the British government and are known as **gilts**. Gilts are thought to be safe from the risk of default as the government will always make the payments even if it has to raise taxes or print money to do so.

In the above example, the return on equities is about **12%** per annum compound over the 67 years in question. Now let's take the family example a little further. If your father had invested in equities at the end of 1949, he would have achieved a **better** return of about **14.4%** per annum compound over the next 47 years. If you had decided to invest in equities in 1969, you would have received an **even better** return of about **15.8%** per annum compound over the next 27 years.

In all the time periods, the return on equities has handsomely exceeded that on gilts. Even from 1969 to 1996, when gilts enjoyed their best performance compared with equities, the return on equities was still 4% per annum compound greater than that on gilts. An extra return of 4% may not seem much, but let's put it this way - the equity investor would have a fund nearly **3 times larger** than the investor opting for the perceived security of gilts.

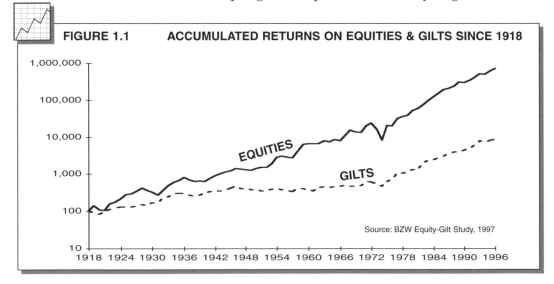

FIGURE 1.1   ACCUMULATED RETURNS ON EQUITIES & GILTS SINCE 1918

Source: BZW Equity-Gilt Study, 1997

During the 20th century, the experience in the United States, home to the world's largest capital markets, has been very similar, with the long term return on equities being good and much higher than that on fixed interest bonds. One market expert, Siegel, has managed to extend the US data on stock and bond returns as far back as 1802. He found that equity returns substantially exceeded fixed-interest returns over the whole period.[2]

EQUITY RETURNS VERSUS INFLATION

An important factor we haven't considered yet is inflation. Everyone knows that prices have shot up over the years. In 1929, £100 was a fairly substantial amount of money. If we allow for the effects of inflation, was our hypothetical grandfather really so clever investing in equities or might he have been better advised to spend his money before it lost its value. In fact, the effects of inflation do **not** by any means wipe out the attractive returns on equities.

If the effects of inflation are allowed for, £100 at the end of 1929 was the equivalent in purchasing power to £2,563 at the end of 1996. So over the 67 years from 1929 to 1996, investing in equities would have transformed £2,563 into £197,578 in terms of real purchasing power. Or in other words, the purchasing power available would have increased by over **77 times**.

In rather miserable contrast, investing in gilts would have transformed £2,563 into a meagre £6,089. So in this case, 67 years of patient investing would have resulted in just over a twofold increase in purchasing power. Rather than investing in gilts, grandfather might as well have enjoyed spending his money!

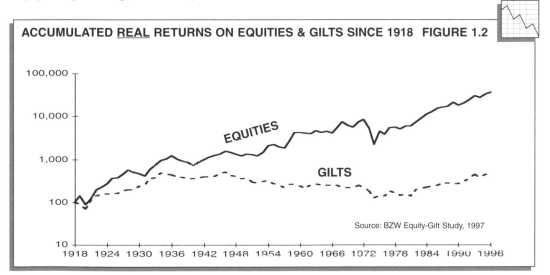

ACCUMULATED <u>REAL</u> RETURNS ON EQUITIES & GILTS SINCE 1918 FIGURE 1.2

Source: BZW Equity-Gilt Study, 1997

EQUITY RETURNS VERSUS OTHER INVESTMENTS

Individual investors have a variety of investments, other than UK equities and gilts, available to them. Many people have a large proportion of their money in the bank or building society. Much of the population regard their house as much as an investment as a place to live and enjoy, while gold has often been regarded as the ultimate store of value over the ages.

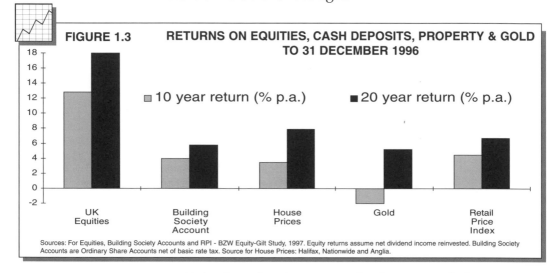

FIGURE 1.3   **RETURNS ON EQUITIES, CASH DEPOSITS, PROPERTY & GOLD TO 31 DECEMBER 1996**

▣ 10 year return (% p.a.)   ■ 20 year return (% p.a.)

Sources: For Equities, Building Society Accounts and RPI - BZW Equity-Gilt Study, 1997. Equity returns assume net dividend income reinvested. Building Society Accounts are Ordinary Share Accounts net of basic rate tax. Source for House Prices: Halifax, Nationwide and Anglia.

It is clear that investors who have avoided equities, in favour of other investments, over the last 20 years have missed a major opportunity. Investors **do** need to diversify by holding a spread of investments as well as allowing for their own circumstances, but anyone interested in long term investment should consider equity investment very seriously.

WHY HAVE SHARES PERFORMED SO WELL?

The reader may be wondering why the equity market has done so well over the years. The biggest reason is that, in the long run, companies gain from the increasing prosperity of the national and international economy and individuals holding equities in companies share in these gains. The general increase in prosperity may be fairly imperceptible in the short run but it becomes very clear when longer time spans are examined. For example, if we consider the state of the nation in 1929 compared to the present day, it is obvious that general prosperity is now far higher. There has been dramatic progress in almost every field of economic life. Here are a few illustrations:

 Computers did not even exist in 1929 but have now transformed the efficiency of most industries and personal computers are a standard consumer item.

 Cars were rare in 1929 and only for the very wealthy, whereas today ordinary families with two cars are commonplace.

 Air travel was in its infancy in 1929 and has now grown into a huge industry.

 Most homes possessed no more than a radio set in 1929, but are now full of consumer electronic equipment.

 The chemical industry has transformed everyday life by introducing a large range of plastics and artificial fibres.

Whilst this list could be extended almost infinitely, the key point is that most industries are vastly more productive than they were in 1929 and many totally new ones have been created. Consumers have benefited from this progress and have the resources to purchase the products. Equity investors are entitled to a share of company profits and so have directly benefited from this growth. There is no sign that this economic progress will not continue in the long run and one would expect equity investors to continue to profit from this.

Another aspect of the excellent past performance of equities has been their role as a hedge against inflation. Equities provide a degree of protection against inflation which fixed interest securities, such as gilts, do not. As their name implies, such securities provide a return which is fixed in money terms. This means that the return becomes less valuable if the value of money is reduced by inflation. In sharp contrast, equities represent a share in a business which has the opportunity to increase its prices to reflect inflation and which also controls physical assets which may also increase in value with prices. Whilst an inflationary environment may not be particularly good for equities, it will **not** be as potentially disastrous as it is for fixed interest securities.

IS IT ALL TOO GOOD TO BE TRUE?

CLOSE-UP

The worst year in this century was 1974 when the total return on equities was – 49.4%.

The previous paragraphs certainly make long term equity investing seem attractive but is it all too good to be true? The drawback of looking at past long term statistics is that they do not highlight the ongoing risk that stock market investment involves. The market can fall as well as rise. On a daily basis, stocks are almost as likely to fall as they are to rise. On a yearly basis, the total return on the UK stock market has been negative in about a quarter of the years since 1923.

In the long run the market has always recovered and provided very attractive returns to people who have been patient. However, all the major market falls will have been very painful indeed to people who were unprepared for the possibility of such drops. Investors who need to raise money in the market after a drop, or who panic and sell their holdings fearing the possibility of even greater losses, can suffer very badly. The most inexperienced investors are often caught like this. These investors are often drawn into the market after a period of exceptionally good performance and have little appreciation of the risks involved.

Consider, for example, the experience of many people who invested in the market for the first time just before the October 1987 stock market crash. They lost around a third of their money in two days. Some of them panicked, withdrew their money and have regretted the whole thing ever since. Similar tales of disaster, some of them now bordering on folk memories, are associated with other dramatic market falls such as the 1929 Wall Street Crash, the 1974 debacle in the UK, the decline in Japanese markets in the early 1990s and the recent problems in the Far Eastern markets. Chapter 2 covers the history of these infamous market downturns. Despite the good long term performance of the market, it is a fact that many people have invested near a market peak in the past and consequently have been financially and psychologically bruised by the out-turn.

Obviously, given the preceding disaster stories, stock market investment deserves to be treated with a degree of healthy caution. It is easy to see why many people are so frightened of the risks involved that they forgo the large potential rewards of stock market investment. Their fears are perhaps overdone, even though we can be fairly sure incidents like those mentioned above will recur in the future.

However, there are ways to quantify and control the risks involved, allowing investors to take advantage of the rewards without taking risks that are too large. The remainder of the book will cover the more sophisticated of these methods in detail. For the moment, here are a few salient points:

 All investors need to accept the possibility that the value of their shares may sometimes go down in the short-run and possibly quite substantially. If they cannot face this, equity investment is not for them. In concrete terms they certainly should **not** invest any money needed to meet short term commitments.

 For most investors, it is wise to invest with a reasonably long time period in mind unless you are willing to accept a substantial loss if things go badly wrong in the short term.

 It is sensible to commit money to the market gradually over a period of time to avoid the possibility of investing it all at a bad time.

 If you are investing in the market for the long term, it is not sensible to be constantly worrying about the value of your investments.

Some investors will still be worried about the stock market. They might argue that the fact it has always recovered from setbacks in the past does not mean it will always recover in the future. There must be a possibility of some sort of financial catastrophe that would wipe out stock prices.

This view may be logically correct but, in practice, the main markets have proved very robust. The UK and US markets have operated through many recessions, the Great Depression, the 1970s' Oil Crisis and two world wars. It has even been calculated that the markets of Germany and Japan, countries which were defeated in World War II and suffered massive physical destruction, have provided attractive real returns in the period since 1926.

It is perhaps possible that some future government of the extreme left might adopt a policy of wealth confiscation but in the present political climate, with even the ex-Warsaw pact countries and China adopting free market policies, this possibility seems extremely remote and much less likely than it has been for most of this

CLOSE-UP

Between 1926 & 1995, the average real compound annual return on equities was 5.9% in Germany and 4% in Japan.[3]

century. In the event of such a doomsday scenario, it is unlikely that any other form of savings or investment would fare any better than shares.

IS STOCK MARKET INVESTMENT JUST GAMBLING?

There is a common misconception that stock market investment is no more than glorified gambling. It could be considered to be a gamble in the sense that the outcome is not certain. However, not much in life is certain. For instance, farmers are not accused of gambling when they plant a crop even though they don't know for certain how large the final crop will be when it matures or even what the price will be.

Even if the analogy with gambling is accepted, there is a big difference between investing on the stock market and pure gambles (such as betting in casinos or on horses). The difference is that **with stock market investments one can expect to win**. People playing conventional games of chance will generally lose money. Let's look quickly at a few examples:

 When playing the French version of Roulette on single number bets, the casino takes on average 2.7% of each bet. In the American version (with a double and single zero), the house edge is 5.3%.

 In Blackjack, even for people playing their cards correctly, there is a house advantage of something under 1%. In practice, most people don't play their cards correctly and the house edge can be 5% or more.[4]

 Racecourse bookmakers make a profit of around 3.5% to 5% on bets. Off-course bookmakers, with less competition and less informed customers, generally make a much larger profit of around 20%.[5]

 The National Lottery is a terrible gamble from the point of view of profitability, with only 50 pence out of each pound spent by participants going towards the prize money.[6]

In contrast, in the stock market most people have made money most of the time. In mathematical terms, the expected return to be gained from stock market investment is positive.

CAN THE MARKET BE BEATEN?

In our analysis so far we have examined the market as a whole. The past returns in the market have undoubtedly been very attractive but is it possible to do better than this? There are two potential ways of beating the market - **market timing** and **share selection**.

Market Timing

Given that the market rises and falls, an obvious method of trying to beat it is to hold shares when the market is rising (in a bull market) and to sell shares and hold a safe investment, such as cash, when it is falling (in a bear market). Nothing could be simpler in principle. If an investor could actually get his timing perfectly correct, the rewards would beggar belief.

David Schwartz, a well known market statistician, has calculated that over the period from 1919 to the end of 1994, if a hypothetical investor had invested in the stock market and had the ability to hold shares throughout each bull market and also to jump out of shares and put his money in the bank throughout the exact duration of each bear market, he could have grown a £1,000 nest egg to an unbelievably large figure of over £400 million, before taxes and commission.[7]

These figures, of course, cannot really be taken seriously. Nobody could ever possibly time the market perfectly for any prolonged length of time. Perfect ability to time the market is akin to the philosopher's stone of investment, it would be the key to vast wealth but is probably impossible to find. The figures do, however, give an indication of the potential rewards of good market timing. Information which would lead to the avoidance of even one bear market would be very valuable and a great deal of effort does go into research on market timing. We will review the different methods of market timing and their effectiveness later in the book.

ORIGINS

The origins of the terms 'bull' and 'bear' are probably lost in history. They were certainly in use as early as the 17th century in Holland. One theory of their origins is that the frenzied crowds trading stocks resembled those seen watching bull and bear baiting. Another theory is that the terms derived from the bull and bear symbols in the Druid Oracle. These represented character traits which may have related to the emotions associated with rising and falling markets.

Share Selection

The market is, of course, made up of individual companies and we will now turn our attention to these. Over any given period of time some shares will do better than the market as a whole and some worse. The market is a very dynamic arena, the shares that make up the market constantly vary as new companies are formed, companies merge and some companies fail. Many of the most familiar stock market names of today would be unknown in their present form to the investor of even twenty years ago.

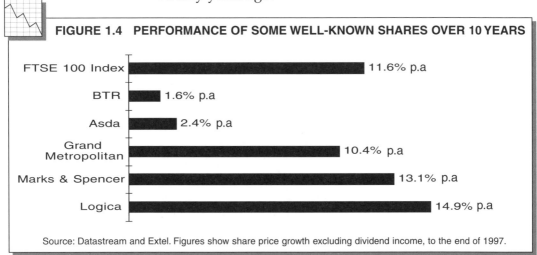

FIGURE 1.4   PERFORMANCE OF SOME WELL-KNOWN SHARES OVER 10 YEARS

FTSE 100 Index — 11.6% p.a
BTR — 1.6% p.a
Asda — 2.4% p.a
Grand Metropolitan — 10.4% p.a
Marks & Spencer — 13.1% p.a
Logica — 14.9% p.a

Source: Datastream and Extel. Figures show share price growth excluding dividend income, to the end of 1997.

The increases in the share prices of some companies over the years have been quite outstanding. The share prices of other companies have shown only mediocre gains or even heavy losses. One of the main themes in equity investment has always been the drive to identify which shares are going to be the best performers in the future and this is a theme we will return to many times.

CONCLUSION

In general, most people see stock market investment as a black art that they know little about. Many people have unrealistically optimistic or pessimistic expectations about stock market investment or perhaps just a fear of the unknown. This chapter has started to introduce the facts that will dispel much of the mystery and enable you to put the returns you can expect and the risks you may take into better perspective.

LESSONS TO BE LEARNT

 Shares have produced very good returns if held for long periods.

 The long term returns on equity investment have still been very attractive even after allowing for inflation.

 The long term returns on equity investment have been better than on most alternative investments available to investors.

 The main reason for the success of equity investment is that it allows investors to share in the long term increases in national and international prosperity.

 The stock market is undoubtedly risky in the short term and investors need to be prepared for this.

 It is possible to beat the stock market. There are two ways to do this - market timing and share selection.

 Market timing involves attempting to hold shares when the market is rising and to hold safer investments when it is falling. This is potentially very rewarding but it is not easy to get the timing right.

 Share selection involves attempting to hold shares which will perform better than the market. There are many ways to identify shares which will be good performers and these are examined later on in this book.

CHAPTER 2

The History
of the
Stock Market

M ost human endeavours are based on learning from experience. As we pointed out in the introduction to this book, there is a limit to what can be learnt about the detail of stock market investment without actually getting some practical experience. However, the record of the past performance of the stock market can provide a good grounding in how equity prices might be expected to behave. Before venturing into the stock market, it is wise to try and understand where the market has come from and where it might be going in the future.

In this chapter, we will be walking through the history of the stock market and learning a few salient lessons along the way. We will discover the ways in which particular historical events have influenced the market and this will provide us with a guide to what to look for in the wider world of economics and current affairs. When we reach the present day, we will see how the world's equity markets are becoming increasingly interdependent. This will lead us to having a quick look around the globe to catch up with the current state of play on the other major world exchanges.

SMALL FISH IN A BIG POND

In general, the private investor wishes to use the stock market as a tool. He or she rarely feels any great compulsion to own equities as an end in itself, but rather is looking to preserve or increase their wealth, whilst having some fun along the way. This tool, however, is not the sort you can fully control. Individual investors have real control over only a very small part of the operation of the market - just their own investment strategies, share selections and timing decisions. The stock market is fundamentally a communal activity. If you ever had the misfortune to sit through an economics lesson at school, you were probably told that a 'market' is just a place where buyers and sellers meet.

The UK stock market has its origins in the coffee houses of 17th century London where those who wished to invest or raise money bought and sold shares in joint-stock companies such as the East India Company, the Royal Africa Company and the Hudson's Bay Company.[1] As the volume of shares traded in these joint-stock companies began to increase, the number of brokers also grew and eventually they moved into a property on Threadneedle Street. In 1773, they voted to name the building the 'Stock Exchange'. Meanwhile, over on the other side of the Atlantic, dealing in securities sprang up among the houses and offices of those merchants and bankers who lived on Wall Street in lower Manhattan. In 1792, a handful of dealers came together to form the forerunner of the New York Stock Exchange.[2]

Back in Britain, the industrial revolution of the 19th century greatly increased the demand for business capital. New inventions and industrial processes presented ever increasing investment opportunities. Over 20 stock exchanges sprang up around the UK which eventually amalgamated into the London Stock Exchange we know today.

Although the structure and scale of the market have changed over time, many of the forces at work are the same today as they have been down the years. In this chapter, we will be focusing on the lessons to be gained from movements in the general level of share prices. It should be remembered, however, that when commentators talk about market movements, they are actually talking about the overall collective position of a large number of players and of many different shares. Imagine something like your local swimming baths on a crowded school day. The swell and choppiness of the water is driven by the collection of many individual actions. So what types of

ORIGINS

The concept of share ownership first emerged in 1553 when an adventurer called Sebastian Cabot founded the first 'joint-stock company' in which public shares were issued. This company - called the 'Mysterie and Companie of the Mercant Adventurers for the Discoverie of Regions, Dominions, Islands and Places Unknowen' - was formed to defray the costs of an expedition to discover the Northeast Passage, which Elizabethans believed led to the Orient and the Indies.

forces have moved the market over the years and what are the significant lessons the private investor can learn?

THE GREAT CRASH OF 1929

Despite the best efforts of Conservative governments in the 1980s, share ownership has yet to become very popular with the average man in the street. Outside of the 'Square Mile', the vagaries of the market are not a common topic of conversation to be shared over a pint at the local pub. As a result, much of the news and debate concerning the stock market frequently passes most of the general public by. It takes events of significant magnitude to stir the popular interest. Such monumental occurrences, though rare, stick in people's memories and perhaps colour their perceptions of personal equity investment.

Perhaps the most famous of all was the Great Crash of October 1929 when billions of dollars were lost on Wall Street in a single day, paving the way for the Great Depression of the 1930s. The lesson everyone has taken away from this episode is that shares can be risky and prices can fall very rapidly. While this is a lesson well worth noting, the crash of 1929 needs to be seen in the context of the bull market of the 'Roaring Twenties'.

The key lessons of the Great Crash are those of both 'boom' **and** 'bust', highlighting the dangers of reckless speculation and investing money which is not spare.[3]

The 1920s were a thriving time for America. Production and employment were high, prices relatively stable and company earnings growing. Security prices began to move ahead during 1924 and grew steadily throughout 1925. Following a brief set back in 1926, the market surged ahead the following year. These were exciting and adventurous days. As Charles Lindbergh flew the Spirit of St. Louis out of Roosevelt Field and set a course for Paris, he left behind a stock market making its own dash for new stratospheric heights. The rise in prices continued throughout 1928 as the speculative boom got underway in earnest. As the market surged forward everyone wanted a piece of the action. By the Summer of 1929, the stock market not only dominated the news, but had also permeated American culture.

ORIGINS

The roots of the 1927 US bull market have a British connection. In 1925, the Chancellor - one Winston Churchill - returned Britain to the Gold Standard, which fixed the rates of exchange between gold, the dollar and sterling. In Spring 1927, the Bank of England lobbied the US to ease its monetary policy to protect the value of the pound. The resulting actions of the US Federal Reserve led to a lot more money being freed up for the pur chase of shares.

The lessons of the boom market are twofold:

! A speculative market loses touch with reality. It stops considering the economics of wealth creation and how shares reflect what companies are actually doing. During times of speculation, investors focus solely on the fact that prices are rising without considering the reasons why.

! It reveals the dangers of investing money which is needed for other commitments. In 1920s' America, lots of shares were being bought 'on margin'. People took out loans using equities as collateral. As long as the equities kept rising, the loans were secure and nobody worried. Of course, as soon as the value of the shares dropped below the amount owed, the banks wanted repayment. So speculators had to liquidate their share holdings to pay back the monies due.

In October 1929 the speculative bubble burst. As prices began to fall, everybody either wanted to get out quickly while the going was still good or they were forced to sell to meet loan repayments. The result was panic. On Thursday October 24th, the market degenerated into a wild, mad scramble to sell as crowds clamoured outside the Exchange. (It is one of those ironies of history that Winston Churchill was in the visitors' gallery that day to witness the consequences of his earlier policy.) During the week that followed, prices collapsed as the selling frenzy continued. Things went from bad to worse. Anyone who went back into the market, to mop up a few bargains after the crash, was in for a shock. Despite a brief recovery in early 1930, the market turned down again and fell month after month right through to June 1932 as the Great Depression swept across America.

EYEING–UP THE INDEX

When talking about the general level of share prices and describing the state of the market, commentators frequently use a form of short-hand called an 'index'. For each Stock Exchange around the world, at a given point in its history, there will be a popular index which is used to express the general movements in prices. In 1935 the Financial Times Thirty Share Index (FT30), with a base starting value of 100, was introduced as a general measure of UK share prices. In this chapter we will describe the UK stock market using the popular indices of their time; the FT30 up until 1984 and the Financial Times Stock Exchange 100 (FTSE 100 or most commonly referred to by its nickname 'the Footsie') from then onwards. The reader will be aware that, although the stock market is of major importance to the UK economy, it does not tend to get a great deal of air-time on the evening news bulletins. Instead most broadcasters just sum up the day's business with a quick look at what has happened to the 'Footsie'. On the overseas markets, movement on the New York Stock Exchange is usually summed up using the 'Dow' and business in Tokyo by the 'Nikkei'.

Using the UK indices as a guide, we will examine how the market has performed since 1935 and consider what that teaches us about the way it is likely to behave in the future.[4] We will see that as the market grows in response to the increase in economic wealth, it does not do so in a straight line but rather moves in an irregular pattern seemingly 'driven' by corporate, political, economic and international events. We will discover that what is happening in other parts of the world really **does** affect the price of shares here in the UK. We will learn that all sorts of economic data (and opinions about what the data actually mean) also have an effect.

1935 – 1950: IN WAR AND PEACE

History teaches us that domestic and international events affect the price of shares. Today's events are likely to affect the earnings potential of companies in the future. The market's view of the future and, therefore, the worth of companies, is shaped by current events; some will have a big effect, some lesser.

Probably the most extreme example is where international events threaten the entire economy of a nation and the ability of firms to continue their production. The prospect of war in Europe caused share prices to fall in 1937 and 1938. With the outbreak of hostilities, the Stock Market closed between the 1st and 6th of September 1939, but survived the war intact. In June 1940, the evacuation of troops from Dunkirk, the entry of Italy into the War and the fall of France made the threat of invasion imminent. As a result the Financial Times Index plunged to a low of 49.

The index moved down on news of specific events such as the bombing of Pearl Harbor in December 1941, but as the war news improved, so did the market. By the time Allied troops landed in Normandy in June 1944, the market was making a concerted advance based on the prospects of victory and a post-war regeneration of the economy.

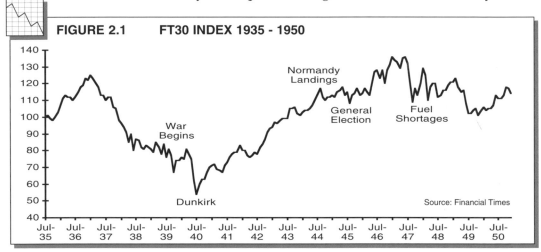

FIGURE 2.1   FT30 INDEX 1935 - 1950

Source: Financial Times

Changes in social attitudes and tastes, brought about by the war, raised the prospect of new commercial opportunities. The war had seen the development of many new technologies which would one day lead to the emergence of whole new industries. Inventions in the field of automotives, electronics, television, textiles and plastics would lead to major industrial developments in the years ahead.

In July 1945 the market was expecting the continuation of a Conservative government under Winston Churchill. The surprise of Clement Attlee's landslide Labour victory caused the market to fall overnight under the fear of nationalisation. The immediate post-war years were days of austerity and of fuel shortages which strangled production and dragged the market lower.

1951 – 1959: A BULL IN A GILT SHOP

As we saw in Chapter 1, equities are only one type of investment and are influenced by the relative performance of other types of investments. The early 1950s marked the start of the first post-war bull market and built the foundations of 'the cult of the equity'. Share ownership was becoming more commonplace by the 50s with shares in familiar high street shops, such as Marks and Spencer, becoming increasingly popular. The economic news of the day was more encouraging and industries such as motor cars, aircraft and textiles were on the up. In April 1954, the FT30 index finally passed its former peak of January 1947 and was steaming upwards, with dividend pay-outs also on a rising trend.

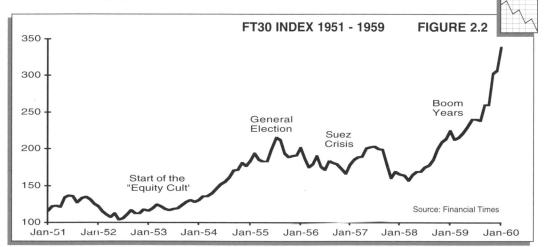

FT30 INDEX 1951 - 1959   FIGURE 2.2

Source: Financial Times

As the performance of equities improved, institutional investors began to change the composition of their portfolios in favour of holding shares rather than gilts. Equities rose by 53% in 1954, for example, whereas gilt prices rose only 3%. The Conservative election victory of 1955 looked like good news for the market and pushed the FT30 through the 200 mark for the first time, which meant the index had doubled over a period of some twenty years.

As the development of 20th century business unfolded, it became clear that the increasingly international operation of companies would also affect the market. By the mid-50s shares in international operators, such as ICI and BP, were

CLOSE-UP

In July 1956 Colonel Nasser seized the Suez Canal. Shares in shipping companies and oil companies fell. Under the threat of oil shortages, the index slumped back to 162.

ORIGINS

Because shares are risky, you'd expect investors to insist on a higher income return from shares than from safe gilts; this difference is called the '**yield gap**'. However, if investors expect rising dividends into the future, shares are worth holding even if their current income return is less than that from gilts - a '**reverse yield gap**'.

benefiting from the attention of American investors. By contrast, the forces operating in the market for gilts were more to do with domestic concerns, particularly rising inflation, and gilt prices fell in the face of higher interest rates. Internationalisation, however, cuts both ways. The value of companies operating on the international stage can be adversely affected by events many miles from home.

After a year of disinflationary measures in 1957, the market was ready to rise again and the stage was set for the 'you've never had it so good' boom of 1959. Production, productivity and exports soared. With all this evident industrial success, investors increasingly believed that tomorrow's dividend pay-outs would be greater than those presently being made. With this expectation, gilts became of much less interest to the average private investor. The bull market in equities swept all before it. Macmillan's landslide re-election provided the bonus of political continuity and, at the end of 1959, the FT30 closed at a whopping 338.

1960 – 1969: THE SWINGING SIXTIES

The 1960s were a swinging time in Britain in more ways than one. The decade saw the equities index rise and fall, recover then dip, make some headway towards the end of the decade only to lose it all again. By the start of the seventies we were back where we started. In fact, the FT30 index would close in 1970 only two points above where it started in 1960! Over this period, managing to keep up with the market would not have proved a very profitable endeavour.

CLOSE-UP

In March 1961, Tetley and Ansells merged with Ind Coope to form the country's largest brewer. In the same year, ICI made a record breaking, but ultimately unsuccessful, bid for Courtaulds.

The overall lesson of the sixties, then, is all about timing. There are any number of events which affected the market upward or downwards. Some of these were shocks having immediate, but not lasting, effects; others perhaps went little noticed at the time but were to have an enduring impact on industry. For example, we can see that share prices are affected by periods of bids, take-overs and mergers. The early 1960s were a time when mergers and consolidations were taking place in a number of industrial sectors.

Where potential bids are concerned, the market does its best to second guess what companies are doing and, consequently, prices frequently move on the basis of the rumour or speculation of bids. News of bids and acquisitions, whether actual or predicted, is short term, new information that the market seeks to absorb. Other news has longer term implications. As we will see in later chapters, share prices should reflect the expected future competitive success of companies, which means keeping an eye on what the competition is up to. Back in 1961, Nissan began producing cars for the domestic Japanese market and for export. Meanwhile Renault was introducing its models to the UK. The emergence of such foreign competition was to have a significant impact on the UK motor industry.

Although the operation of the market is a collective activity involving many people, commentators frequently describe the market as having a single 'mood' or 'reaction'. It is fairly common for commentators to personify the market and give it such emotions as 'excitement' or 'taking fright'. Some of the up and down movements in the index are due to the market making fairly abrupt adjustments to an overall view as to what the realistic level of values ought to be.

For example, in May 1962 President Kennedy intervened in the US economy to stabilise steel prices. Wall Street became scared at Kennedy's perceived 'anti-business' attitude and, on 29th May, the Dow dived nearly 6%. As is so often the case, what panics Wall Street, panics London. The London index fell 18 points to 261 losing nearly 6.5% of its value - its largest one day fall since 1938. The Chairman of the Stock Exchange at the time, Lord Ritchie, advised small investors to "put their heads down and let the wind blow over them".[5] When the market is buffeted by such international affairs, private investors need to keep their heads.

History also shows us that the market will move down in response to political uncertainty. Everyone who is old enough can remember where they were on the 23rd November 1963. The untimely death of President Kennedy sent the Dow downwards. In Britain, the election of 1964 returned Harold Wilson as Prime Minister and James Callaghan as his Chancellor, with a tiny majority. The election result caused the index to dip 5 points.[6] Government economic policy also affects the future profitability of companies. The FT30 index was on the up again during the first half of 1966 to peak at 374 in June. It wasn't to last. Jim Callaghan's July package of deflationary measures took the legs out from under domestic demand and by November, the FT30 index was down to 284.

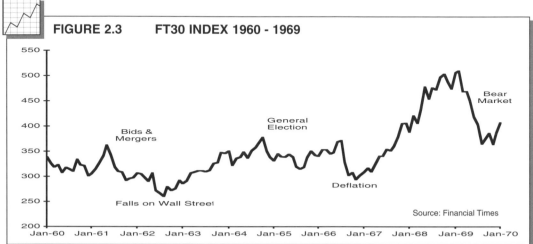

FIGURE 2.3   FT30 INDEX 1960 - 1969

Source: Financial Times

1967 and 1968 were up-swing years for the UK market. As interest rates drifted lower, the market moved ahead. There was another dip in late 1967 with the devaluation of the pound to $2.40 and the subsequent resignation of the Chancellor of the Exchequer, but the market surged ahead again through most of 1968 reaching a peak of 522 in late September. By early 1969, the FT30 was around the 500 to 520 mark, but as the Chancellor tightened up on domestic demand, the bears came out and the market went into free-fall. By July, as Neil Armstrong walked on the moon, the FT30 was back down to below 360.

CLOSE-UP

In 1968, the merger of Westminster Bank and National Provincial Bank formed the National Westminster Bank we know today.

1970 – 1978: OIL ON TROUBLED WATERS

If the prices of shares represent the expected future profitability of companies, then the market has two overlapping and sorry tales to tell from the 1970s - tales of oil crisis and of the turbulent waters of divisive industrial relations. The decade started with the FT30 having popped its head up above the 420 mark again, but against a backdrop of growing industrial unrest and escalating pay claims.

The June 1970 election brought the Conservatives under Edward Heath back to power and, interpreting new government economic policy, the index made some ground until October. In industry, however, things were getting worse. Strike followed strike, wage demands soared and more and more companies were reporting liquidity problems. The market headed downwards. By the end of the year, Rolls-Royce were reporting large losses on the production of the RB211 engine and, in February 1971, they shocked the market by calling in the receivers. The beginning of March that year saw the largest political strike since the General Strike of 1926, as one and a half million workers protested against the Industrial Relations Bill. The FT30 promptly fell to 305.

The government's response was Anthony Barber's expansionist budget and the liberalisation of the consumer credit industry - the start of the so-called 'Barber boom'. Despite the continuing bad news from industry, record post-war unemployment and rapidly rising earnings, the market began to gain ground, reaching 543 by mid-1972. From then on, the very real fear of inflation took over. With the government taking draconian measures to try to control spiralling pay and price rises, inflation, strikes and confrontational wage demands became daily news.

Amidst this sorry tale of political and economic disruption, a storm began to brew in the Middle East. During 1972 and 1973, Libya seized control of the assets of UK and US oil companies within its borders and production of oil was stopped in Libya, Iraq and Kuwait. In Geneva and Vienna, OPEC was debating increasing the price of oil. Then in October 1973, Egypt and Syria attacked Israel - the Yom Kippur war had begun. With the US aiding military operations in Israel, the Arab world reacted against the West. Iraq seized US oil interests in its country and the Gulf States led a series of massive rises in the price of crude.

Back in London, the oil shock arrived just at a time of confrontation with miners and power workers. Ted Heath declared a State of Emergency over the oil and coal crises and share prices plunged. In December 1973, the government introduced a 3 day working week to save fuel.

CLOSE-UP

These turbulent days for industry provide another salutary lesson: when trading conditions turn rough, the level of a company's borrowings can leave it high and dry. At the start of 1975, Burmah Oil ran onto the financial rocks. It had financed recent acquisitions with a massive dollar loan from US banks and could no longer service the debt. The Bank of England bailed out the company, but at a price. The Government took over the majority of its North Sea operations and its holdings in BP and Shell.

The FT30 had opened 1973 above the 500 mark; by mid-December it had dipped to nearly 300. There was worse to come. The political pressure brought to bear by these crises forced the general election of 1974. The shock result - a hung parliament with Labour forming the largest party - caused another sharp fall in the market. With Michael Foot at Employment, Tony Benn at Industry and Denis Healey at the Exchequer, the prospects were for a left-wing agenda of intervention in industry. In the days which followed, the unions exerted massive influence over British industry.

The Retail Prices Index headed for the sky. With spiralling upward pressure on wages, the prospects for company profits and dividends were not good. The value of shares nose-dived further. Labour's re-election in October 1974 brought with it new fears of a programme of nationalisation. Amidst all this industrial uncertainty, the stability of the country's financial institutions began to unravel. The value of shares in Lloyds and National Westminster banks fell below their par value. In November the FT30 was down to 150. It was the worst year **ever** for the market. Over 12 months, the index more than halved. Hard as it may be to imagine today, Britain stood on the verge of social and political collapse.

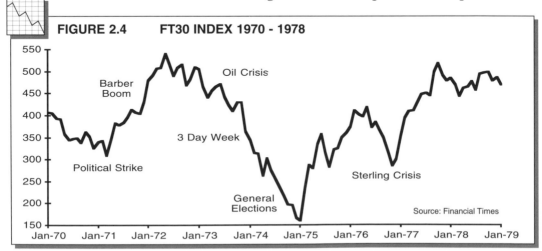

FIGURE 2.4   FT30 INDEX 1970 - 1978

Barber Boom

Oil Crisis

3 Day Week

Political Strike

General Elections

Sterling Crisis

Source: Financial Times

The market bottomed out in January 1975 at 146, looking very cheap indeed. The tide turned. The worst was over and the market began to climb sharply. With it, the story of oil and political turbulence took a new twist.

For Britain, the new focus for oil became the North Sea. Britain was heading towards self-sufficiency in oil and its revenues boosted the Balance of Payments. Having North Sea oil gave Britain an advantage over its industrialised trading partners. The nation's oil wealth and the performance of oil company shares was a stabilising factor in the equities markets at the end of the 1970s.

Despite the set back of the sterling crisis of the Autumn of 1976, the index made it back up to 549 by September 1977. In industry, increasing realism over the nightmare of inflation had dawned and some degree of pay restraint had appeared for a time. It was not to last, however, as the government's pay policy became increasingly unachievable. Despite the government's 5% earnings increase guidelines, the Ford workers' strike of September 1978 produced a settlement of 17%. The spiral was inevitable. The engineering union asked for 33%, the miners for 40% and the public sector workers, seeking parity on pay, started their strike action. The 'Winter of Discontent' had arrived.

1979 – 1983: SOME UNPLEASANT MEDICINE

The election of 1979 was to have major repercussions for the British economy and the stock market. With mountains of rubbish cluttering the streets, the picketing of food deliveries to hospitals and the continued disruption of essential services, the Conservative party's cry for trade union reform found a receptive ear in the public at large. The increasingly likely prospect of a Conservative victory drove the index upwards.

The election result, with Margaret Thatcher taking over the helm, pushed the index to a new all time peak of 558. Almost instantly, however, the realisation dawned on the market of the harsh economic medicine that would be imposed. Geoffrey Howe's first budgets tightened the monetary squeeze and the FT30 struggled to keep its head above the 400 mark.

One lesson to be learnt from 1980s Britain is the way in which interest rates affect share prices. Interest rates were a key economic policy instrument during the 1980s. At the start of the decade rates were rising in all major industrialised nations to attack the problem of inflation. (In Britain, the decade opened with retail price increases still running at some 17% per year). Interest rates in both Britain and the US would be a central element in the movement of share prices during the decade.

Geoffrey Howe introduced his medium-term financial strategy in 1980. The idea was to drive down the rate of money growth over the coming four years and simultaneously reduce the Public Sector Borrowing Requirement (PSBR) from 5.5% of the National Income to just 1.5%. Revenue from North Sea oil would be used to cut the public sector deficit. As interest rates fell in the US and unemployment topped 1.5 million, the credit squeeze was eased slightly as interest rates moved down to 16%. As a result, the FT30 punched up through the 500 barrier and plateaued around that level for the latter part of the year. A set back occurred with the election of Ronald Reagan to the American presidency. US interest rates rocketed to 21.5% and the market feared another funding crisis. In both the US and the UK, shares dropped.

Unemployment began to increase as Britain's traditional manufacturing base began to crumble with the focus of economic activity moving to oil and the service sector. Shares in companies in the oil and financial sectors moved ahead whilst those of traditional heavy industry fell back reflecting the major structural shifts in the economy. Manufacturing, it seemed, had moved out and headed East to Japan and South-East Asia. The recession began to do its work on inflation as unemployment soared. This shake-out of labour onto the dole queues, as industries were rationalised, drove productivity upwards and as a result the index pushed ahead at the prospect of better earnings to come.

The market, however, was buffeted at the mercy of US interest rate policy. Huge interest rates in the US meant a strong dollar and by the Summer of 1981, the value of the pound had dived below the $2 mark. The US reliance on interest rate policy had serious implications for economies across the world. In September 1981, rates moved up again and in the space of a fortnight the index lost 100 points. Similarly as soon as US short term interest rates fell, so did the UK base rate and the index climbed again to over 500.

NUTSHELL

PSBR is the difference between what the government gets in by way of taxes and what it spends in the form of public expenditure. This gap needs to be funded through the sale of government securities.

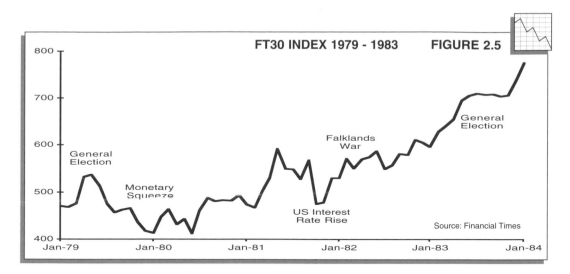

FT30 INDEX 1979 - 1983   FIGURE 2.5

Source: Financial Times

Then suddenly, other considerations took over with the outbreak of the Falklands war. The military and, by extension, the political risks undertaken also showed up in the movements of the market. The decision to send the Task Force saw the index drop; the guarantee of US support in the conflict brought it up again; Argentinean successes pulled it down again, but the impending British victory drove the index up above 590. Then, as quickly as it had become a market issue, the war became history. Consideration of international affairs returned to the level of US interest rates and eyes turned once again to the domestic problems of industrial unrest and stagnation. The easing of the US monetary stance brought UK base rates down to 9% and equities pushed through the 600 barrier. With the success of the war behind them, the government was re-elected in 1983 with a landslide majority of 144 seats. Signs of industrial improvement also provided market momentum and so the FT30 broke through 700 in early Summer and ended the year at 775.

1984 – 1987: YUPPIE MARKET

From 1984 onwards, we swap indices with the introduction of the FTSE 100. The 'Footsie' has become the most frequently used index in the broadcast and press media. At 1st January 1984, the FTSE 100 was set at a base level of

ORIGINS

On 27th October 1986, 'Big Bang' changed the way the stock market worked. It marked the end of the 'open outcry' on the exchange floor as traders moved to computerised trading desks.

1000. It turned out to be a good time to start - from 1984 to 1987 the stock market went into boom. By the end of 1984 the FTSE 100 would have become 1232, a year later it would stand at 1412, and by the end of 1986 it would have become 1679. The index cruised through the 2000 mark in the spring of 1987, having doubled in just over 38 months.

The boom was fuelled by falling interest rates, cheaper oil, large privatisation offerings and pro-industry budgets from Chancellor Nigel Lawson. The collapse of the dockers' and miners' strike in 1984 looked like the last death throes of the industrial disruption that had plagued the country through the 1970s, and inflation at last appeared to be under reasonable control. The general public were given a taste for the equities market in the shape of major privatisations.

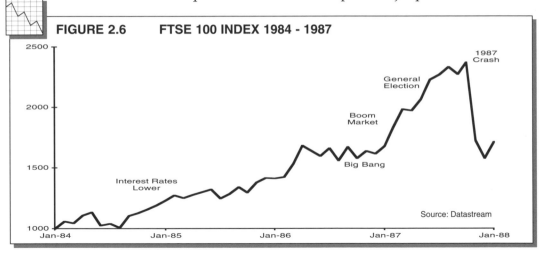

FIGURE 2.6   FTSE 100 INDEX 1984 - 1987

The experience of many private investors putting their toe in the market for the first time was, perhaps, unrealistic as shares like British Telecom all but doubled on their first day of trading. The 1986 budget also introduced Personal Equity Plans (PEPs) to promote equity holding.

As we've already seen in the case of 1920s America, a bull market can reach the point where it feeds off its own expectations of future price rises rather than looking at the fundamental reasons for such growth. Arguably, the UK bull market reached this point in 1986, pushing ahead despite the underlying frailty of the economic base. Besides, there was a general election in the offing and the government were sure to promote growth rather than

CLOSE-UP

The market was also stimulated by record-breaking bids including Argyll's bid for Allied Lyons, Hanson's for Imperial and GEC trying to get hold of Plessey. Once the predators came out, competitive bidding forced prices up.

subdue it. Deregulation of the Stock Exchange also took place in 1986 with 'Big Bang' in the City and brokerage firms being snapped up by UK and overseas banks.

1987 – 1989: CRASH AND BOUNCE

The third week of October 1987 was the scheduled date for the flotation of £7.2 billion worth of BP shares. Manufacturing output was rising, unemployment falling and confidence high. On Thursday 15th October the FTSE 100 closed at 2322. That night London and the South East were devastated by one of the worst storms in living memory, bringing Friday's trading to a virtual standstill. Meanwhile, across the Atlantic, an even more costly storm was breaking.

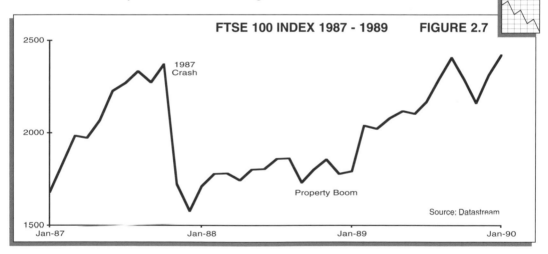

FTSE 100 INDEX 1987 - 1989   FIGURE 2.7

Source: Datastream

At the end of the first week of October, US interest rates had increased and news on the economy looked less than encouraging. Confidence drained out of the New York market and prices started down. In light trading, each large transaction could cause a sudden shift in prices. Sales orders started increasing. Panic set in. On Wednesday 14th October, the Dow dropped 95 points; on the Thursday it lost a further 57. US interest rates moved up an additional 0.5% on the Friday and the Dow nose-dived 108 points. The FTSE 100 responded on the Monday by dropping nearly 250 points. 'Black Monday' delivered the worst ever fall on Wall Street as the Dow crashed a further 508 points or 23% of its value! The FTSE 100 followed suit with a second drop of 250 points to 1802. The Tokyo market also fell by nearly 15%.[7]

Still, just as the bull market had shown a dislocation between capital gains and corporate earnings on the way up, so the impact of the crash seems to have been at arm's length from the real economy. The Lawson boom continued into 1988 with record levels of bank lending, high consumer spending and growing corporate profits; although many private investors, now dramatically aware of the riskiness of equities, transferred their attention to bricks and mortar and the ensuing property boom. The Footsie quickly recovered. It closed 1988 at nearly 1800 and was back above 2300 by the Summer of 1989.

1990 – 1992: RATES OF EXCHANGE

Given that the rest of the industrialised nations were gritting their teeth and bearing the austerity of high interest rates and rising unemployment, in the name of the long term suppression of inflation, the UK boom looked increasingly out of step with its trading partners. With high interest rates abroad, the question of the exchange rate came to the fore and the Chancellor went head to head with Sir Alan Walters about how it should best be answered. To keep it at around the three deutschmarks to the pound level, the Chancellor would have to push interest rates higher. As German rates moved up, UK rates followed suit. In October 1989, with Base Rates up at 15%, the house price boom turned into bust and Nigel Lawson resigned. Fear of the impact of high interest rates was compounded by the rise in the price of oil when Iraq invaded Kuwait and operation Desert Shield went into action.

The solution to the exchange rate policy debate came in October 1990 when the UK joined the European Exchange Rate Mechanism (ERM) at DM2.95. The market welcomed the move by gaining 130 points in two days, but the Conservative leadership crisis which followed drove the FTSE 100 back down to almost 2000. Relief came in the odd form of air supremacy over Baghdad. The swift resolution to the war in the Gulf which followed, removed the old spectre of high oil prices and the FTSE 100 moved ahead again. For the rest of 1991 nobody could decide whether the recession was coming to an end or not. The index plateaued between the 2500 to 2600 mark then dropped away to 2400 prior to the April 1992 election.

The recession in Britain was looking more severe but a cut in interest rates and currency devaluation was restricted because of ERM membership. Those who were anti-ERM blamed the lack of recovery on the government having its hands tied. ERM supporters thought the long hard slog would be worth it as UK interest and inflation levels converged with Germany's. The surprise re-election of the government in 1992 caused the FTSE 100 to leap 136 points. By May, the index was up at 2739. But the recession remained. British consumers had gone to ground, licking the wounds inflicted by high interest rates, negative equity and the fear of unemployment.

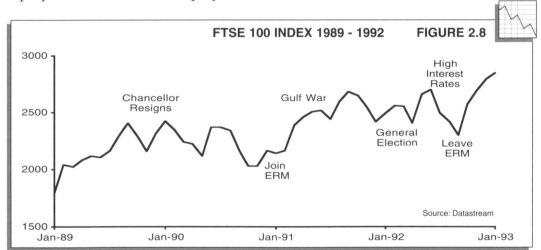

FTSE 100 INDEX 1989 - 1992   **FIGURE 2.8**

Source: Datastream

Unification was causing even higher interest rates in Germany; but meanwhile the US had embarked on a policy of using low interest rates to break out of recession. The pound was caught between a rock and a hard place. Britain had to stick to high interest rates to maintain the exchange rate, while at the same time needing to reflate the economy. The exchange rate was pushing $2 to the pound, but at the same time heading towards its ERM floor against the deutschmark. Interest rate rises seemed inevitable and the FTSE 100 headed for 2300. The foreign exchange markets realised that higher interest rates were domestically untenable and the devaluation of sterling all but inevitable. They sold, adding massive speculative pressure against the price. Base rates rose by 2% on September 16th 1992 and threatened to move to 15%, before the government caved in and left the ERM. The next day base rates were at 10% and the FTSE 100 climbed 105 points.

The ERM debacle wrecked the government's credibility, but at least its policy could now turn around. Interest rates headed down to 7% and the FTSE 100 headed for the sky. It closed the year at 2846.

1993 – 1998: TIME FOR CHANGE

1993 brought the first signs of recovery. Although unemployment was almost 3 million, inflation seemed to be under control and private sector pay was only rising at 3.6%. By the time Kenneth Clarke took over as Chancellor, the economic news was looking more rosy and by the Summer of 1993 investors were gaining confidence. If we really were entering a time of low interest rates and low inflation, then corporate profits were due to rise. Additionally, the Uruguay round of the GATT talks liberalised international trade and the broadening of the restrictions in the ERM freed up European economies from German domestic problems. In August 1993, the FTSE 100 broke through the 3000 mark and closed the year at 3418.

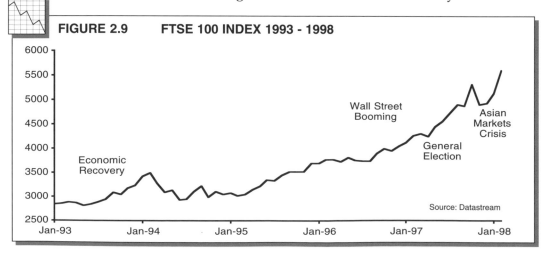

FIGURE 2.9   FTSE 100 INDEX 1993 - 1998

Source: Datastream

The market dipped back in 1994, but since 1995 has gone from strength to strength, following in the wake of a booming Wall Street. The FTSE 100 cruised through 4000 before the end of 1996 and by the time the new Labour administration came to power in May 1997, the index stood at 4445. The 5000 barrier was smashed in the Autumn of that year. In October the index fell sharply on the back of the market crises in the Far East, only to recover again before the end of the year. At the time of writing, the FTSE 100 is again breaking new record highs.

CLOSE-UP

The London Stock Exchange and the Deutsche Börse, based in Frankfurt, are working to harmonise the markets for leading UK and German equities. This step may form the nucleus of a single European stock market.

1998: WORLD MARKETS TODAY

The USA

Wall Street is booming and has been for some time. The main index used to express the state of the US market is the Dow Jones Index of the New York Stock Exchange (NYSE). At the start of 1996 the Dow was a little above the 5000 mark. It pushed through 6000 by the Autumn of that year; cruised through 7000 by the Spring of 1997 and relentlessly surged above 8000 by the July. The index moved sharply down in response to the problems of the Far East markets, but almost instantly shrugged off the contagion and returned to its upward drive. At the time of writing the Dow has reached new record highs at around 9000.

Europe

European exchanges outside the UK play a less significant role in the global equities markets and, as a result, you will tend to hear less about them. Still, the major European markets are also setting new record highs at the time of writing, bolstered by the strength of the US market. The German market is described by movements in either the DAX Index, which currently trades around the 5500 mark, or the Commerzbank Index at around a fairly similar number of 5200. The Paris market is quoted using the CAC40 Index which has climbed from the 2000 level in the Spring of 1996 to over 4000 today.

Japan

Japan has been in a bear market for some 8 years, with no end apparently in sight. The key measure used for the Japanese market is called the Nikkei 225 Index. The Japanese market boomed between 1982 and 1989. At its peak in December 1989, the index was pushing towards a level of 40000. Its collapse has been both spectacular and sustained. In the course of 1990 the index shed 39% of its value and by 1992, it was some 60% lower than its 1989 peak. During the most recent years the Nikkei has continued to trend downwards. Still struggling after the collapse of the 80s bubble, some of Japan's financial institutions were too fragile to withstand the 1997 Asian markets' crisis. Some of Japan's largest brokerage firms collapsed and the Nikkei tumbled below 15000. At the time of writing the index is floating around the 15300 level.

Hong Kong

Hong Kong has historically also been a major centre for international securities trading. The index usually quoted to describe the state of the Hong Kong market is called the Hang Seng Index. The Hang Seng has been through a far more recent boom and bust than the Nikkei. At the start of 1996, the Hang Seng was almost exactly at 10000. By July 1997, it was way up, having passed the 15000. Then between August and October 1997, the crisis in the financial markets of the Far East economies washed across Hong Kong. The international exchange rate of the Hong Kong dollar, which was pegged to a high US dollar, came under attack from currency speculators. To maintain the value of its currency, interest rates rose sharply and the stock market nose-dived. By the end of October the Hang Seng was down at the 9000 level.

Asian Contagion 1997

You will doubtless be aware of the economic and financial turmoil which swept across the Asian Pacific rim in 1997. The crisis occurred in some of the fastest growing Asian 'Tiger' economies. The rush for economic growth can sometimes store up trouble for the future. In the Tiger economies, the flood of foreign investment pushed up asset prices and Western investment banks injected funds into huge infrastructure projects such as new cities, roads and railways. Additionally, most of the region's currencies were pegged to the strong US dollar and as a result their export trade was becoming less competitive. These sorts of links served to intertwine the state of the region's economies. When Thailand allowed its largest finance company to collapse and its currency to float sharply downwards, the rules of the game changed for investors in the Far East and stock market values began to unravel. Malaysia, Singapore, Indonesia and Hong Kong all came under pressure from currency speculators. Across the region, governments were forced to cancel infrastructure projects, troubled banks collapsed and equity prices and currencies tumbled. Despite being the world's 11th largest economy, South Korea needed to be bailed out from defaulting on its foreign debts. The repercussions of the financial turmoil fed out to Japan, the USA and Europe.

CONCLUSIONS

The history of the general level of share prices provides a good overview of the market from which to consider undertaking personal equity investing. We have seen how political and economic events have affected the market over the last six decades and learnt some important lessons about what forces tend to drive share prices in general. History shows us that current events influence the prospects of companies succeeding profitably in the future and, therefore, alter the market's assessment of what each company is worth today. You need to keep our eye on the latest news of political, economic, technological and corporate affairs if you are to understand the market's movements more fully. Watching the FTSE 100 and the indices of other international exchanges will give you a feel for the state of play of the equity markets around the globe.

LESSONS TO BE LEARNT

 Speculative boom markets can lose touch with the underlying fundamentals of wealth creation.

 Investing money which is committed elsewhere can mean having to sell shares at a bad time.

 Share prices fall in response to political and economic uncertainty.

 Due to the nature of international business, UK share prices are affected by events around the world.

 Share prices are affected by company bids, mergers and acquisitions and also by rumours of such events.

 Share prices will fall if future costs of production, including wage rates, rise.

 Share prices respond to expected changes in interest rates. Higher interest rates mean higher borrowing costs, less investment and lower profits.

 As economies and equity markets around the globe become increasingly interdependent, movements on other world markets affect the stock market here in the UK.

PART TWO

THE BASIC FACTS

CHAPTER 3

Shares and Events

As we saw in the introduction, stock market investment is as much an art as it is a science. One of the most frustrating aspects of the art of stock market investment is the often indecipherable use of specialised terminology. Here's just one example. Shares are quoted at their bid and offer prices. What are these, you rightly ask? Well, the bid is the price at which the market will buy a share from you and the offer is the price at which it will sell it to you. So all you have to remember is that **bid equals buy** and **offer equals sell** from the perspective of the market; not as easy as it seems, when all the rest of the jargon has to be stored away and remembered. One purpose of this chapter is, therefore, to start to 'bust' some of the more common jargon of stock market investment. It has to be accepted, however, that the investment industry is full of jargon and a finance dictionary is a necessary tool if the financial pages are to be read in earnest.

A further and more important purpose of this chapter is to introduce you to the key characteristics of stock markets and the 'events' that might be faced by shares. Part of being a successful investor is to understand the forces within stock markets and the major events that your shares might confront. One way of thinking through these issues is to consider a share following a life-cycle through a changing environment. Indeed, the structure of the chapter could be categorised as the life and times of a share. More specifically, the chapter covers the following:

THE WORLD OF THE SHARE	■ The funding of companies - equity (shares) versus debt ■ Stock market characteristics ■ Stock market indices and sectors
THE LIFE-CYCLE OF A SHARE	■ The birth of a share - New Issues ■ The decision to issue dividends ■ How a company issues more shares - Rights Issues ■ Large and small company shares ■ Mergers/take-overs/de-mergers ■ Share suspensions and company failure

A detailed biography of a share could fill a book in itself and this is one way of seeing the in-depth histories of individual companies. Here we offer more of an executive summary, if a rather extensive one.

THE FUNDING OF COMPANIES

Although some would argue that the prices of shares are more to do with the sentiment of the market than the actual nature and performance of companies, it strikes us that it is brave, if not downright foolhardy, to invest in shares without a basic understanding of the fundamentals of company finance. While Chapter 5 goes into a reasonable amount of depth in analysing company accounts, the purpose of this section is to consider briefly some basic terminology.

The starting point for understanding financial terminology is to remember that business, in outline, is extremely simple:

Any business needs money (funds) to buy assets to enable it to make more money (profits).

Businesses can obtain funds from three broad sources - equity (shares), debt (loan finance) and retained profits (once a business has been running successfully). Of course, for some assets, immediate cash is not needed because they are granted on credit terms - a good example is that raw materials are usually provided on credit terms. Let's now consider these three sources of funds separately.

Equity or Share Capital

A business can obtain funds by issuing ordinary share capital and inviting others to invest as shareholders and the owners of the business. The chief characteristics of ordinary share capital are:

 No interest has to be paid on shares and the shareholders have no legal entitlement to any return on their investment in shares. Rather, they have rights to what is left (it may be nothing!) each year after all the other claims (debts, costs and taxes) have been met. If there are any residual amounts left, the directors can decide to keep them in the business as reserves (retained profits) or divide them up amongst the shareholders in the form of dividends.

 Shareholders have no rights to take their money out of the business. What they can do, is sell their shares to others - one purpose for listing a company on a stock market.

 Share certificates are issued with a nominal or face value (sometimes referred to as the Par value). For example, they may be given a face value of £1 of equity share capital.

 Shares have no fixed value, they are only worth what others will pay for them. This could be a lot or it could be a little.

 Therefore, equity capital is risky. Shareholders are not guaranteed a dividend, nor are they guaranteed any particular value for their shareholdings.

We will deal with more complex forms of shares (preference shares and convertibles) in the next chapter. Given the above characteristics of ordinary share capital, it should be apparent that its valuation is far from straightforward; essentially future dividend payments and capital gains are unknown and have to be forecast and given the uncertainty involved, it is not at all clear how these future gains or losses should be evaluated.

Debt (loan capital)

Debt or loan capital is the other source of external funds that a business can access. Its basic features are:

 There is a date when the loan capital is due to be paid back. The loan is re-payable at its original money value - irrespective of the cashflow performance of the business.

 The repayment of the loan by the end of its term is a legal charge on the company. If the company is unable to meet this, the lender is entitled to put a receiver into the company and if needs be, force the sale of the assets or securities of the business.

 Similarly, the interest is a legal charge which has to be paid when it is due.

A further form of debt finance is corporate bonds. Unlike bank loans which are not tradeable, corporate bonds (debt securities) are tradeable or negotiable. The same company can issue a variety of different types of bonds, in which case there is a rank order of repayment should it become insolvent (the term bankrupt applies to individuals, not companies). Debentures are repaid first, then secured loan stocks and, finally, unsecured loan stocks. The inherent features of debt finance make it a riskier source of funds for a business. Given this, shareholders should take note of the mixture of debt and equity used to fund a business.

NUTSHELL

A **secured** loan is backed by the assets of a business. If the business defaults on the loan, the provider of the loan has a claim over the assets of the business.

Retained Profits (Reserves)

The third source of funds available to a company is the profits retained in the business. These retained profits are equivalent to additional equity capital and they share the same essential characteristics. The one potential benefit to companies of retained profits, however, is that they can be used for internal purposes without the need to go to outside providers of funds.

One final point to bear in mind is that while it is good financial practice to match the maturity (i.e. short, medium and long term) and the nature (i.e. risk and flexibility) of funds to the types of activity - for example, bank overdrafts should not be used for long term investments in fixed assets such as plant and machinery - the only logical connection between the sources and uses of funds is that they must be equal. This simple point is worth bearing in mind when analysing companies: if a company has undertaken a set of activities, where have the funds come from? Such a thought might have provided insights into Polly Peck and the Maxwell companies.

STOCK MARKETS

Although the previous chapters have reviewed the history of the UK stock market, the purpose of this and the next section is to consider some of the detailed mechanics of the stock market.

When you buy a share, it gives you rights to the residual performance (after all the other charges, interest on loans, paying the tax man, etc., have been met) of the company for as long as you hold the share. This being the case, the better the expected future performance of a company, the higher should be its current share price. If the stock market is efficient, which means that information flows concerning the future performance of companies are dispersed and quickly impounded into investors' assessments and actions, then the current share price of a company should reflect its future performance and there would be little in the way of excess returns to be made. As described in the previous chapter, however, share prices do diverge from underlying fundamental performance values and there are a number of famous instances to illustrate this point such as Tulipmania and the South Sea Bubble. In other words, the price movements of stock markets may be as much a reflection of the beliefs and actions of investors as the performance of companies.

One aspect of the famous instances of share prices diverging markedly from underlying fundamental values is the colourful expressions used as descriptions. Such words as Tulipmania, bubble, panic and crash immediately evoke images of frenzied and irrational buying and selling behaviour.

ORIGINS

The Netherlands became a centre of the cultivation and development of new tulip varieties after the tulip's entry into Europe from Turkey in the mid 1500s. Professional growers and wealthy flower fanciers created a market for rare varieties in which bulbs sold at high prices. By 1636, the rapid price rises attracted speculators and prices of many varieties surged upward from November 1636 to January 1637. In February 1637, prices suddenly collapsed and bulbs could not be sold at even 10% of their peak values.

Examples such as Tulipmania indicate that market prices need not reflect underlying fundamental values but rather may be driven by the price speculation of market participants. Why is this important? Well, if market prices are driven by fundamental values then there should be a degree of stability in price movements. Consider classic cars. For many years, classic cars were the domain of enthusiasts who appreciated the fine detail and craftsmanship of a bygone era. They enjoyed tinkering with their beloved machines and taking their pride and joy to classic car rallies to share their appreciation with others of a like mind. In this market, prices were driven by the fundamental values that enthusiasts placed upon the various types of cars. Naturally, the old Jaguars had higher prices than the old Fords. The prices were determined by the perceived intrinsic values of the cars and not by the notion that money could be made. In other words, the cars were bought for themselves and not as an investment that would make a 'fast buck'. Then suddenly, everything changed. Classic cars became seen as a means of making quick money. People started buying them, not because they appreciated the finer points of engineering, but because they thought prices would keep on rising and they could make a quick and easy profit. The market of car enthusiasts was suddenly swamped by price speculators. Now the problem with the speculators was that they cared not a jot about the real underlying value of the cars, but only the money they could make. This lack of a firm anchor in fundamental values allowed prices in the speculative market to quickly spiral upwards. 'Current' price rises were seen as signalling future price rises and as the money piled in to reflect such expectations, the expectations became self-fulfilling - classic cars were indeed an easy way to make money.

However, such upward speculative spirals do not go on forever. There comes a point when the prices are so far adrift from fundamental values that individuals start to wonder whether prices can keep on rising. There only needs to be some doubt in the minds of potential speculators for the bubble to burst. As soon as such doubts cause sufficient hesitation in the mind of speculators, prices will not rise as previously and the doubts now become self-fulfilling. Of course, once prices stop rising, there is always the worry that prices may fall and it is at this point that speculators will want to take their profits by selling their investment in a classic car. Suddenly, there is a glut of classic cars on the market as speculators rush to beat the expected price declines - not surprisingly, prices spiral downwards. In fact, they will spiral downwards to the point where the enthusiasts think they are worth buying - yes, they should eventually settle on prices which reflect underlying fundamental values. You may be wondering why we have described the market for classic cars. Well, stock markets are a mixture of the same basic forces but it is easier to think of the intrinsic values of classic cars than it is for shares.

Moving on to consider shares, there are investors who try to invest on the basis of the perceived fundamental values (the potential profit generation) of companies and there are investors who speculate on share price movements. The movement of individual share prices and the movement of the overall market reflect varying combinations of fundamental and speculative investment. In making sense of overall stock market price movements, you have to decide whether they reflect changes in fundamentals or speculation. If it is the latter, you will also need to consider exactly where on the speculative cycle the market might be.

Let's consider the UK stock market during the first half of 1998. The market broke two records. First, the FTSE 100 index hit its highest level ever and second, the total market value exceeded £1 trillion. With such records being broken, a number of newspaper articles started to sound alarm bells. Investors were seen as getting itchy feet, 'all good things must come to an end' statements were being made. Questions concerning the timing of the downturn were being asked. In trying to answer such a question, there was no shortage of analysis of the factors that had given rise to the boom and whether they could continue. The price rises were seen as reflecting the potential for mergers and take-overs, especially within the banking and telecommunication sectors. However, no such take-overs had taken place during the first half of 1998 and shares in banks had been rising purely on the back of expectation. The institutional investors were being blamed for 'merger mania' and this was seen as a factor causing the boom in

CLOSE-UP

E-Type Jaguars were priced at £6,000 to £15,000 in the early 1980s. At the peak of the classic car boom, the mid to late 80s, they had spiralled from £50,000 to £60,000.

prices. How long such expectations would last was a question at the back of every shareholder's mind.

A second factor was straight forward supply and demand. Demand was seen as increasing through people putting more money into unit and investment trusts and through increased saving via pension funds. More money was chasing a fixed number of shares. Some analysts were arguing that this factor may indeed keep the market moving upwards. Pension funds had been keeping cash back and this is a situation that might not be sustainable. There are predictions of further pension fund injections into the market. Bill Mott, head of UK equities at Credit Suisse, has said,

"There will be a meteoric boom. I think the market could hit 7,000 this year (the market was just above 5,000 at the start of 1998), so investors should definitely not sell out."

A further factor seen as pushing the market upwards is the general health of the economy. Interest rates are not overly high and may indeed fall, and inflation is under control.

Against the positive fundamental factors of demand out-stripping supply and a fairly healthy economy, there is the potential for the 'army of private investors' created by the demutualisation of building societies to judge the market as having 'topped out' and it being the appropriate time to sell. In other words, has the boom reached a point where there is rising doubt within the minds of both private and institutional investors that it is not sustainable? Will negative expectations dominate positive expectations and the sound fundamentals of the economy? Is the stock market now a money bubble and is it about to burst? Sadly, it is the nature of stock markets that such questions cannot be answered unequivocally. The markets are characterised by risk and every investor has to make judgements when to invest and when to dis-invest. It is the purpose of this book to help you make such judgements on as solid a foundation of knowledge as possible.

So far, we have talked about stock markets in general terms and I expect most of us have in mind the main market (also known as the official list). This is the market where the likes of BP, Halifax and Tesco are to be found. It is generally a market of well established, well known and reasonably large companies. A feature of the main market is that there is no shortage of information on which to make a judgement concerning individual shares.

There are more 'junior markets' where the companies are usually considerably smaller and younger than those on the senior or main market. The best known, and the one you may consider, is the Alternative Investment Market (AIM). AIM was established to make it easy for small, young and growing companies to raise external finance. With this in mind, the AIM rules place no restrictions on market capitalisation, length of operating record or percentage of shares in public hands. In contrast, the official list normally requires a company to have published accounts for at least three years prior to its listing. There are also other requirements such as the continuity of management over the period covered by the accounts and that the management have collectively appropriate experience.

Instead, AIM operates on the principle of disclosure, allowing investors to choose whether to put up money based on the careful analysis of the merits of companies, having made allowance for the higher risk associated with AIM companies. AIM's objective of providing a market accessible to a wide range of companies is reflected in the list of sectors represented. These range from hi-tech and biotech, to leisure, right through to the more traditional engineering sectors. The market value of companies varies from under £2 million to over £200 million, although the majority of companies fall between the £5 million to £30 million range. It is important to note that companies from a range of backgrounds have joined AIM. In particular, an increasing number of owner-managed or family-run businesses have chosen AIM because it enables them to obtain new funding to grow the company without having to lose control. Most owners release between 20% and 30% of their shares, allowing them to remain in charge and create a sufficient market to attract investor interest. The amount of money raised by a company can vary widely and depends on the objectives of the company and its attractiveness to investors. Typically, fund-raising falls in the £2 million to £10 million range although a few companies have used the market to raise sums of less than £1 million. At the other end of the scale, the largest amount raised so far has been £54 million by Prism Rail. Against

ORIGINS

Launched in June 1995 as a replacement for the Unlisted Securities Market (USM), **AIM** has established itself as the market of choice for small and fast-growing companies. More than 300 companies now have their shares traded on the market giving it a total value in excess of £5.7 billion. More importantly, as a measure of the appeal of the market to outside investors, it has raised £1.6 billion from external investors.

this positive background, AIM has had its share of detractors who have questioned the quality of some of the businesses coming to the market and the number of profit warnings. There have also been questions regarding the motives behind some of the AIM flotations. None the less, once you are aware of the risks involved, investing in AIM companies can provide a good return.

MARKET INDICES AND SECTORS

While the previous chapters used the FT30 and FTSE 100 indices to analyse the history of the UK stock market, this section details these and the other major indices on offer.

In understanding the available stock market indices, we need to consider what an index actually is. Well, an index is a summary measure of what is happening to a group of similar entities (share prices, mortality, unemployment, etc.). So the FTSE 100 index tells you what is happening to the share prices of the top 100 companies listed on the London Stock Exchange.

NUTSHELL

Indices tell you about average performance and, therefore, provide a benchmark to assess the performance of individual shares.

FT 30

The oldest ordinary share index, the FT 30, was established in 1935 by the *Financial Times*. It covers the share prices of 30 of the largest companies in the UK in industry and services. Like all indices, the FT 30 began from a base number. So the number you see in the financial pages is not an average of actual share prices. Unlike the other indices discussed below, the FT 30 has no clear rules about which companies qualify to be included. None the less, this index allows investors and academics to judge the long term performance of the UK stock market.

FTSE 100

It was started in 1984 and gives investors an up-to-the-minute picture of stock market performance at any time of the day. It is a real time index of the 100 biggest (in terms of their overall share value; also known as market capitalisation) companies listed on the stock exchange. The FTSE 100 is a weighted average mean index so that the influence of each share is weighted according to the market capitalisation of the company. So a 20% rise in the share price of a £6 billion company has twice the impact on the index as the same rise in the share price of a £3 billion company. The FTSE 100 began at a base of 1000 in January 1984 and was hovering around a level of 6000 during the second quarter of 1998.

> **NUTSHELL**
>
> **Market capitalisation** is calculated by multiplying the number of shares in issue by the current share price.

FTSE A All Share Index

Started in 1962, it is the main measure of investment performance. It is calculated just once a day and fund managers generally use it as a benchmark of their own performance. Its title is, however, somewhat misleading. It actually only includes about 900 of the 2,000+ shares traded on the stock exchange. However, in terms of share value (market capitalisation), the All Share captures over 95% of the market and it covers more than 99% of the total volume of shares traded.

Between the FTSE 100 and the All Share there are a range of other indices, each representing a different group of shares.

FTSE 250

This covers the next 250 biggest companies after the FTSE 100. Its bottom size limit is £250 million and its upper limit is £1.5 billion.

FTSE Actuaries 350

Combines the FTSE 100 and the 250 and is a real time index of large and medium sized companies designed to mirror the All-Share sector figures.

FTSE SmallCap

This covers smaller companies (about 550) with market capitalisations of between £40 million and £250 million. The SmallCap index is calculated at the end of each day.

There are also a range of more specialist indices produced by the *Financial Times*; for example, the FTSE Gold Mines Index. The best way to become accustomed to the various indices, is to spend some time browsing through a *Financial Times*. To show what can be gained from such information, we graph just two of these indices below.

FIGURE 3.1

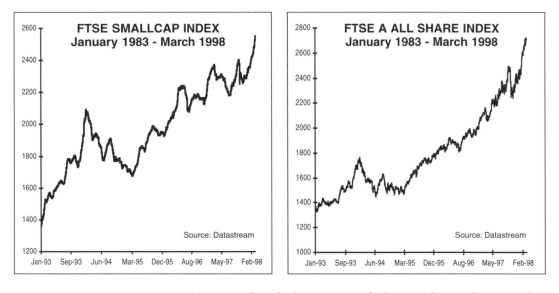

A more detailed picture of the stock market can be gained from considering individual sectors. The *Financial Times*, the Stock Exchange and the Institute of Actuaries combine to produce an index for each of the 36 sectors of the stock market. To make it easier for investors, companies with similar business interests are grouped together, for example, Sainsbury and Safeway are both to be found in the Food Retailing Sector. Although grouping companies with similar business interests together in a sector makes comparisons easier, it is important not to over use such comparisons. While companies in the same sectors normally have a lot in common, this isn't always the case. Some sectors are more diverse than others and include companies with a wide range of interests. For example, what do recruitment agencies, dry cleaners, computer service companies all have in common? Well, they are all listed in the 'support services' sector. Interestingly, IT firms do not have a whole sector of their own, despite their growing importance in modern economies (consider the enormity of the Year 2000 problem and the work involved with EMU). Somewhat surprisingly the total market capitalisation of IT companies on the London Stock Exchange represented less than 1% of the FTSE All Share Index towards the end of 1997. It normally requires 1% or more of total market capitalisation for a new sector to be created. In fact, keeping an eye on the overall composition of sectors can be an instructive process. For example, prior to the mid 1990s, companies such as SmithKline Beecham and Glaxo were listed in the 'Health and Household' sector along with firms that made fabric dyes and baby products. However, the rising importance of pharmaceutical companies led to a separate sector in January 1994. While pharmaceutical companies have been removed from the 'Health and Household' sector, clothes manufacturers such as Claremont have been added. In general, watching the moving make-up of sectors might give an insight into profitable longer term trends.

Finally, although companies are grouped by sectors (the business from which a company derives more than 50% of its profits) in the *Financial Times*, there are other interesting groupings that an investor may want to consider. Some shares can be classified in terms of how they move in relation to the economic cycle. Food retail share prices tend to be quite resistant to economic downturns (people still need to buy food) and not surprisingly, such shares are known as 'defensive' shares. Included in share portfolios, they help to defend against potential downturns. In contrast, 'cyclical' shares tend to follow the economic cycle; companies in the building and construction industries are good examples of this type of share. Further types of grouping might be by the size of the company (this is, of course, captured partially by the various indices discussed above) or by the age of company (this is reflected to a minor degree by the difference in age between the well established firms on the senior market and the frequently younger firms on the AIM). Essentially, you pick your focus and choose your markets, sectors and indices accordingly.

NEW ISSUES OR INITIAL PUBLIC OFFERINGS

Given that we have now covered the broad environment of shares, it is time to start considering the life-cycle of a share. As for any life-cycle the obvious place to start is with the birth of a share. As we discussed earlier, shares are born when a limited company is formed and as few as two £1 shares may be issued at this point. This initial formation of companies is normally of little interest to the wider share buying public because the shares are usually retained in a small number of private hands. Of far more interest is when a company is brought to a stock market for listing. It is this process of the birth of a listed company that is the focus of this section.

There is little doubt that money can be made from investing in new issues. However, before we look at the mechanics of a 'new-listing' investment strategy, there is a need to understand the various ways by which a company can gain a stock market listing.

Offer For Sale

This is the only general form of new listing method that gives the private investor a decent chance of obtaining shares. With this approach, a set number of shares at a set price per share are offered to both private and institutional investors. You will be familiar with this method because it has been used for the privatisation issues of the public utilities. If the shares are undersubscribed then the surplus is normally taken up by an underwriting merchant bank. On the other hand, if an issue is oversubscribed, then you may not get all the shares you applied for.

Offers For Subscription

This method, often used by investment trusts and very similar to the offer for sale method, has one important difference. Here, if the level of subscriptions does not meet a pre-specified level, then the sale does not go ahead - an important insurance policy when launching an investment trust!

Tender Offers

A further variant on the offer for sale method is where subscribers state the number of shares they would like to buy and at what price. Once the tender is closed, a 'strike price' is determined on the basis of the tender bids received. Those subscribers who tendered at a higher price than the 'strike price' will receive an allocation of shares; although the allocation received by an individual investor may not equal the number of shares requested.

Placings

In contrast to the variants on the 'offer for sale' method, which give private investors a chance to get in on the action, placings are usually directed at institutional investors. The listing company places its shares in the hands of institutional investors and the private investor is only able to buy the shares once they start to be traded on the market, which, as we will see, may be too late to make any short term gains. Occasionally, a company will place its shares with a financial intermediary and private investors may be offered the opportunity to buy the shares before they start to be traded. Sadly, for the private investor, placings are a cheaper route for floating a company than an 'offer' method. Not surprisingly, therefore, more companies are choosing this route to a stock market listing.

Introductions

This happens when a company already has a lot of shareholders and it simply wants to list itself on the stock market. If the stock exchange requirements are met by the company, it lists its existing shareholders and there is no opportunity for new shareholders to buy into the company.

Now that you understand the various methods for listing a company on the stock exchange, how should you go about deciding whether to buy into a new share issue? Well, the obvious place to start is the company's prospectus. Although not usually the most exciting of documents, it should contain information to answer the following types of questions.

 What does the company intend to do with the money raised?

 What proportion of the shareholding is to be retained by the original entrepreneurs?

 Who are the advising agents (accountants, investment bank, etc.) and what do they have to say?

 What is the business of the company and what is its financial history?

 And, most importantly, what are the company's trading prospects and its forecast financial position?

A prospectus should contain both a financial summary of the company (revenues, profits, etc.) and investment statistics - dividend yield, price-earnings ratio and the stock market value of the company. These summaries should be underpinned by more detailed tables of the financials of the company and in-depth discussion of its business prospects. Equally important, the prospectus should give details on who will run the company and their own stake in the business. Similarly, there should be a discussion of the funding structure of the business. Remember, however, that a prospectus has its limitations. It is bound to show business and investment opportunities in the most optimistic light allowed within the rules of the Stock Exchange. Have you ever come across a pessimistic marketing campaign apart from Reggie Perrin's campaign for 'Grot'?

So you like the look of a new listing from its prospectus and you have decided to buy some of the shares, assuming you are permitted to do so. What can you expect?

First, don't assume you will get all the shares you have applied for: the more interesting issues are often oversubscribed. Second, don't assume you will make a quick profit. Although the privatisation issues have been markedly underpriced and private investors could have made exceptional early gains, this does not always apply to the new issues that private investors can get their hands on. However, it is true that new issues are generally underpriced.[1] There are lots of potential reasons for this being the case. For example, to make sure the issue is an early success, for underwriters to avoid bearing the costs of undersubscription or as a reward for the potential uncertainty of the investment. The evidence also suggests, however, that the gains from underpricing are short-lived (normally a matter of the first day) and that the longer term (up to 1 year) performance of new issues is less than that of the established market.

Although the evidence varies around the globe, it is not difficult to achieve an average first day rise of between 10 and 15% and the following rules offer the best way forward for the private investor:

 If you can buy the issue before trading begins, sell your shares during the first day of trading.

 If you can only buy the share from the market after trading has begun, be prepared to hold the shares for quite a long period, if losses are to be avoided.

 Minimise the investment risk by doing your homework on new issues - successful investing really requires stock selection. Check the prospects!

Information regarding new issues and their short term performance can be found in the *Financial Times* and the *Investors Chronicle*. Don't be fooled by the success of the privatisation issues. Prospecting for gold in new issues is hard work!

THE DIVIDEND DECISION

NUTSHELL

A **dividend** is the amount of a company's profit distributed to ordinary shareholders. It is expressed as either a percentage of the nominal value of a share (that is the face value of a share, say £1, rather than its market price), or more commonly as an absolute amount per share.

After you have bought a share in a company, the next 'event' you are likely to be faced with is the dividend decision of the company. The amount of the dividend is decided by the board of directors depending upon the profitability of the business and the need to retain earnings to fund future projects and so on. However, even where present profitability is poor, directors may decide to maintain dividend payouts at previous levels because the prospects of the business look good. In fact, it is not unknown for businesses to fund dividends out of reserves. This may reflect the belief of the directors in the strength of future business prospects or it may be a mechanism to defend the share price. From their own perspective of avoiding a take-over, it is always in the interest of directors to maintain the share price of their business. Given the large amount of academic evidence which supports the view that the stock market reacts negatively to the announcement of a dividend cut, it is not surprising that directors are keen to maintain levels of dividend payout.[2]

Where dividends are paid out of profits, and this should normally be the case, corporation tax will already have been deducted, as will payments to holders of preference shares and debentures. Furthermore, dividends are paid to shareholders after deduction of income tax at the lower rate. Larger companies may pay dividends bi-annually (or even quarterly) and these are known as interim dividends, with the last dividend declared in the financial year being known as the final dividend. If you buy a share **cum-dividend**, then you are entitled to receive the next dividend when it is due. If the share is **ex-dividend**, then you do not have rights to the next dividend; it belongs to the seller of the share. One further aspect of dividends is that they can be paid via the issue of further shares (the idea of scrip dividends) rather than as cash. This has the advantage to the company of retaining cash in the business but it has the disadvantage of being more expensive in terms of administration costs. The important issue with regard to scrip dividends is their effect on the existing share price; the issue of further shares may well have a negative impact!

Now that we have defined what is meant by the payment of a dividend, we need to cover a bit more financial terminology in relation to dividends.

Dividend Yield

You will often see this term used in the financial press. It is defined as:

$$\frac{\text{full-year dividend per share} \times 100}{\text{price per share}}$$

This is a measure of the annual percentage return a shareholder receives from dividends, based on the current share price. It is **not** the total actual return earned by a shareholder for a company because it ignores any annual capital gains or losses from holding the shares. It is also based on the current share price which need not be the price the shareholder paid for the share. Furthermore, the *Financial Times* quotes the dividend yield in gross terms (before tax) and what this means for the cash actually received by an individual (that is after tax) will depend upon his or her tax rate.

Dividend Cover

This is the number of times by which available profits after tax cover the dividend payment. It is defined as:

$$\frac{\text{total profits available for ordinary shareholders}}{\text{dividends paid to ordinary shareholders}}$$

In one sense, it is a measure of the 'risk' involved with investing in a particular share. This is because it indicates how far earnings could fall before dividends need to be cut.

Now that we have covered some of the basic terminology of dividends, it is time to consider how they should be interpreted. We mentioned above that directors may maintain dividend payout rates because of the potential negative consequences for share prices of reducing dividends. We also stated that such actions on the part of directors have substantial empirical support - share prices do react adversely to a reduction in dividend payouts. This, however, takes us straight to the heart of the dividend controversy that has dogged academic finance since the early 1960s. Miller and Modigliani made the extremely elegant observation that in a world characterised by high information flows and where there is an absence of tax effects and transactional costs, value comes from the use of assets, not how they are funded.[3] In other words, share prices should reflect the future profitability of a business and this comes from the use of the assets, not how the assets have been funded. Essentially, the dividend policy of a company should not affect its share price, but the empirical evidence indicates that share prices do indeed react! How can we explain this divergence between theory and evidence? There are at least three sets of theories which explain why dividend policies may indeed be important.

The Traditional View

This argues for high dividend payout ratios. According to this perspective, shareholders prefer immediate dividends over less certain and more distant capital gains, which should happen if the cash was reinvested in the business instead of being paid out as dividends.

Tax Differential View

NUTSHELL

Individual investors have an annual **capital gains tax allowance** of £6,800 in the tax year ending 5 April 1999.

A second theory reaches the opposite conclusion. It argues that shareholders prefer capital gains over dividends, because most people will have an unused capital gains allowance. Thus although capital gains and dividends attract the same marginal tax rate, dividend income will be taxed because any personal allowance will usually have been used up; whereas most people do not use up their capital gains allowance. Furthermore, it is easier to manage the use of capital gains as it is the investor who decides when to sell his or her shares; whereas, dividend payments are under the control of the company.

Signalling View

Finally, this perspective sees dividends as important because they signal to investors changes in management's expectations about the company's future earnings; in theory, management will only be willing to increase dividends if they are confident about the future prospects of the business.

Of course, the dividend policy of an individual company may be the result of it trying to balance the competing forces described in all three of the perspectives outlined above. If this is the case, then it will be difficult to offer a precise interpretation of any given dividend policy. Perhaps, the best that can be concluded is that companies take dividends seriously and so does the market. Watch out for any impending reductions!

RIGHTS ISSUES

A rights issue is an issue of new shares which existing shareholders have a right to buy - in fact, they have first refusal. Normally, ordinary shares are offered but sometimes **convertible preference shares** and the like may be made available. The number of new shares offered and their price will be determined by how much the company wants to raise. The price will normally be lower than the market price of the existing shares but this does not mean that they are a bargain. For example, in a 3:1 rights issue, every existing shareholder has the right to buy 3 new shares for every existing share he or she holds. Clearly, with this size of rights issue, there is going to be a significant dilution of the value of each individual share. In fact, if the money raised adds no value to the profitability of the business, the value of your new shareholding, assuming no stock market sentiment or reaction, should only change by the amount of money paid over for the new shares. Of course, the stock market does react and the value of the new shareholding may well be different from that of the old shareholding plus the money paid for the new shares. It will depend on how the market thinks the extra money raised by the company will be put to use. Before we go on to consider the evidence, we need to describe briefly some of the basic mechanics behind their issue and how they might be interpreted.

As a shareholder of a company with a rights issue, you will receive notification of the offer being made. At this point, there are several ways forward:

You may decide to take up the issue. You simply send off your money and you increase the number of shares you hold without paying commission or stamp duty.

 You may decide that you don't want to take up the issue - you can ask your broker to sell your rights. The value of 'nil-paid' rights depends on the after rights issue price of the shares and the rights issue price (the amount they are being offered at) of the shares.

 If you decide not to take up the issue or sell your rights, the company will eventually sell your rights for you and send you the money. The problem with this approach, is that the company may sell a lot of unused rights in a block and this may have a negative impact on the market price. On the up-side, however, is the fact that they may achieve very favourable brokerage costs.

CLOSE-UP

Forthcoming rights issues are published in Saturday's *Financial Times*. A date is set when the issue goes ex-rights (designated **xr** in the share service table) and after this date the buyer does not receive rights.

Now that we understand some of the options on offer with regards to rights issues, how should they be interpreted? In considering this, you need to ask yourself a couple of questions.

? Why is the company wanting to raise more money? Here are a few possibilities. One of the most common reasons is to fund the acquisition of a company. You need to consider how the acquisition fits the strategy of the company. Is it paying a reasonable price and how is the stock market likely to react to the acquisition? A second reason is to bail the company out of its present difficulties. In this type of situation you need to look at the recent performance of the company and its likely future performance. This is similar to being asked to fund recovery. Basically, you have to ask yourself whether anything has changed with the company or market to suggest that the new monies will be any better used than the previous ones.

? In line with the previous question, you need to consider whether the money will make any difference. Is sufficient being raised to overcome previous difficulties and move the company onto fresh pastures?

The above questions are concerned with the fundamental soundness of the business and this is important if you intend to hold the shares for the long term. If they are being held for the short term, you will be more concerned with the market reaction to rights issues. Here, there is an absence of convincing evidence either way. As the price of the new shares being issued is normally lower than the market price of the existing shares, the share price of a company should fall, all other things being equal, after a rights issue and this is usually the case. What we are unable to tell is whether the price reduction is warranted given the prospects of the company. This is a situation where you will have to make your own judgement.

Before moving on, we need to consider briefly stock splits. The idea behind a stock split is that it makes the shares more marketable. People seem to prefer holding twenty £1 shares than one £20 share and it is easy to understand why; it gives greater flexibility as to how they might buy and sell their holding. In contrast to rights issues, there is a fair amount of empirical evidence regarding the reaction of the market to stock splits. They seem to occur after there has been an increase in share price and there is a further price rise after the announcement of the split. This positive price effect may well reflect the fact that stock splits are associated with an increase in dividends. In other words, stock splits are good news (at least in the short term) for the investor. Sadly, there is an absence of evidence concerning whether they can be predicted.

> **NUTSHELL**
>
> A **stock split** increases the number of shares in a company but without raising any new funds; in this sense they are like scrip dividends. The procedure is relatively straightforward. For example, if shareholders currently hold £1 shares, the company may suggest that each £1 share is replaced with two 50 pence shares.

IS SIZE IMPORTANT?

Although this is not really an event but more of a process, it is important to consider whether the performance of a share is related to the size of a company. This is equivalent to asking whether the performance of blue chip stocks is better or worse than small companies? It was commonly accepted in the 1980s that small firms outperformed their larger brethren in terms of the stock market. The picture is now not so clear. Let us consider the two camps on this topic.

> **ORIGINS**
>
> The term 'blue chip' refers to shares in well established, large companies. The name derives from the highest value chip in poker.

The Big Firm Camp

The evidence of the 1990s suggests that larger firms have outperformed smaller firms. This raises two interesting questions. First, why has the small firm effect of the 1980s and before gone into reverse in the 1990s and second, is the reversal likely to continue? In answering these questions, we can turn to the work of Dimson and Marsh of the London Business School.[4] Their work suggests that before the 1990s the real dividend growth of small firms was almost twice that of large firms. Not surprisingly, investors were attracted to such firms and prices were accordingly pushed up. Since that start of the 90s, however, the real rate of growth in dividends of small firms has only been a quarter of that achieved by large firms. What are the reasons behind this reversal of fortunes? Those sufficiently long in the tooth will well remember the gross inefficiencies of the large corporates in the 60s and 70s. More recently, large firms have downsized, cut costs and focused on being both effective and efficient. Furthermore, there is a greater weighting of large listed firms in those sectors that performed well in the 90s, such as pharmaceuticals and financial services.

The Small Firm Camp

During 1998, a number of advisors have stated that small firms will come back into vogue - it is just a question of when. The basis of this belief in small firms comes from a number of arguments. First, it is easier for small companies to achieve a given growth rate because of their small scale starting position. Due to market limitations, it is more difficult for ICI to achieve a given growth rate than 'xyz Small' chemical company - elephants don't gallop. Second, in contrast to the above, small firms are seen as populating the high growth and high technology sectors. Third, just a minor change in fund management attitudes would lead to a massive injection of cash into the small firm sector. Fourth, there is an indication that the larger firms are looking for a part of their growth from acquiring promising small firms in their sector. Similarly, there is a lot of venture capital money sloshing around Europe and it will not be too long before small listed firms become targets.

The above has outlined the perspectives of both camps and it is up to you to make your choice. Assuming you have decided to go with the small firm camp, what sort of investment model should you follow? Well, the first thing to note is that small firms can go disastrously wrong very quickly and it is critical to be aware of the background to the company. With this in mind, let's now look at one approach to investing in smaller companies.

We have already said it is important to understand and evaluate the potential of a small company and this forms the basis of the approach. Essentially, it is a 'value' investing approach to buying small company shares. It selects shares that look to be relatively 'undervalued' to their real longer term potential. The approach, therefore, requires careful analysis of the company and patience in holding the shares once they have been bought. Against this background of solid business and company analysis are there benchmarks that could be usefully followed? Some advisors have proposed the 'double seven' method of small company investing. This involves investing in companies with a PE ratio of around 7 (or below) and a dividend yield of 7% (or above). A PE of 7 should leave quite a lot of room for appreciation through sound management. Whereas a dividend yield of 7% (or above) is valuable in itself and it also provides a support to the share price. John Lee of the *Financial Times* published an article in 1997 that highlighted Black Arrow, the office furniture supplier, as a good solid investment. It had a high dividend yield, it was cash rich, it had a low PE and good solid management. It was indeed a good investment, almost doubling its share price across 1997/early 1998!

The above has highlighted some financial indicators (low PE, high dividend yield and even the idea of being cash rich) but it has also mentioned the idea of solid management. It is the quality of management that will deliver the eventual value that you are looking for. Are there any indicators that can help in assessing or even warning about the quality of the management? The first thing to note for small firms is that they are quite likely to still be managed by the original entrepreneur and/or his family. In this situation, the businesses are likely to be competently run and this will often continue under the management of the next generation. Beyond the second

> **NUTSHELL**
>
> The **price/earnings** (PE) **ratio** is the quoted price of an ordinary share divided by the most recent year's earnings per share. Earnings per share are defined as the profits that are potentially distributable to shareholders, divided by the number of issued shares.

generation, you need to be a bit more careful - there is evidence of companies faltering once they pass through the third generation of the family; as the saying goes, 'clogs to clogs in three generations'. There is also a need to be careful when a management team is 'imported' with large company experience. They often seem to lack the skills and understanding needed to run smaller concerns. Essentially smaller firms (in terms of their cultures, lack of systems, etc.) are different from large firms and they need management who understand their specific requirements. Sadly, it often is not overly easy for the private investor to gain a handle on a company's management. Usually the only decent information is contained in the flotation prospectus and you need to check the performance of the team since then and what changes there may have been in the management team. It is also worth checking (as mentioned earlier) that the management team itself has a good number of shares in the company. A strongly committed and well incentivized management team is not a bad starting point!

MERGERS, TAKE–OVERS AND DE–MERGERS

The stock market has periods when mergers and take-overs seem to be the fashion of the day. We have been going through such an episode in the mid to late 90s. The question for the private investor is whether mergers and take-overs benefit them in the short and long-run and whether they can be predicted. Although mergers and take-overs are not identical activities, the evidence to date has tended to use the terms interchangeably.

In terms of short term gains, the evidence is unequivocal - a large amount of academic evidence for both the US and UK indicates that shareholders in target firms earn sizeable positive returns during take-over announcements. In regard to pure mergers, shareholders from both firms tend to do well.

Jarrell et al provide insights into the size of the returns from takeover for the US market.[5] For completed take-overs, the shareholders of target companies gained 19% during the 1960s; 35% in the 1970s, and 30% in the 1980s. Bradley et al report similar results for the periods 1963 to 1968 and 1981 to 1985.[6] The gains to target shareholders are replicated in the UK studies. Franks et al[7] report abnormal returns of 26% and Firth[8] reports gains of 29% in the announcement month itself. In other words, shareholders in take-over target firms earn substantial short term gains.

These gains, however, do not appear to be sustained in the long run. In a survey of six US studies, Jensen and Ruback find systematic declines in bidder share price of approximately 5.5% in the year following the take-over.[9] This finding has been supported by a number of other US studies. In contrast, Franks et al fail to find evidence of negative performance.[10]

Although the debate on post take-over performance is equivocal in its conclusions, on balance the evidence suggests that the high positive returns to target shareholders around the time of announcement are reversed in the year following the take-over or merger for the shareholders of the combined enterprise.

The above suggests, therefore, that it is best to take short term gains from mergers and take-overs and move on to other ventures. There are a number of reasons why post merger/take-over performance may not live up to the expectations at the time of the announcement.

 The cultures (in all their many dimensions) of the two organisations may be such that any real integration is impossible.

 Even if real integration is achievable in the long term, there are bound to be some fairly hefty short term (1-2 years) adjustment costs.

 Ignoring the difficulties of merging organisational cultures, there is always the technical problem of merging IT systems, business processes and so on.

 Even if all the above can be overcome, one should never forget the problem of trying to meld a senior team out of two sets of corporate egos. Evidence suggests that up to 50% of the target firm's management in a take-over may be replaced within two years of the take-over.

The evidence suggests that take-overs are good for target firm shareholders in the short term and mergers are good for both sets of shareholders in the short term. This raises the question whether they can be predicted. To date, there has been little work on the prediction of mergers but there have been efforts to establish the characteristics of take-over targets.

Here is a check list of signals to watch out for:

 The company's earnings record is generally worse than those of its immediate competitors.

 There is a loss of confidence in the management's ability to generate profits and the share price falls substantially.

 The management has been forced to cut its dividend payments.

 The company has a low market value compared to the book value of its assets. This means that assets can be bought cheaply and this provides some security for the bidding firm.

 The firm has reasonable gearing (debt). Bidding firms do not tend to like to take on firms with 'messy', complicated and expensive funding structures.

The above is not a complete set of potential signals of a take-over target but they seem to be the most robust. Finally, don't forget that some sectors go through merger or take-over booms as companies seek to gain the economies of scale they supposedly need to compete in their respective marketplace. At the moment this is the argument underpinning merger and take-over talks in the pharmaceutical and financial services industries.

Before moving on to the next section, we should touch on the issue of de-merger. Given the longer term problems, mentioned above, associated with bringing organisations together, it is not surprising that some decide eventually to de-merge. The 1980s and 1990s have been decades when a number of businesses have tried to get back to their core business. The key question for the investor is how the share price performs after such activities. From the de-mergers at BAT, Racal, Courtaulds and ICI, it is clear that de-merger is good for shareholders, at least in the short term. There seems to be a 'de-merger' honeymoon period of up to almost a year - some last longer, as was the case for the de-merger of Courtaulds Textiles from Courtaulds in the early 1990s, which lasted almost two years. Overall, the conclusion is simple. De-mergers offer opportunities to make a profit, especially if action is taken as soon as the de-merger becomes known. If you are already a shareholder of a company that is going to de-merge, enjoy the profits but keep a close eye on the share prices of the two organisations. Don't be lulled into a false sense of security, as your price gains could soon go into reverse.

COMPANY FAILURE AND SHARE SUSPENSION

The worst event to confront an investor is the failure of a company he or she has shares in and the eventual suspension of the shares. Obviously, if failure could be predicted, at least to some degree, then the severe costs of share suspension could be avoided. We will tackle this issue once we have considered the mechanics of share suspension.

If a company is having severe problems or it is going through significant re-organisation, the directors will normally ask the Stock Exchange to suspend dealings in its shares. This is intended to protect the shareholders while the company sorts itself out. The truth is that most companies do not come back from suspension.

In considering the collapse of a company, there are three potential routes:

 Administration - this happens when a company has severe problems but there is a chance of recovery. When the court appoints an administrator, it gives the company a breathing space. The appointment protects the company from being wound up without the court's permission. The court can also stop creditors reclaiming assets used as security or equipment covered by lease, etc.

 Receivership - a secured creditor, most commonly a bank, will appoint a receiver. The bank will often have its loans secured against specific assets. In theory, the receiver could just sell the asset securing the loan but more commonly, he/she will keep the company going long enough for the appointing creditor to retrieve the money it has 'invested' in the business. The remaining creditors argue over what is left.

 Liquidation - this is the final death knell of a company. A liquidator is appointed to wind up the company and realise its assets.

The obvious question that now needs answering is whether company failure can be predicted? There is a voluminous academic literature that has attempted to tackle this issue.[11] Although a number of failure models have had a degree of predictive success, there is a lack of consensus as to what are the defining predictors of corporate failure. For the private investor, the best that can be hoped for is as follows:

- If external funds are being raised - are they being used to build the business or bail it out of problems?

- Are margins being maintained compared to those of competitors?

- Are sales being maintained?

- Is the business generating cash?

- Is the management team stable?

- Is the business being over-extended?

- Are the accounts being prepared on a timely basis?

The above is not a complete list but it should be sufficient if you are dealing with businesses of a reasonable size. Keeping an eye on the identified indicators when following the business news should give adequate warning to avoid major disasters. Of course, with very small firms, the news is not so informative and the speed of collapse can be very rapid indeed. Remember, the gains from investing in smaller companies can be remarkable, as can be the losses!

LESSONS TO BE LEARNT

This rather long chapter has attempted to cover a range of topics that every investor should be aware of. Rather than summarising all the points raised in the various sections, we will draw out the overall lessons to be learned from the chapter.

 The business of investment is full of jargon. Even the experts having difficulty in keeping track of it all. Buy a finance dictionary.

 Despite its apparent complexity, business is extremely straightforward. It raises funds to buy assets in the hope of making profits. Do you understand where the funds have come from and what they have been spent on? If this is not clear - start to have doubts.

 The stock market price of a company is driven both by fundamental business values and stock market sentiment. For a given business, it is always worth attempting to identify which of these is driving its share price.

 In addition to the official list of the stock market (also know as the main market), there is the Alternative Investment Market. Here the listing requirements are less stringent in the hope of attracting younger and smaller firms. Although the gains to be made from investing in companies listed on AIM can be substantial, so can the risks.

 The various aspects of the stock market performance can be gauged from the different published indices. The performance of individual companies can be assessed via comparison with these market indices or the general performance of the sector that the company belongs to.

 Some shares move with the economic cycle - cyclical shares such as building; some shares move counter to the cycle - defensive shares such as foodstuffs.

New issues (new companies coming to the market) tend to show a price inflation effect on the day of issue but thereafter they tend to under-perform. It is not always easy for private investors to gain access to new issues.

 Dividend reductions are not taken lightly by companies and investors should always consider what lies behind a specific dividend reduction.

 If a company is undertaking a rights issue, ask what it is to be used for.

 Stock splits are generally good news for the investor. They are normally associated with a rising share price.

 Small firms used to outperform large firms in terms of the returns that could be made. This situation has been reversed in the 1990s. The unanswered question at the moment is whether small firms can again outperform large firms.

 We suggested that one method for guiding small firm investment is the double 7 approach. Pick firms with low PE ratios (below 7) and high dividend yields (above 7%). It is also worth noting their cash position and the recent performance of the management. In addition, what generation is the management and is it well incentivised?

 Mergers and take-overs are good news for investors in the short term but care has to be taken with the long term.

 There are some indicators that can be used to predict a take-over target - poor earnings record, share price reduction, a cut in dividend payments, low market to book value and a reasonable level of debt.

 De-mergers tend to lead to share price gains.

 Share suspensions are generally bad news for investors. There are some simple, if not overly effective, predictors of failure.

CHAPTER 4

Alternative Investments

In the previous chapter we considered the 'life and times' of a share; that is, the stock market and the major events that may confront shares. While most private individuals will be primarily concerned with investing in ordinary shares, there are a number of alternative securities (traded investments) available. This chapter describes, as briefly as possible, the more commonly known alternative investments. The mechanics of a number of these alternatives (especially the more exotic derivative instruments) are rather complex and it is not the intention of this text to go into a 'full blown' detailed analysis of their make-up. Rather, we give enough detail for you to assess whether these types of investment may be more suited to your particular needs and attitudes towards risk than ordinary shares.

PREFERENCE SHARES AND CONVERTIBLES

As we learned in the previous chapter, ordinary shares convey a number of rights. For example, ordinary shareholders are the owners (residual claimants) of a company and this gives them a vote at the annual general meeting (AGM). Being the residual claimants of the business, ordinary shareholders are likely to receive the largest slice of any profits but they are also last in line if things go wrong.

CLOSE-UP

Unlike other preference shares, **participating** preference shares give investors a portion of profits as well as a fixed annual payment.

Holders of preference shares are not the residual claimants of the business and, therefore, do not participate in the full profit potential of the business. Instead, they accept a predetermined return which is similar in notion to a fixed interest payment. Preference shares, in general, give their holders priority over ordinary shareholders in terms of receiving a dividend but they may have no (or limited) voting rights. Furthermore, there are cumulative and non-cumulative preference shares. With a non-cumulative preference share, any dividends not paid by the company are gone forever whereas with a cumulative preference share, any dividend arrears are accumulated and carried forward.

The above has described the most common variants of preference shares but there is a range of more 'exotic' variations. These can be described briefly as follows:

 redeemable preference shares - will pay the holder the nominal value of the share at some future date.

 zero coupon preference shares - pay no dividend but will be redeemed at a fixed value at a given date in the future. The benefit of this type of share is that any gains are subject to capital gains tax and not income tax - a useful feature if you have some unused capital gains tax allowance.

stepped preference shares - offer a pre-determined dividend which increases by a given percentage every year.

A final type of preference share is the **convertible preference share**. Such shares allow the holder to convert them into a pre-specified number of ordinary shares. There are also other forms of convertibles, such as convertible loan stock. In general, convertibles are fixed interest investments that can be converted into ordinary shares at some future date.

WARRANTS

While convertibles give rights to convert loan stock or preference shares into ordinary shares, warrants give rights to buy ordinary shares at a fixed price for specified time periods. Although the price of a warrant is obviously linked to the price of the underlying ordinary share, it is essentially separate through being independently traded. Before we go on to explain how they might be valued, it must be stressed that warrants are more complex than ordinary shares and suffer greater volatility.

To understand warrants, let's consider an example. Imagine a warrant which allows you to buy one ordinary share at an exercise price of £2.00 at any time up to 31st December 2002. If the ordinary share is currently trading at £2.50, then the warrant should be worth at least 50 pence because this is the gain that could be made through exercising the warrant. However, given that warrants are traded on the stock exchange, it would be unusual for the price of a warrant to exactly equal its current intrinsic value. Most warrants, not surprisingly, trade at a price above current intrinsic value - if not, there would be an immediate opportunity to make money and this would be arbitraged away. However, this raises the question why individuals are willing to pay more for warrants than their current intrinsic values, especially as warrants do not pay dividends and they offer reduced shareholder rights; for example, you cannot attend annual general meetings.

As an illustration, suppose for the above example that the warrant price is currently 75 pence (against a current intrinsic value of 50 pence derived from a £2.50 current share price and a £2.00 exercise price). There are two reasons why the traded price of a warrant should be at a premium to the current intrinsic value; these are **time value** and **gearing**.

NUTSHELL

The **intrinsic value** of a warrant is the current price of the underlying share minus the price at which the warrant lets you buy the share.

NUTSHELL

If a security is traded in two different markets, and its price in each market is not identical, it is possible to buy the security in the market with the lower price and simultaneously sell it at a profit in the market with the higher price. This process is called **arbitrage.** Arbitraging causes the price of the security to adjust until it is the same in both markets.

Time Value

The market may be willing to pay 75 pence for a warrant with a current intrinsic value of 50 pence (hence, paying a premium of 25 pence) because it believes there is sufficient time up to 31st December 2002 for future intrinsic values to exceed the current price of 75 pence. If the share price rose in the future to £3.00, then every warrant bought for 75 pence with an exercise price of £2.00 would yield a gross profit of 25 pence. Clearly, as we move closer to 31st December 2002, then the traded price of the warrant should more closely approximate the current intrinsic value because there is less time for future intrinsic values to diverge from current intrinsic values. In other words, the longer the period of time under consideration, the more chance there is for future share prices to diverge from current share prices; hence, warrants have a time value and this should be greater the longer the remaining exercise period under consideration.

Gearing

The second reason why investors may consider warrants is their gearing property. This means that investors can gain exposure to the movements in a share price for a smaller outlay than buying the share itself. Let's continue with the previous example. Suppose the ordinary share is trading at £2.50 and the warrant with an exercise price of £2.00 has a traded price of 75 pence. Imagine that the ordinary share price jumps to £3.50. For the investor who bought the ordinary share at £2.50, this represents a very worthwhile potential gain of 40%. However, the investor who purchased a warrant could have gained over 100%. This can be calculated as follows: against a cost of 75 pence for the warrant, it yields a **gross** gain, in intrinsic value, of £1.50 (£3.50 - £2.00). Given the market price of the warrant will be above its instrinsic value, the gross gain in market value will be over £1.50. Therefore, this offers a **net** gain of over 75 pence (£1.50 - £0.75) for every warrant bought. So warrants allow you to buy into potential share price gains at a lower cost. Of course, there is also the possibility of magnified downside losses. If the share price reduced to £2.00, the ordinary shareholder who purchased at £2.50 would have suffered a notional loss of 20%, whereas, the warrant holder would have a warrant currently worth nothing in terms of exercise value (£2.00 current price - £2.00 exercise price) and he or she would have suffered a current notional loss of 100%. Thus, warrants magnify both the gains and losses to be made from movements in ordinary share prices.

In conclusion, warrants are a riskier investment than ordinary shares but you 'pays your money and takes your choice'. However, this is not as simple as it might be. If you like the sound of warrants, it is not easy to assess which ones you should go for without quite a bit of leg-work. The *Financial Times* does not publish the exercise price or the exercise period for warrants, so it is a bit like dancing in the dark. The really committed warrant hunter would either need to access the company accounts or talk to his or her friendly stockbroker.

FUTURES AND FORWARDS

In this section we consider futures and forwards.

Futures

Because all variants of future contracts have the same underlying principle, we will concentrate on the FTSE 100 index future. If you enjoy a gamble this could be the investment for you!

Essentially, you buy for a down payment (known as an initial margin) of £2,500 a contract which specifies the level of the FTSE 100 index at some future date. In early 1998, it was possible to buy future contracts for March (5680), June (5740) and September (5816). If the actual index at these dates is higher than the contract, then the investor could have made some money. Let's take the June contract as an example. If the FTSE 100 index was 5940 on the appropriate day in June, then the investor could have made (5940 minus 5740) 200 points in profit. As each point is worth £10, then this equates to £2,000 profit. Of course, if the actual index had turned out to be lower than the futures price, then losses would have been incurred at the same rate as profits.

There is an additional need to understand the notion of a **margin**. We mentioned above the need to make a down payment of £2,500 (initial margin) as a means of undertaking a FTSE 100 index futures contract. This is common to futures contracts in general. Buyers and sellers in a futures market place initial levels of collateral (£2,500 in this case) for each open contract. This initial margin is returned with interest when the position (contract) is closed out. However, profits and losses on the open

NUTSHELL

A **futures contract** gives an investor the opportunity to buy or sell an equity, index or commodity at a specified price at a given date in the future.

CLOSE-UP

In addition to providing the opportunity to speculate, futures contracts can also provide much needed certainty. For example, the farmer who wants to guarantee a price for his wheat while it is still growing, can sell it at a specified price for a given delivery date via a futures contract. This avoids the vagancies of selling the crop, once it is grown and harvested, in a current market - also known as a spot market.

contract (when it is still in operation) are calculated daily. If the contract makes a profit during the day (that is, the actual index is above and moves up against the futures index 'price') then this is added to the initial margin. On the other hand, if losses are made, they are subtracted from the initial margin. These daily additions or subtractions to and from the initial margin are known as **variation margin**. However, the level of the initial margin must be maintained throughout the time the contract is open. Finally, it is equally possible to 'bet' that the actual index will be less than the futures index! Remember, the futures index is the market's best guess at what level the actual index will be at a given date in the future. You can 'bet' (sell a futures contract) that the actual market undershoots the expectation of the market (the futures' index level).

Forwards

Due to the size of the minimum transaction (£500,000+) with Forward Rate Agreements (FRAs), they are unlikely to be of much practical use to most investors. It is, however, worthwhile having at least a nodding acquaintance with the basic concept.

Although there are a variety of types of forward contract, we will use interest rate forwards to illustrate the concept. A Forward Rate Interest Agreement is simply a formal agreement between two parties (normally a company and a bank) that at a given date in the future, one party (the company) can borrow a stated amount of money for a specific period of time at a given rate of interest. Therefore, in this example, the company would know for certain, by the use of a Forward Rate Interest Agreement, what the cost of a loan would be for a future business contract. Unlike futures which can be bought and sold in varying amounts through the market, FRAs are one-off formal agreements between two parties.

OPTIONS

In contrast to Forwards, which are essentially only of any use to large corporates or very wealthy individuals, options are available and of use to the average investor. It needs to be stressed, however, that they can be one of the most complex of investments (although they needn't be) and it is best for the investor to try them only once he or she has a reasonable understanding of how they work. As we have already touched upon an 'option-like' investment with our discussion of warrants, the initial description of the principles underpinning options should not be too onerous. Also, because of the Nick Leeson affair, options have been described and discussed by the whole range of the financial press (although it should be noted that the unwise and unchecked use of futures was the primary undoing of Barings).

Those investors who eventually become interested in options will most likely deal with traded options on shares and market indices handled by LIFFE (the London International Financial Futures and Options Exchange). These traded options are of two basic types, **Calls** and **Puts**, and this section describes their underlying structures. It is not the intention of this section to detail the more complex combinations of options, as these can be found in the many specialist texts on the topic. Rather, the section offers a discussion of the basic option types and the practicalities that will have to be confronted if they are to be used as part of an investment portfolio.

NUTSHELL

The purchase of an **equity option** gives the investor the right to buy or sell the underlying share at a pre-determined price for a specified period of time.

ORIGINS

In spite of the advent of the Chicago Board of Trade as a market for futures in 1848, **LIFFE** did not open until 1982.

Calls

A call is an option to **buy** a stated package (number) of a company's shares at a pre-determined (exercise or strike) price for a specified period of time, after which the option will expire. Let's consider a real example. As ASDA sits at the top of the LIFFE Equity Options list in the *Financial Times* we will focus on this option. In early 1998, the actual price of ASDA ordinary shares was 188.5 pence and there were two basic options quoted in the *Financial Times*; an ASDA 180 pence option and an ASDA 200 pence option. The 180 pence call option would allow an investor to purchase an ASDA share for 180 pence and the 200 pence call option would allow an ASDA share to be bought for 200 pence. For each of these options there were three specified time periods as shown in Table 1 overleaf.

Table 1 - Call Options		April	July	October
ASDA	180	15	21	26.5
(188.5)	200	4.5	11.5	18

As can be seen from Table 1, it was possible to buy an ASDA 200 pence call option for the period up to April for 4.5 pence per share. This means that for 4.5 pence, you could buy an option to purchase an ASDA share for 200 pence. With an actual share price of 188.5 pence, this might have been a good bet. If the price went up to say 250 pence before April, this means that an investor could exercise the option, buy the share for 200 pence and then sell it to the market for 250 pence; giving an overall gross profit of 45.5 pence (250 pence - 200 pence - 4.5 pence). If, however, the actual share price did not reach 200 pence, there was no obligation to buy the share and lose money - this is the potential power of buying an option. For a given premium (4.5 pence in this case), an investor could buy into all of the potential upside benefits but bear none of the potential downside costs (apart from the possibility of losing the initial premium).

Call options can be:

 In the money - the exercise price of the option is less than the current price of the underlying share.

 At the money - the exercise price of the option equals the current price of the underlying share.

 Out of the money - the exercise price of the option is above the current share price.

CLOSE-UP

A further factor which affects the price of an option is the **volatility** of the underlying share; the higher the volatility, the greater the chance that the share price will move sufficiently for profits to be made.

With a 'current' share price of 188.5 pence, the ASDA 180 option would be 'in the money', whereas the 200 option would be 'out of the money'. Not surprisingly, 'in the money' options are more expensive.

Table 1 also indicates that options become more expensive the longer the time period under consideration. For example, the October 200p option costs 4 times the April option (18 pence as compared to 4.5 pence). This is because options have time value. The longer the period of time under consideration, the greater the probability that the actual share price will exceed the option exercise price by any given margin; there is more chance that a share price will increase by 10 pence if a month is being considered as compared to a minute!

Puts

So far we have considered call options (the right to buy a share at a given price). There are also put options which give the holder the right to **sell** at a given price. So if you believe that the price of a share is on the way down, you could make money by buying a put option. Table 2 lists ASDA put options available in early 1998.

Table 2 - Put Options				
		April	July	October
ASDA	180	4.5	8.5	11
188.5	200	15	19	21.5

The same logic applies for puts as for calls, except puts give a right to sell a share at a specified price, whereas calls give a right to buy. Not surprisingly, given the 188.5 pence current share price, the 180 pence puts (out of the money) are cheaper than 200 pence puts (in the money). For with the 200 pence puts, you have the right to sell at 200 pence but you can currently buy for 188.5 pence, whereas, with the 180 pence puts, you can only sell at 180 pence but the share costs 188.5 pence to buy in the current market place.

Trading Option Contracts

So far, we have talked about buying a single option, for example 4.5 pence for an ASDA 180 pence April put. However, options are offered by LIFFE in contracts of 1,000 shares (in the case of equity options) or £10 per index point for the FTSE 100 index option. This means that if you had bought the above ASDA put, it would have cost £45 (4.5 pence x 1000) for the contract. Furthermore, although we have talked about exercising the option and buying or selling the share to make a profit in the market, there is no need to do this in traded options. With traded options, you can just sell the option. The option price moves in such a way that the profit you make by selling it is very similar to the profit to be made by exercising the option. A further point to be borne in mind is that there are costs in addition to the initial premium purchase price. First, there are brokers' commission charges and these are generally more expensive than normal share dealings; they can be as much as 2% with minimum commission charges of as much as £50. Second, the bid-offer spread on traded options is generally higher in percentage terms than is the case for ordinary shares.

Option Prices

Now that we understand the underlying principles of call and put options, and the likely committed costs, there are two remaining issues to be considered - how do we assess whether the price of the option is fair and what practical steps might be used to formulate a solid strategy towards investing in options?

We have so far mentioned that the value of an option is a function of the length of the option period and the volatility of the underlying share. These ideas were formalised by Black and Scholes in the 1970s and their model now forms the backbone of most commercially available software-based option pricing models.[1] Of course, even with the help of such sophisticated software tools, the private investor should never lose track of the basic questions - what chance is there that the actual share price will exceed the exercise price of the option plus the other per unit costs (premium, dealing commissions, etc.) and does the expected out-turn justify the cost of the option?

Before reaching the above decision point, however, there are a few prior steps that need to be considered if investing in options is to be a part of your overall investment strategy. First, there are over 70 shares with options available and when you consider that each share will have a number of call and put options with various exercise prices, this is an awful lot of options to consider. At this stage it might be best to select options for shares for which you have some background knowledge and understanding. Such understanding should give you some insights into the potential volatility of the share and, therefore, the

CLOSE-UP

The Black-Scholes option model sees the potential value of an option as a function of the volatility of the underlying share, the current price of the share, the exercise price of the option, the remaining period before the option matures and the risk-less rate of return.

probability that the option will exceed the exercise price plus the unit costs.

Second, once you have selected the option which is of potential interest, then you need to remember that options are highly geared investments. If your investment is £2,000 in options, then you can potentially forfeit this entire amount with a reasonable degree of probability. Although such a loss is also possible if you invest £2,000 in ordinary shares, it is far less likely to happen. Thus, when investing in options, there is a clear need to understand what amount of money you are prepared to lose. Third, it is relatively easy for options to move in and out of the money and it is best if you decide what losses and gains you are prepared to accept, then watch the market on a regular basis and stick to your specified decision strategy. It is easy to end up making a loss on options by being fooled into a false sense of security by the appearance of short term notional profits. Although the Barings fiasco is not directly applicable to private investors, it is always worth keeping at the back of your mind.

BONDS

The emphasis of this chapter so far has been on alternative equity investments. It is now time to consider 'traded loan' investments such as government bonds (gilts) and non-government bonds. As the mechanics of these various investments are essentially similar, we have decided to focus on government gilts. These are the types of bond that most investors will first turn to as an alternative to equities.

Gilts

When the British government needs to borrow money it issues gilts. As they are issued by the government, it is not surprising that they are considered to be one of the safest investments available. Gilts fall into the following categories:

- **shorts** - redemption periods of up to 5 years.

- **mediums** - 5 to 15 year redemption periods.

■ **longs** - over 15 years.

■ **undated** - no fixed redemption date.

■ **index linked** - where the return on the investment is linked to the inflation rate.

At the end of each of the various redemption periods, the government repays the holder the par (face) value of the gilt which, with the exception of the index-linked gilts, is £100. So, unlike holding a share which offers no guarantee that it will be worth anything, a gilt has a definite value of £100 if it is held to redemption.

Gilts also offer another form of certainty, in that they pay a fixed rate of interest (unlike the 'variable' dividend payments of shares). This fixed rate of interest is known as the coupon and is expressed in terms of the par value of the gilt. Let's consider some real examples as shown in Table 3.

Table 3 - UK Gilt Prices								
			Yield				52 Week	
	Coupon	Year	Int	Red	Price £	+ or −	High	Low
Shorts (lives up to 5 years)								
Treasury	$15^1/_2$%	1998	14.83	6.87	$104^1/_2$	$-^1/_{32}$	$113^{13}/_{16}$	$104^1/_2$
Exchequer	$12^1/_4$%	1999	11.64	6.95	$105^9/_{32}$	$-^1/_{32}$	$110^{11}/_{16}$	$105^9/_{32}$

The first column of the table gives the names of the various gilts but these are relatively unimportant to the investor. The second column gives the coupon (the rate of interest) of the gilt. For the Treasury gilt shown in the first row of the table, the coupon is $15^1/_2$%. This means that a holder of one of these gilts (with a par value of £100) would receive £15.50 for each year it is held. However, most gilts pay interest every six months, so the holder receives half the coupon twice a year. The next column give the redemption year of the gilt (1998 for our Treasury example).

The next two columns for yield are a bit more complicated to understand. Before turning to these, however, we need to understand a basic feature of gilts. If a gilt could be bought at the time it was issued at its par value and held until redemption at its par value, then the return to be made from the gilt is a simple reflection of its coupon

- its rate of interest. However, gilts are rarely bought at their par value and, therefore, the coupon is not a true indicator of the effective rate of interest earned. Furthermore, if a gilt is not bought at its par value, then there will be a capital gain or loss if it is held to redemption. These ideas are captured under the two yield columns of Table 3.

Interest Yield: this shows that the effective rate of interest (yield) to be derived from the coupon (15½% in our Treasury example) depends upon the price paid for it. The *Financial Times* shows the interest yield as the coupon divided by the current price of the gilt which may, of course, be different from the price you paid for it. Thus our 15½% coupon translates into a 15½ ÷ 104½ = 14.83% interest yield.

Redemption Yield: this indicates the total return if the gilt is held to redemption. It includes capital gains and losses made at redemption as well as the coupon income. Therefore, if you bought the gilt at a higher price than its par value, you will make a capital loss at redemption and in this case the redemption yield will be lower than the interest yield. In our Treasury gilt example, the redemption yield is 6.87% as compared to the interest yield of 14.83%. Please note that the redemption yield is defined, as is the interest yield, on the current market price of the gilt - not the price which you may have paid.

The remaining columns indicate the current price of the gilts (the mid point between buy and sell), their price change and their high and low prices during the past 52 weeks. Now that we understand gilts and the terminology associated with them, all that remains is to discuss the forces which determine their market prices. Basically, there are three factors to consider - interest rates, inflation and the redemption date.

Interest Rates: given that the effective interest rate of a gilt is its coupon divided by its price, then if interest rates rise elsewhere in the economy, the price of the gilt must fall if the coupon is to stay attractive. In a competitive market this will happen because as interest rates become higher elsewhere, the demand for the gilt (with its fixed coupon) will fall and, therefore, so will its price. On the other hand, if interest rates fall elsewhere, then gilts become more attractive and their prices should rise. So, rising (falling) interest rates should lead to falling (rising) gilt prices.

[!] Inflation: however, the pricing of gilts is not as straightforward as so far suggested. In general, gilt prices seem to be determined more by long term interest rate expectations than short term interest rate fluctuations. Imagine the following scenario. Short term interest rates have been rising and this is expected to dampen inflation in the medium term. If this is achieved then interest rates can be expected to be lower in the medium term. If these expectations drive gilt prices, then medium and long-dated gilt prices should rise because they are relatively more attractive. But note, we would have rising gilt prices at the same time as rising short term interest rates. Therefore, the mechanics of gilts price determination may well be more to do with longer term interest expectations than short term interest rate fluctuations. If longer term interest rates are expected to fall (rise), then gilt prices should rise (fall). Not surprisingly, however, this is not quite the full picture. Most gilts pay their coupons across quite long periods of time and are redeemed at some point (often relatively distant) in the future. If the real worth of these payments is likely to be eroded by inflation, then gilts will become less attractive. It needs to be noted that although longer term expectations regarding interest rates and inflation tend to move together, they do not have to! Therefore, there is a need to try to assess the relative weight (as compared to longer term interest rate expectations) of inflation forecasts on the current thinking of the market.

[!] Redemption Date: as gilts move closer to their redemption dates, their prices will move towards their par values.

Finally, remember that private investors do not pay tax on capital gains from gilts. Therefore, gilts which offer more money from their capital gains than their coupon payments are especially attractive to higher rate tax payers who have used up all of their capital gains tax allowance. A gilt trading below par should appeal to such investors.

CONCLUSION

There are quite a few alternative investments to ordinary shares that you may want to consider. We would suggest, however, that you take your time and understand as fully as possible their make-up and how their various risk characteristics suit your own attitudes towards risk.

LESSONS TO BE LEARNT

 Preference shares, in all their many guises, generally offer a more certain investment than ordinary shares.

 Convertible preference shares give the right to convert them into a pre-specified number of ordinary shares. There is no need to exercise the right.

 Warrants give the right to buy ordinary shares at a fixed price for a specified time period. There is no need to exercise the right.

 A futures contract gives the obligation to buy/sell a commodity or a share index at a specified price at a given date in the future.

 The basic mechanics of call and put traded options are similar to warrants in that the investor buys the right to buy (a call) or sell (a put) a share at a pre-specified price for a given period.

 Traded options are more valuable the greater the remaining exercise period and the higher the volatility of the underlying share price. Both of these factors increase the probability that the actual share price will move sufficiently for it to be profitable for the investor to exercise the option.

 When we considered bonds, we focused on gilts. These are seen as one of the safest of investments because they are issued by the government when it wants to raise funds.

 Gilts are normally issued at a par value of £100 and this is what will be returned to the investor if the gilt is held until redemption. The exception is index linked gilts.

 Gilts offer a fixed rate of interest (the coupon) and this is expressed as a percentage of the par value of the gilt under consideration.

 Gilt prices are determined by basic market forces. If they are deemed to be more attractive, their prices will rise. If they are seen to be less attractive, prices will fall.

CHAPTER 5

The Analysis of Company Accounts

It is not difficult to understand why a great number of private investors shy away from conducting company analysis. It takes a long time to understand the 'mumbo-jumbo' of accounting speak and actually conducting an analysis of a company is not a two-minute affair - although modern on-line data facilities have cut the time needed to a fraction of what it used to be. It is perhaps not surprising, therefore, that investors seek to find more understandable and less costly approaches to making investments; for example, the use of unit trusts and investment trusts, buying and selling shares on the sole basis of share price movements (see Chapter 8 for a detailed discussion of the technical analysis or chartist approach to investment) or following the lead of the share price tipsters. Even if you adopt an approach that is not critically dependent upon a full understanding of the financial make-up of companies and their financial performance, it is always worth having a working knowledge of financial statements and the ability to make sense of financial press reporting. Being able to make sound interpretations of financial matters at least provides a cross-check to the conclusions drawn from other approaches to investing.

Now that we have explained why it is worth any private investor mastering the basics of financial statement analysis, we have to find a structure that allows it to be described in a single chapter rather than the more usual approach of dedicating an entire book to the subject. With this in mind, the chapter is structured as follows. In the first section, we discuss the importance of understanding the sector a company belongs to and the major events of a company's recent history. Without a full appreciation of the peculiarities of a company and its sector, it is difficult to be confident that sound conclusions are being drawn from the available financial statements. Once you are confident that you understand the context of a company, it is time to take the second step of over-viewing the past two or three years of the financial statements of the company and its nearest couple of competitors. To achieve this overview step, you have to have a familiarity with the meaning of accounting terms and the make-up of financial statements. This step should alert you to any major unusual movements in the company's activities and finances. This overview part of the process is tackled in the second section. The third part of the process is to go into more detail on those items that have already been highlighted as being important and/or unusual. This often means trying to gain understanding by both disaggregating the accounting terms through a careful reading of the notes to the financial statements and by aggregating the single accounting terms into key indicators and ratios (for example, profits divided by the funds invested in the business). The final step in this approach to financial statement analysis is to evaluate all the available and gathered evidence and reach a conclusion as to whether the particular share under consideration is a good buy - this is tackled in the concluding section. The current approach to company analysis was developed by Phil Moon and Ken Bates[1] and it can be summarised as follows:

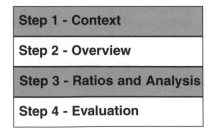

| Step 1 - Context |
| Step 2 - Overview |
| Step 3 - Ratios and Analysis |
| Step 4 - Evaluation |

If you remember to adopt the CORE approach to company analysis, you won't go too far wrong.

CONTEXT

To make sense of a company's financial performance there is a need to understand its context both externally and internally. On the most general of levels, different sectors are not affected equally by economic forces. For example, exchange rate movements will have a greater impact on manufacturers of exports than home retailers. Equally, different sectors will have varying internal dynamics; the retail banking sector has recently had a period of 'merger-talks', this has not been the case for the house building sector. As well as the need to consider the context of the appropriate sector, there is also the need to appreciate the specifics of the company. As we will see, it is difficult to understand fully a number of years of accounts without being aware of the key changes that have taken place within a company. In tackling the issue of context we have the three sub-headings of external profile, internal profile and data sources.

External Profile

The first thing to note under this sub-heading is that the activities of different sectors are likely to result in very dissimilar financial profiles. For example, the activity of banking is likely to result in a substantially different financial profile from that of a chemical company. The business of banking is about borrowing and lending money and the financial profile of this type of company is dominated by the sheer impact of these activities. Compare this to the financial profile of a chemical company which is, not surprisingly, usually dominated by the need to have large amounts of physical plant. In essence, it is difficult to understand what is special and/or unusual about a company's financial profile unless there is an appreciation of what could be considered normal for the sector as a whole. Therefore, before conducting any form of financial analysis of a company, make sure you have thought through and researched what a normal profile should look like for that particular type of business.

The second aspect of external profile is to consider how far the sector may have been and may be affected by the major sources of external change. It is easiest to think through these issues with the use of STEP analysis; that is, how is the sector affected by sociological, technological, economic and political forces. For example, to understand the past and the future of the house building sector, there is a need to appreciate the potential impact of an ageing population and the move to single parent and single individual dwellings. To have a good handle on the past and future of financial services, there is a need to understand the impact and potential impact of the changing nature of information technology. Similarly, it is difficult to make much sense of the dynamics of the car industry without considering the global nature of car manufacturers and the status/health of the various major economies. Finally, a number of sectors are dependent on the political environment. Take farming as an example. For years UK farming has been driven by the European agriculture policy and recently, by the governments' handling (Tory and Labour) of the BSE crisis. In summary, take a long hard look at the sector in question and the broad forces which act upon it and spend some time thinking through how the activities of the sector should be reflected in the financial profiles of companies.

Internal Profile

As well as the sector having specific features which need considering, individual companies have histories and characteristics that also need to be borne in mind. Companies are dynamic organisms with many aspects - cultural, organisational, managerial, technological, etc. - to their functioning through time. To understand how the financial profile of a company has changed and is likely to change across time, there is a need to spend effort on recognising the key events and features of a company's recent history. In addition to analysing the physical activities of a business, much can be gained from also trying to understand how the business has been or is being driven by its senior management team. For example, most of the business success stories of the 20th century can be explained by the drive and ambition of single individuals - Ford, General Motors, Virgin, Microsoft, etc. In fact, it might be fair to say that the market backs the senior management team as much as it does the output of the business. In summary, spend some time analysing the activities of the company and its senior management team.

CLOSE-UP

Apricot computers moved from being a supplier of computer hardware to a computer service company. This will have had a major impact (reduction) upon its stock position . Tesco attacked Sainsbury at the top-end of the food retailing sector by building new out-of-town supermarkets. Similarly, Tesco invested heavily in the electronic management of its distribution and stock systems. These fundamental changes to the business will have had important influences on its balance sheet, with the relative proportion of land and buildings increasing and that of stock decreasing.

Data Sources

We cannot stress too highly the importance of this first step of the process. It is worth expending some effort trying to obtain as good a feel as possible for a sector and its key constituents. This is why professionals specialise on individual sectors - it is just too time consuming trying to make sense of a whole range of different sectors. Thank goodness, however, the electronic age has made this part of the process so very much easier. Let's start with what is available at a good civic business library. We normally start the process of building up our understanding of context by referring to Mintel Reports and Key Notes. Both of these provide excellent summaries of individual sectors. These can also be supported by the *Financial Times'* reviews of sectors and by finding the relevant trade journals. All sectors have their own journals and these are often very illuminating of recent events and changes. Remember, with the advent of CD ROMs, it is often easy to search on key words. For example, the *Financial Times* CD ROM service is a fantastic source of sector and business news. Furthermore, most of the CD ROM and on-line business data services provide sector statistics and these should inform your thinking on an individual sector.

Once you have built up your knowledge of the key features of a sector, it is time to turn to the company in question. Here you can use McCarthy Cards, the Extel News Service, the *Financial Times* CD ROM, the web-sites of the broad-sheet newspapers and the web-site of the company itself. These are just a few of the ways that you might gain information concerning a sector and a company. It is also possible to subscribe to a whole series of specialist services. We would recommend, however, that you first try your local business library and the web before these subscription services.

POINTER

Most large conurbations have excellent business libraries and it is a sound investment spending a bit of time getting to know their services. Such libraries will often have good paper based and on-line services for sectors and companies.

POINTER

There is now a veritable industry providing investors with company and sector data. The pages of the *Financial Times* and the *Investors Chronicle* carry advertisements for these types of service.

OVERVIEW – FINANCIAL STATEMENTS

The second part of the CORE approach to company analysis is to form an overview of the financial statements of the target company and its close competitors. Overview, in this situation, means a feel for what is different/special about the company's financial profile as compared to its 'normal' state of affairs and its close competitors. To achieve this 'overview' objective, this section considers, as simply as possible, the structure and meaning of balance sheets, profit and loss statements, and cash statements. If the terminology involved becomes too much, just remember the three key questions:

where's the money coming from;
what has it been spent on; and
is the business a net cash generator in the medium term?

With these basic questions in mind, let's now turn to the substance of this section.

The Annual Report

The first thing to turn to in a company's annual report is the chairman or chief executive's review. Find the part of the review that comments on the future outlook of the company. Although this often does not tell you much that can be defined as useful, occasionally it does. You need to decide whether it is blandly optimistic (as they usually are) or that there really is some 'meat in the sandwich'. It is also worth considering how far the outlook statement reflects recent external comment on the company. Basically, companies are driven by their senior executives and the outlook statement is one (albeit highly imperfect) opportunity to try to gauge their thinking. A further aspect of annual reports is that they now describe directors' remuneration and shareholdings. Here the rules of interpretation are fairly straightforward. If a director is to be highly motivated and aligned with shareholders, then ideally he/she should have substantial shareholdings relative to salary. If they really believe in the company, why haven't they bought the shares? A similar but weaker argument can be made for options. Directors holding options should be aligned with shareholders because they also gain from increases in share price. Where options differ, however, is that directors don't normally buy options but rather they are granted as part of the general remuneration package. Hence, options allow directors to benefit from upside share price gains but there is no real downside pain through share price declines. Essentially, granting options to directors is not quite the same as them buying shares!

Finally, the annual report contains the summary financial statements and their notes. Don't be 'fazed' by the detail of the statements and the normally voluminous notes. As we will see, the logic of the statements is fairly straightforward and it just requires a bit of patience to make sense of the notes. Once you have been through a few sets of accounts, you will be surprised how easy it is to use them.

The Balance Sheet

Remember that the first two questions to always have in mind when analysing companies is where does the money come from and what has it been spent on? These can be answered (not always as clearly as we would like) by the balance sheet. Before we look at an outline balance sheet, it is worth noting a couple of points.

First, balance sheets are normally based upon an historic cost notion of value. This means that assets are recorded at what they cost, with fixed assets bearing a depreciation charge for wear and tear. The advantages of this approach are its objectivity and its ability to record where the money has gone. Its disadvantage, however, is that the money paid for an asset need not reflect its current worth. Imagine a company had bought a machine for £1,000 and had written it down to zero value through 4 years of depreciation at 25% per annum. In the balance sheet it would have zero book value but it could easily be the case that it is still doing good service for the company; in other words, it has value. Equally, imagine a company had bought a piece of land for £2 million; it could be the case that rapid property inflation had driven the market value of the land to £5 million. This would not be shown in the balance sheet unless the company had undertaken a revaluation of its land and buildings. So care needs to be taken in seeing the balance sheet as a measure of asset values; it really just records what they cost and this need not equal value.

Second, the accounts are drawn up on a going concern basis. This means that the values shown in the balance sheet are based on the premise that the company will continue as a going concern. This is important because asset values are normally drastically reduced if they are the subject of a forced sale through liquidation.

Now that we have covered these issues, let's turn to an outline balance sheet. As we have described the meaning of the accounting terms within the structure of the balance sheet, it is important that the following is read carefully.

NUTSHELL

The **balance sheet** is a snap shot at the end of the financial year which records how the business has been funded and what assets have been bought with the funds.

FIGURE 5.1

Outline Balance Sheet

£ million

Fixed Assets

Patents, brand values and goodwill. Usually difficult to value objectively. ⟶ Intangible assets 75

Includes land, buildings, plant, fixtures and fittings, etc., recorded at historic cost (or revaluation) less accumulated depreciation. ⟶ Tangible assets 1661

Investments in associated and other companies. ⟶ Investments 25

1761

Current Assets

Valued at the lower of cost or net realisable value. ⟶ Stocks and work in progress 835

Customers who have bought goods on credit. ⟶ Debtors 320

Investments 200

Cash at bank and in hand 72

1427

Also known as current liabilities. Will include trade creditors, other creditors (e.g. Inland Revenue) and short term borrowings (e.g. bank overdrafts, bank loans). ⟶ **Creditors**: Amounts falling due within one year (1400)

Current assets less current liabilities (or creditors). ⟶ **Net current assets** 27

Fixed assets + current assets, less current liabilities. ⟶ **Total assets less current liabilities** 1788

Will include loans and leases etc., which are due for repayment after more than one year. ⟶ **Creditors**: Amounts falling due after one year (270)

Provisions made for future costs (e.g. future redundancy costs resulting from reorganisation.) ⟶ **Provisions for liabilities & charges** (40)

1478

Capital and reserves

The ordinary share capital at nominal value. ⟶ Called up share capital 170

The difference between the issue price and the nominal value of newly issued shares. ⟶ Share premium account 220

The amount by which fixed assets may have been revalued. ⟶ Revaluation reserve 210

Accumulated retained profits. ⟶ Profit and loss account 900

Equity shareholders' funds 1500

Funds provided by the minority shareholders of subsidiary companies owned by the group. ⟶ **Minority interest** (22)

1478

This has covered the key aspects of a balance sheet and if you spend a bit of time working through it, you should have a reasonable feel for what should be included. However, the biggest problem facing the investor is that no two companies use the same basic format. If you understand the basic principles, then this is not too much of an issue.

Remember that the basic principle is: **Assets = Funds;** because you can't buy assets without funds. This can then be broken down into: Fixed Assets (FA) and Current Assets (CA) = Current Liabilities (CL) + Long Term Liabilities (LTL) + Shareholder Funds (SF).

So we have different types of assets being funded by a variety of funds. This can be shown in the following simple column form of Balance Sheet.

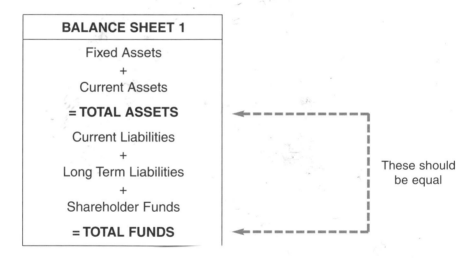

However, it is far more common to have the following two types of balance sheet.

In variation 2 we have current liabilities on the asset side of the balance sheet as a subtraction from current assets. As indicated, current assets less current liabilities equals the net working capital (cash + stock + debtors – creditors) of the business. This is, possibly, the most common form of balance sheet.

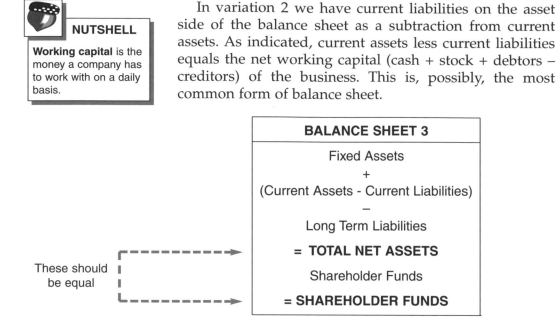

These should be equal

BALANCE SHEET 3
Fixed Assets
+
(Current Assets - Current Liabilities)
–
Long Term Liabilities
= TOTAL NET ASSETS
Shareholder Funds
= SHAREHOLDER FUNDS

With this third form of the balance sheet, the long term liabilities, as well as the current liabilities, are subtracted from the assets of the business. Therefore, all that is left on the funding side of the balance sheet are the shareholder funds. This form is quite useful as it identifies quite starkly what would be left to shareholders after all liabilities have been met.

Remember, that in reviewing the financial statements of a company and its competitors, you are likely to come across different balance sheet formats and you need to be able to adjust them into a common format that you feel comfortable with.

Outline Profit and Loss Accounts

In contrast to the balance sheet which takes a snapshot of a business at a single point in time, the profit and loss account reports how well (in terms of profit and loss) the company has been trading over the previous year. It needs to be noted, however, that profits can be 'created' by accountants and they should never be seen as being equal to additional cash generation. That is why some analysts concentrate on the cash generation of a business rather than its profitability. None the less, the profit and loss account can be informative, so long as care is taken to ask the right questions.

FIGURE 5.2

Outline Profit and Loss Account	
	£ million
Turnover	5814
Cost of sales	(3880)
Gross profit	1934
Operating expenses	(1519)
Operating profit	415
Exceptional items:	
Profits/(losses) on the sale or termination of operations	(2)
Costs of a fundamental reorganisation	(4)
Profits/(losses) on the disposal of fixed assets	5
Profit on ordinary activities before interest	414
Net interest payable	(25)
Profit on ordinary activities before taxation	389
Tax on profit on ordinary activities	(115)
Profit on ordinary activities after taxation	274
Minority interests	(2)
Preference dividends	(2)
Profit for the financial year attributable to ordinary shareholders	270
Dividends	(120)
Retained profit for the year	150
Earnings per share:	
basic	41.0p
before exceptional items	41.8p

Annotations (left column):

- May be broken down into turnover from continuing operations, acquisitions made during the year and operations discontinued during the year. → Turnover
- Direct costs, such as raw materials, products for resale, production labour and direct overheads. → Cost of sales
- Will include selling and administrative expenses split as above. → Operating expenses
- These items must be shown on the face of the profit and loss account. → Exceptional items
- This is profit (or loss) after exceptional items. → Profit on ordinary activities before interest
- The net interest received and paid. → Net interest payable
- Profit after interest. → Profit on ordinary activities before taxation
- The amount of corporation tax payable on the profit made. → Tax on profit on ordinary activities
- In the case of subsidiary companies which are not 100% owned, the share of the profits due to the minority shareholders. → Minority interests
- Paid to the holders of preference shares. → Preference dividends
- Profit after the deduction of minority interest. → Profit for the financial year
- Dividends payable to ordinary shareholders. → Dividends
- Amount of profit retained in the business and added to reserves in the balance sheet. → Retained profit for the year
- Profit attributable to ordinary shareholders divided by number of ordinary shares issued. → basic
- Companies often provide alternative measures of EPS (for example, profit calculated before the deduction of exceptional items). → before exceptional items

You need to keep an eye on a number of factors when reviewing profit and loss accounts.

[?] Is turnover growth keeping pace with the sector and the company's major competitors? Also, has turnover growth been achieved organically or bought through acquisition? If it is the latter, will the acquired company maintain its turnover once it is fully integrated into the overall company?

[?] How well is the company managing its gross margin (gross profit divided by sales)? This should be compared across time and to the margin achieved by competitors. If the margin is too high, it may be damaging sales and/or sales growth. Check. If it is too low, it may reflect a poor pricing policy, a poor product mix and/or not sufficient control of the direct cost base. Each of these possibilities should be checked as far as it is possible.

[?] Are the indirect overhead costs being sufficiently well managed? There is a habit of 'successful' companies 'over-growing' their indirect central administration. This needs watching.

[?] How far do current profits reflect one-off events - profits made on the sale of a major asset, re-organisation costs, etc.?

[?] Do the profits look sustainable given the state of the company, the competitive nature of the sector and the overall health of the economy? This is not an easy question to answer but it is the question at the heart of company analysis!

Cash Flow Statements

It should come as no surprise that cash flow statements can provide additional insights. In fact, as intimated above, some analysts see such statements as the corner-stone of good company analysis. The cash flow statement allows the investor to establish whether the company is generating or consuming cash. Major changes in the company - such as capital expenditure, acquisitions, asset disposals, etc. can all be examined in terms of their cash consumption/generation.

NUTSHELL

The **Cash Flow Statement** sets out movements in cash during the accounting year and, unlike profits, it is almost impossible to create cash flows out of thin air!

Also, it indicates how any cash surplus is being used or how any shortfall is being funded. As for the previous sub-sections, we present below an outline cash statement.

FIGURE 5.3

Outline Cash Flow Statement

£ million

Cash effects of transactions relating to the operating activities. A note will reconcile the operating profit to this figure.	Net cash inflow (outflow) from operating activities	670
Includes interest and dividends received and interest and preference dividends paid.	Returns on investment and servicing of finance	(55)
UK corporation tax and overseas tax paid and/or repaid.	Taxation	(75)
Includes the purchase or disposal of fixed assets (other than as part of businesses acquired or sold) and the purchase or disposal of investments.	Capital expenditure and financial investment	(185)
Cash flows related to the acquisition or disposal of business undertakings (e.g. subsidiaries, associated companies).	Acquisitions and disposals	(140)
Dividends paid to ordinary shareholders.	Equity dividends paid	(110)
Includes the withdrawals from/payments into short term deposits and the purchase and sale of short term investments.	Management of liquid resources	(60)
Include receipts from issuing shares, increasing loans and payments to repurchase shares and repay loans.	Financing	(115)
Sum of the above cash flows.	Increase/(decrease) in cash	(70)

An analysis of the above table indicates that the company is generating cash from its operating activities. The sections dealing with returns on investments and servicing of finance, taxation and investing activities reveal whether cash is being absorbed or generated from non-operating activities. In this instance, the funds generated or absorbed by investing activities in terms of acquisitions or sales of subsidiaries and the purchase and disposal of fixed assets are of particular interest. Overall, the net cash flow from operating and non-operating activities is positive. However, the payment of dividends, the management of liquid resources and the financing activities of the company led to a net decrease (70) in its cash position.

RATIOS AND ANALYSIS

It is never easy deciding on the best way to present the analysis of financial statements. This is because the three financial statements of balance sheet, profit and loss and cash flow are, by nature, inter-related. We have decided, however, to split the inter-related analysis into three separate subsections reflecting the individual financial statements. Before we move on to consider the analysis of balance sheets, however, we need to discuss some issues that are relevant to the analysis of financial statements in general.

The first thing to note is that a business is a multi-dimensional entity and it is not sensible to draw conclusions from a single financial item in isolation. For example, you might note that the debt funding of a business has increased markedly. This may or may not be a negative; it all depends on why the funds have been raised. If the debt has increased because the business saw a profitable opportunity to raise its fixed asset base, then this is a positive rather than a negative. Second, as already noted, the published accounts are based upon an historical cost valuation base and this may give a poor approximation to market and/or 'real' values. Third, financial statements include aggregated figures. For example, for many companies, the overall turnover figure is an aggregation of sales figures from many different types of business. It is quite possible that the overall turnover figure is hiding bad news from a particular sector. You, of course, may never be able to find out the detail behind the aggregated figures but it is always worth having a sceptical frame of mind when analysing financial statements. Part of the reason for spending a fair bit of time on the context part of the process is to gain some insight into what might lie behind the published aggregate figures. Finally, it is worth remembering that a financial profile of a company should reflect the sector that it belongs to. For this reason it is difficult to derive simple mechanical rules of company analysis.

The Analysis of Balance Sheet Items

Now that we have given you the appropriate 'health warnings', it is time to turn to the analysis of balance sheet items. Remember that a lot of the detail you require will only be found in the notes to the accounts.

Fixed Assets

Remember that fixed assets are items that a business means to keep (normally for more than a year). They include such items as plant and machinery, fixtures and fittings, and land and buildings. With the exception of the last, they are recorded at what they cost, less accumulated depreciation. In contrast, land and buildings may be revalued to reflect current market values. In addition to these tangible fixed assets, there may also be intangible fixed assets, such as patents, goodwill and brand values. There are some specific questions which need considering for each of these individual items of fixed assets, as well as more general questions.

? **Plant and Machinery** - are the values written down to zero, or is there evidence of the plant being updated? Are the depreciation policies in line with sector norms? Is the spending on new plant in line with the key competitors? Is the capital intensity (sales divided by plant and machinery) of the business comparable to the rest of the sector? Essentially, if the business is in manufacturing (as compared to services), do you feel that there has been sensible investment in plant and machinery and is it generating the necessary sales and profits?

? **Fixtures and Fittings** - similar arguments apply as to those given under the plant and machinery heading. The importance of this item will vary by sector, with it being very important for high street retailers.

? **Land and Buildings** - here the obvious questions to ask are: when was the last revaluation and, on current market values, is the company comparable to its closest competitors? By now, you must be asking how close competitors are to be defined. Well, they should normally be of a similar size (in either sales, employees or market capitalisation) have a similar range of business interests and a similar geographic spread. Please note, this is not always as easy to achieve as it sounds.

[?] **Patents** - is it the type of business where patents might be important, for example, a genetic engineering company? If so, are they shown in the accounts? How have they been valued? Are they being amortised (depreciated)? If not, what is being assumed about their long term value?

[?] **Brand Values** - are these an important part of the company's value? For example, consider how important the brand Burger King is for Diageo. Are the brand values shown in the accounts and how have they been estimated?

[?] **Goodwill** - occurs when a company pays more for another business than its net asset value. Most UK companies write this 'excess' payment straight off to reserves. The notes to the accounts will tell you how much goodwill has been written off. The real question here is whether the total price paid for a business (therefore, inclusive of goodwill) was warranted given the long term net addition to the overall profits (or net cash generation potential) of the business.

In general, you should consider the following types of question:

■ Is the investment in fixed assets similar to that of the close competitors? If not, why not?

■ Is the make-up of fixed assets comparable to that of the competitors. If not, why not?

■ How are the assets being valued?

■ Are they generating sufficient sales and profits?

Current Assets and Current Liabilities

The next part of the analysis of balance sheets is concerned with current assets and current liabilities. Here there are two basic issues to consider:

Liquidity - does the company have sufficient liquid current assets to meet short term liabilities?

 Working Capital Management - given the costs of working capital, are the individual components of cash, debtors, stock and credit well managed?

Liquidity

The issue here is whether there is any threat that the company could be forced into liquidation because it is unable to meet short term liabilities (creditors). So the starting point is to try and assess the short term liability position of the company. This can be achieved as follows. Consider the size of the year-end creditors and the amount of any short term bank loans that might need repaying within a given period; some notion of the average credit period for the sector will tell you how much time the company has before it needs to pay its creditors. Furthermore, we will show below how the company's own past credit period can be derived from the accounts. At this stage, you should have a feel for the short term financial commitments of the company.

The next step is to calculate the short term financial resources available to the company. First, what is the cash position of the company? Second, given the defined period of interest derived from the credit position of the company, how much of the year-end debtor values can be turned into cash? This depends on the ability of the company to turn debtors into cash and this can be derived from the company's accounts (see below). Finally, given annual turnover, what new sales are likely to be made and turned into cash in the period of interest, allowing for the debtor collection policies of the company?

As you can imagine, the above can take a bit of calculating and there is still a fair amount of guess work involved. For this reason, analysts tend to use short-hand liquidity ratios and we will describe the two most common.

$$\text{Current Ratio} = \frac{\text{Current Assets}}{\text{Current Liabilities}}$$

$$\text{Quick Ratio} = \frac{\text{Current Assets} - \text{Stock}}{\text{Current Liabilities}}$$

Analysts are supposed to like a Current Ratio to have a value of 2 or above and Quick Ratio (where the less liquid asset of stock is removed) to have a value of 1 or above. But clearly, care needs to be taken in using such broad brush measures. First, large companies can afford to run liquidity ratios at far lower levels than mentioned. This is because they have market power compared to most (if not all) of their suppliers. Imagine a small food manufacturer taking on one of the big supermarket chains because its invoice had not been paid. Second, it should be obvious that the ratios hide the important detail. It could be the case that a company has low levels of the ratios but the current assets are dominated by cash because the business is highly cash generative. Third, as we will see shortly, efficient working capital management will lead to 'low' liquidity. This is not a problem if the management of working capital (cash + debtors + stocks − creditors) also involves keeping an eye on the liquidity position of the company. As for other aspects of company analysis, the best that can be hoped for is to compare the liquidity position of the company, via the above ratios, with its recent past and to its close competitors. If there appears to be a problem, then the detailed analysis we started this section with may need to be gone through.

Working Capital Management

The management of current asset and current liabilities is a tricky business. A business needs sufficient cash and stocks to meet the daily demands of the business. Similarly, it needs to offer credit terms to its customers that are competitive with the rest of the sector. In terms of suppliers, it does not want to pay them too quickly but it still wants a loyal set of suppliers. All of the above business needs have to be balanced against the costs of running high balances of cash, debtors and stocks and low balances of creditors (suppliers who supply on credit terms). Over the past decade, there has been an increased emphasis on working capital management through improved cash systems (consider the movement of cash and 'cash equivalents' through the tills of supermarkets to interest earning accounts), better stock control (just-in-time distribution systems) and improving credit management systems (debtors are vetted and chased by computer based systems).

Not surprisingly, therefore, it is difficult to compare current working capital management practices with those of even 5-6 years ago. The best that can be hoped for is to compute the following ratios and see if they are improving/deteriorating for the company of interest and how they compare to its close competitors.

$$\text{Stock Turnover} \quad = \quad \frac{\text{Cost of Sales}}{\text{Average Stock}}$$

The purpose of the above ratio is to establish how often the company turns its stock over in a year. The numerator should ideally be the cost of sales (this does not include a profit margin, as is also the case for stock values) but often you will be forced to use the sales figure for the year because this is all that is available. The denominator is the average of opening and closing stock for the year. So imagine that the sales figure was £1,000 and the average stock for the year was £250; this means that the company would have turned over its stock 4 times in a year (or $365 \div 4 = 91.25$ days).

$$\text{Debtor Days} \quad = \quad \frac{\text{Sales}}{\text{Average Debtors}}$$

As with the stock turnover ratio, we can calculate the average time it takes for a company to collect its debtors. If the sales figure was £1,000 and the average debtors ((opening + closing debtors) $\div$ 2) was £100, then the company would turn its debtors over 10 times in a year ($365 \div 10 = 36.5$ days). Finally, we can make a similar calculation for creditors.

$$\text{Creditor Days} \quad = \quad \frac{\text{Cost of Sales}}{\text{Average Creditors}}$$

As for stock turnover, the numerator of creditor days should be cost of sales (the creditors supply raw materials, etc., **not** sales) but we will stick to using the sales figure in the current example. So if the average creditors for the year ((opening + closing creditors) $\div$ 2) was £50, then the company would have turned its creditors over $1000 \div 50 = 20$ times ($365 \div 20 = 18.25$ days).

With all of the above, care needs to be taken with respect to the peculiarities of the sector. For example, a stock turnover figure would not make much sense for a bridge builder or a hotel. Neither of those activities is concerned with selling stock. The bridge builder completes major projects and the hotel sells space. Similarly, it would be plain daft to calculate a debtor turnover ratio for a pure cash business; for example, selling Christmas trees to families.

Sources of Funds or Gearing

The final part of analysing the balance sheet is to consider whether the funding of the company is 'risky or safe'. The basic idea here is that if a company has used a lot of debt to fund its activities, there will be commitments to meet interest payments and capital repayment and we need to be sure that these can be met if the profit and, more importantly, the cash generation of the business turns downwards. This topic is normally called 'Gearing' (Leverage in the US) and it is highly confused because textbooks and analysts use different terms to mean the same thing. To avoid this confusion, we will go back to basic principles. The first thing you need to identify is the debt position of the company. This is normally taken to equal the long term liabilities of a company but in reality, short term borrowings should also be included. To ignore short term borrowings would be to mis-represent the total debt of a company and this is especially the case for smaller companies. Once the debt position has been established it needs to be compared to the equity funds of the business. We define this as shareholder funds which equals issued share capital plus retained profits (reserves). Thus, we are able to compute the following gearing ratio:

$$\text{Gearing} = \frac{\text{Debt}}{\text{Shareholder Funds}}$$

Now, the obvious question to ask is how you should interpret any given gearing ratio? At the outset, a ratio greater than 100% might be considered high but as always, the ratio cannot be interpreted in isolation. First, the significance of any gearing level depends upon the relationship of the company with its debt providers. Second, if the company has stability in its cash generation, it will be able to carry a higher debt level. This moves us onto a second way of looking at the funding structures of companies. The real concern is whether a company is generating sufficient profits to meet interest payments. Here, there is normally the following form of ratio:

$$\text{Interest Cover} = \frac{\text{Profit before Interest and Tax}}{\text{Total Interest Payable}}$$

You should consider how far profits can decline before the company is unable to meet its debt commitments. Note, it is perfectly possible for a company to have a high balance sheet gearing ratio (debt/shareholder funds) but also have a high level of profit generation compared to its debt payment commitments. But, this is taking us into the profit and loss account and it is, therefore, time to move onto the next section.

The Profit and Loss Account

Although we have already covered the basic elements of profit and loss accounts, we need to go into a bit more detail before we go further with our analysis. The easiest way of tackling this issue is to work our way down a profit and loss account - you might like to refer back to the outline profit and loss account.

At the top of a profit and loss account there should be gross profit (although sometimes companies just report operating profit - see below). This is an important measure of profit as it measures sales turnover minus cost of sales. If there are major changes in this measure of profit, (although it fluctuates on a yearly basis) you will want to know why. A rapid rise in gross profit should be reviewed just as much as a rapid fall. Competition normally prevents such marked changes and it may be worth spending some time assessing whether the change reflects sustainable business reality or is a short term 'accounting fix'. After gross profit, we next come to operating profit which is effectively gross profit minus central overhead charges. This is a key measure of profit because it is arguably the best overall indicator of how well the core of a business is doing. However, most analysts tend to focus on profit before interest and tax which is operating profit less exceptional charges. In the outline profit and loss account, the exceptional charges were captured under the headings of profit/losses on the sale or termination of operations and/or the disposal of fixed assets and the costs of a fundamental reorganisation. It is clearly debatable whether such costs should be taken into account, given their exceptional nature, when assessing the relative operating performance of a business. Of course, if a company is in the habit of chopping and changing its activities, then such exceptional items are likely to be run of the mill events and on this basis they should be considered. As always, there is no easy answer to this issue and the best that can be hoped for is that you analyse the accounts of the target company and then reach a decision to include/exclude exceptional items in the measure of operating performance. Once you have reached a decision, you must remember to apply the adopted measure consistently.

The next measure of profit is profit before tax; thus interest has been deducted from the profit before interest and tax measure of performance; particularly significant for companies with high levels of debt. In such a situation, changes in interest rates can have a major impact on the company and, therefore, it is worth keeping an eye on this measure of profit. We then move down the profit and loss account and come to profit after tax. For a shareholder this is a key measure of profit because it is what is available for distribution to the owners of the business. Of course, a company has to meet the obligations of preference shareholders and minority interests and this moves us down to the profit that is attributable to ordinary shareholders. From this figure a company decides how much to distribute to shareholders as dividends and to retain in the business.

From an individual shareholder perspective, the important figure is the dividend per share and this is obtained by dividing the total amount of dividends to be distributed by the total number of shares issued. It is not unknown for companies to have major share issues (rights issues) and this potentially dilutes the dividends per share. Finally, the bottom of a profit and loss account indicates a figure known as earnings per share (EPS). This is equal to profit after tax (the profits that are potentially distributable to all shareholders) divided by the number of issued shares. Although this is an important ratio and one that is frequently talked about by the financial press, it is arguable whether it is more informative than the ability of a company to provide its shareholders with a healthy dividend per share. Earnings per share measure the potential of a company to reward its shareholders, while dividend per share measures the actual reward paid out to shareholders (in addition to any capital gains through share price increases).

Now that we have covered the various measures of profit, it is time to turn to the commonly used profit ratios. It has to be accepted that there is a lot of confusion with regard to what

CLOSE-UP

Although there are given rates of corporation tax, companies vary in their ability to manage taxes. To gauge the extent of the tax management divide the tax charge by the profit before tax figure. Then compare this with previous years. If there has been a marked improvement in the tax charges of the company, be wary - it might just be a one-off and the figures for the next year could suffer.

are the most appropriate measures of profit performance. We will stick our necks out and plump for two.

In terms of trying to measure the basic performance of a business, the best, most commonly used measured is:

Return on Total Assets (ROTA) = $\dfrac{\text{Profit before Interest and Tax}}{\text{Total Assets}}$

This tells you how the total assets of a business are being used to generate operational (after exceptional items) profits. It is also often instructive to break ROTA down into its two key constituent parts:

$$\frac{\text{Profit before Interest and Tax (PBIT)}}{\text{Total Assets (TA)}} = \frac{\text{PBIT}}{\text{Sales}} \times \frac{\text{Sales}}{\text{TA}}$$

The first ratio (PBIT/Sales) measures the profit margin and the second measures the ability of a business to generate sales from its asset base. As we know, the overall profitability of a business is a function of its ability to generate sales volume and margin on its sales, and occasionally it is worth knowing how a company compares on each of these aspects to its close competitors.

The second commonly quoted profit ratio is:

Return on Equity = $\dfrac{\text{Profit after Tax}}{\text{Shareholder Funds}}$

This measures the profit that is potentially distributable to shareholders as a proportion of all the funds that they have a claim on (issued share capital plus reserves).

Market Ratios

We should now consider a couple of the stock market ratios that are used to evaluate company performance. For although we have so far emphasised the importance of being able to interpret company accounts, there is also information to be gained from comparing the accounting items of a company to its current share price and the number of shares it has in issue. As we have already covered earnings per share (EPS), we will focus on the price/earnings (PE) ratio and dividend yield.

The Price/Earnings (PE) Ratio

The PE ratio (the share price divided by the company's earnings per share) has a special place in analysts' tool-kits. It allows them, at a glance, because PE ratios are published in the *Financial Times*, to compare the share prices of different companies. It is important to note, however, that the earnings per share denominator of published PEs is based on the most recent published earnings of the company. Of course, given that investors are more interested in the future than the past, prospective PE ratios might be more useful. Here a company's current share price is divided by its expected earnings for the coming year. Allowing for the difficulties in forecasting earnings, a low prospective PE (relative to the sector and close competitors) would indicate that on an equivalent earnings basis, the price of the target company's shares is less than its comparators. This could, however, indicate one of three things. First, as a lot of people would conclude, the share is underpriced. Second, and this is no more wrong than the first option, that the share is correctly priced. The quality of the earnings of the company (in either level or volatility) is such that the market has correctly priced the shares below that of the sector and close competitors. Third, it may even be the case that the shares are overpriced. We know for a fact that sectors come into fashion (for example, bio-tech stocks in the mid to late 80s) and one consequence of this is massively inflated PE ratios. Part of the reason for such high PEs is the market's expectation of high earnings generation from the sector and/or the company. Time and again, the market's expectations have shown to be based more on faith (or possibly hype) than substance. In this situation the shares would, in retrospect, have been shown to be overpriced.

Dividend Yield

The dividend yield of a company is defined as the dividend per share divided by the current share price. It is always worth bearing in mind that PEs and dividend yields are both related to the current price of a share. Since share prices are determined by the aggregate actions of investors in the stock market, PE ratios and dividend yields need not tell you about the fundamental strengths or weaknesses of a company, but possibly only how the company is perceived by the market. This, of course, raises a key issue. If share prices are merely a reflection of market sentiment, why should we be concerned with the fundamental strength of companies? It is this argument that lies behind J.M. Keynes oft repeated statement that success on the stock market is a bit like guessing the outcome of a beauty contest. Where Keynes was wrong, however, is that, unlike beauty contests, the stock market is not a one-off event, rather it is a continuous process supported by the reporting of business realities (here we include the reporting of company news as well as accounts) and this conditions how far share prices can be determined purely by market sentiment. In essence, what we are arguing is that the realities of day-to-day business place an eventual brake on the extent to which fantasies can determine share prices; in other words, bubbles always burst!

We are reminded of the saying, 'you can fool some of the people some of the time but you cannot fool all of the people all of the time'. It is for this very reason that it is worth considering the fundamentals underpinning the cash generation of a business.

The Importance of Cash

Although the above sections detailed the different measures of profit that might be used to judge the performance of a company, this chapter has emphasised that profits are open to manipulation, whereas cash generation is not. This, in itself, is a good reason for focusing on cash. There is, however, an even better reason; that is, at the end of the day, the long term performance and value of a company are based upon net cash generation and not profits. After all, shareholders need cash to buy their goods, not some accountant's fictional notion of profits.

Now clearly, the fundamental determinants of business value (net cash generation) is not a small or easy topic. If it was, how could we explain the 80s' and 90s' phenomena of stock market and management gurus, the armies of highly paid consultants and MBAs that now populate western corporations, and the many bookshops now devoted to the subject? We couldn't. In this book we devote Chapters 10 and 13 to outlining some of the basic frameworks of thought on the subject. With these future chapters in mind, here we describe briefly how one company's (Boots) emphasis on cash generation, rather than the more usual accounting and/or stock market measures (such as earnings per share), has allowed it to focus more clearly on the fundamental determinants of business value.

In 1990 Boots converted to value-based management and the basic principle at the core of their approach is to maximise the long term net cash generation of its businesses. So the express purpose of Boots is to manage sustainable net cash generation and not the more common short term earnings of the business. Boots' system of maximising net cash generation starts by the company analysing the competitive position of its businesses via the application of Porter's 'five forces' model (more of which in Chapter 10). This allows the identification of the important alternatives facing the businesses. Once these alternatives have been identified, they are evaluated in terms of their net cash generation potential. If an alternative fits in with the strategic direction of the company and it adds value (that is, it is a net cash generator including taking account of the cost of capital), then it should be pursued. With this approach, every alternative is evaluated with the same measuring tool. Thus, there is no distinction between capital and revenue expenditure and this should in itself provide a clarity of corporate thinking. Of course, the one 'problem' with this approach is that it emphasises long term value creation and the company needs to be willing to ride out the hiccups that are bound to occur with short term earnings.

Companies have, for quite some time, measured individual projects on a cash generation basis and all that is being suggested with the value-based management approach is that the overall corporate activities be evaluated in the same way. The problem for the City and individual investors, however, is that measures of the net cash generation potential of companies are not published. In fact, this approach to assessing company performance takes a fair bit more effort than those based on published PEs, etc. As we will see, however, in Chapters 10 and 13, the effort may well be worth it!

EVALUATION AND CONCLUSION

This chapter has so far described the first three parts to the CORE approach to the financial analysis of companies. We started by discussing the importance of understanding the context of a company. Here you need to review the salient characteristics of the sector and the recent history of the company. We noted that there is a wide range of available information sources to tackle this part of the process. The second part of the process is an overview of the financial statements of the target company and its close competitors. You will normally need two to three years of recent statements. Here you are looking for any major changes or unusual events. Once you have obtained a feel for which items of the accounts might warrant closer inspection, the third part of the process moves into more detailed analysis. We described the importance of focusing on individual accounting items, as well as forming aggregate financial ratios. You need both to form a full picture. We also stressed the importance of identifying the net cash generation abilities of companies. Cash, unlike profits, cannot be readily created by accountants. The final part of the CORE process is to bring together the evidence from the first three steps and form some sort of overall evaluation. This last step is no easier than the first three steps and how it is approached depends on the individual investor. Imagine you had been analysing a company in the pushchair and pram market. How might you draw together a final evaluation? You might try to see if your impressions were supported by analysts' reports or recent news items. You might bounce your conclusions off some close colleagues and this is one of the benefits of belonging to an investment club. You might know people in the industry and they could form a useful sounding board. Or you might know people who have been customers or suppliers of the business. With all of the above, you are testing your analysis against alternative and recent perspectives. You can do no more! Of course, the power of really good fundamental analysis of companies is that you might know more than any of these alternative perspectives. The purpose of Chapters 10 and 13 is to develop these fundamental thinking skills further.

LESSONS TO BE LEARNT

 Always spend as much time as it needs to understand the context of a company.

 Take an overview of the accounts to highlight important and/or unusual changes.

 While financial ratios can help you to understand the performance, never forget to check your conclusions against the individual accounting items.

 Remember that companies are multi-dimensional entities and no single accounting item should be considered in isolation.

 The net cash generation of a company is a far more reliable indicator of performance than profits.

 It is worth spending some time thinking through which models might best explain the cash generation ability of a given business - a topic we give a lot more time to in Chapters 10 and 13.

PART THREE

ACADEMIC PERSPECTIVES
ON
MARKET BEHAVIOUR

CHAPTER 6

Statistics
and the
Scientific Approach

This chapter looks at what a scientifically based approach can offer to the study of the behaviour of the stock market. Scientists can put a man on the moon, split the atom and perform genetic engineering. By comparison one might think that predicting whether the stock market is going to go up or down should be a trivial task if rigorous scientific methodologies are employed. In fact, predicting share prices raises some difficult problems not encountered in the physical sciences. Market reactions are not based on physical phenomena which can be assumed to be stable over time. Scientists know, for example, that the speed of light in a vacuum or the gravitational constant are not going to change every time they perform an experiment. By contrast, market movements are determined by the interaction of many different investors who might well change their behaviour from time to time. It is an open question as to whether people, in general, do change their behaviour over time, or whether one could justifiably take the view that 'human nature never changes' and so mass behaviour is reasonably stable. In this chapter we assess how much a strictly scientific approach can offer to the practical stock market investor.

STATISTICS AND PROBABILITY

ORIGINS

The mathematical approach to uncertainty has a very long pedigree - as early as the 15th century Italian mathematicians were studying probability.[1] The earliest applications of probability theory were fairly narrow and not entirely altruistic. The main aim of the early exponents of the science was to improve their chances of winning at dice games like craps.

One of the most notable features of stock market behaviour is its apparent uncertainty. A whole branch of mathematics based around probability and statistical theory has been developed in order to quantify and deal with uncertainty. Over time it has been recognised that uncertainty is a feature of most aspects of life and probability and statistical theory are now successfully used in almost every field of modern scientific research and in many practical fields. In fact the importance of statistics can hardly be overstated. No new medical treatment or drug can be introduced without first being subject to statistical testing for efficacy and safety. The insurance industry is based entirely on the practical application of statistics to calculate premiums correctly. New military equipment is evaluated by statistical methods. In manufacturing, statistics are used in quality control. Marketing and market research are increasingly statistically based. Statistics are used to aid decisions in education, economics, engineering, meteorology and many other fields. The list of statistical applications could go on and on. Given its great success in so many fields involving uncertainty, it is natural that academics have turned to statistics and probability theory as the basis for their investigations into the stock market.

The essential principle of statistics is to make inferences based on the observation of the available data. When applied to the stock market, statistics can be used to analyse past share price returns to find the answers to some basic and important questions about the nature of the market.

Statistics and probability theory can be a highly technical and difficult subject. This is not a mathematical text book and we have no intention of boring or confusing you by going into too many technicalities. What we intend to do is introduce some important practical issues regarding market behaviour and then show how they can be resolved by statistics and how the conclusions should be borne in mind by a practical investor.

HOW ARE EQUITY RETURNS RELATED OVER TIME?

The question of how share price returns are related over time is vital to every investor. If share price returns are highly related over time, this would be highly profitable knowledge as future share prices could be predicted from past share prices. For example, if a good day in the market was almost sure to be followed by another good day, it would be fairly easy for investors to start to make a profit out of this. Even obscure relationships could be highly useful. If the share price movement today could be related in any way to price movements over, say, the last month or the last year, this would be well worth knowing.

When addressing this issue it is helpful to gently introduce some statistical terminology. Two events are said to be **statistically independent** if the probability of the occurrence of one is unaffected by the occurrence or non-occurrence of the other. The share price return in a particular period would be said to be independent of the return in an earlier period **if** knowledge of the return in the earlier period is of no use in predicting the return in the later period.

Many of the most common gambles involve independent events. The outcome when tossing a coin does not depend on whether the coin came up heads or tails last time it was tossed and when throwing a die, the outcome does not depend on the number that came up last time the die was thrown. Similarly when playing roulette, the outcome does not depend on the outcome the last time the game was played. In the gambles just described, knowing what happened in the past would be no guide to the future. Some other common events are clearly not independent. For example, in most card games, the cards that a player may receive late in the game will not be independent of the cards that have already been dealt.

The examples given so far are not very problematic in that the independence of the events can be easily determined from examination of the physical circumstances surrounding them. When a coin is tossed fairly, it is clear that it is not physically influenced by any other events and so it will be independent of other events.

However, in many other situations it is by no means so clear as to whether we would expect events to be independent or not. For example, if it rained yesterday it is not obvious whether it is more or less likely to rain today. Or if a football team won its last match does it mean it is more or less likely to win its next match? The stock market falls into this category of ambiguous situations where it is not obvious whether one would expect price movements to be independent or not. To resolve these problems statisticians look directly at the data; by investigating the history of share price movements they can determine whether they are independent or not.

The Random Walk

ORIGINS

The term '**random walk**' is believed to have been first used in an exchange of correspondence between Karl Pearson and Lord Rayleigh which appeared in *Nature* in 1905.[2] The correspondence concerned the following problem: if one leaves a drunk in an empty field on a dark night and then wishes to find him some time later, what is the best strategy?
The solution is to start at the point where the drunk had been left and walk away in a straight line in any direction. The reasoning behind this solution is that this point is an unbiased estimate of the drunk's future position if he is staggering along in a completely random fashion.

If share price movements were independent over time, past price changes would be of no use in predicting future price changes. Price changes would behave in this respect as if they were generated by throws of a die. In this case, share prices would be said to follow a random walk. The first tests of whether security prices followed a random walk were carried out by the French mathematician Louis Bachelier in his PhD thesis which was published in 1900. He found that the prices of French government bonds were consistent with the random walk model.[3] In the thesis, he derived many of the mathematical properties of random walks. It is a measure of his achievement that he anticipated some of the later work by Einstein into the behaviour of particles subject to random shocks. Bachelier suffered the misfortune of being too far ahead of his time. The stock market was not really considered a suitable topic for academic study in France at the turn of the century and his findings were effectively ignored. He struggled to establish an academic career and never attained any acclaim in his own lifetime.[4]

Half a century after Bachelier's thesis, the random walk idea was revisited by a distinguished British statistician, Sir Maurice Kendall. In 1953, Kendall found changes in security prices in a number of stock groupings and commodity markets to behave almost as if they were generated by a suitable die or roulette wheel. For example, regarding the price of wheat on the Chicago commodity market he commented, 'the series looks like a "wandering" one, almost as if once a week the Demon of Chance drew a random number from a symmetrical population of fixed dispersion and added it to the current price to determine next week's price'.[5] Thus Kendall's findings essentially supported the random walk model.

Interpretation of the Random Walk

The proposition that share price changes follow a random walk can certainly seem a rather startling idea. On first meeting the idea many people interpret it as showing that the stock market is virtually on a par with a casino. It also seems to be an uncomfortably nihilistic concept. It seems hard to accept that no matter how much study and analysis are performed, the future prices of shares are not predictable. There is, after all, a whole industry in the City of London based on the prediction of future share prices; are we to believe that all this effort is a waste of time? The famous, Nobel prize winning economist, Paul Samuelson, was able to provide a logical rationale for the random walk in an academic paper in 1965.[6] The essence of the idea he presented is that there are so many intelligent, well informed investors competing in the market that all the relevant information available about a share will already be reflected in its price. When new information arrives, it is reflected in prices very quickly. If a company announces disappointing earnings or launches a take-over bid for another company, investors cannot afford to delay in acting on this information or they will lose out to their competitors. Prices will move rapidly to reflect the new information as investors buy or sell shares to reflect the news. New information arrives randomly and so share prices move in a random fashion. This argument is quite reassuring in the sense that it bases the situation in logic and rationality.

Prices may move in a random manner but this is actually because they are determined in a way that is highly rational. The argument is also, at least to some extent, a reasonable description of market activity. It is certainly true that the market is a highly competitive place and prices do move quickly in response to new information. However, it is something of an open question as to the extent to which the theory provides a complete explanation of market behaviour. As we will see in the following chapters, there are many other ways of looking at the markets and the behaviour of people in them.

Alternatives to the Random Walk

The random walk model of the stock market is a very simple statistical model. It captures some important market features; namely, that it is a very difficult task to predict future share price movements from past patterns in share prices and the even more fundamental fact that there is a large element of chance in share price movements. However, economists and statisticians have considered alternatives to the basic random walk model which may improve the theoretical and practical understanding of market behaviour.

Mean Reversion or Mean Aversion

ORIGINS

Mean reversion was first formalised by the 19th century British scientist, Francis Galton. Galton carried out a famous experiment to study the relationship between the heights of sons and their parents. He found that although parents who were taller than average also had tall sons (and short parents, short sons), the sons tended to be closer to the average height of the general population than their parents. In other words the height of the sons regressed to the mean height of the general population.

Mean reversion, which is also known as 'regression to the mean', is a well known concept both within statistics and in everyday life. (In statistical terminology the average is known as the mean.) The idea of mean reversion is a very familiar one to most people. The concept is encapsulated in such popular expressions as 'what goes up must come down' and 'pride goes before a fall'. There are many concrete examples of mean reversion to confirm the clichés. For example, the economy never booms forever, not every summer is a good one, even the most successful football clubs don't win the league every year. The idea of mean reversion is so familiar and comfortable to many people that they automatically assume that it must apply to the stock market. When shares have gone down, they assume they will go up again. When shares are high, they assume they must fall.

Mean aversion is in a sense the opposite concept to mean reversion. Broadly speaking it is the concept that things which have moved away from their mean have a tendency to move still further away. For example, if the heights of individuals display mean aversion instead of mean reversion, tall people would have children even taller than themselves and short people children even shorter than themselves. This situation fortunately does not exist as it would result in a population of giants and midgets. Natural examples of mean aversion are, in fact, hard to find. However, a lot of stock market trading is conducted on the intuitive supposition that some sort of mean averting process underlies share price movements. Traders who buy fast rising shares in the hope that they will continue to rise or who sell falling shares because they expect them to continue to fall, are acting in accordance with this view.

Figure 6.1 below shows a diagrammatic representation of random, mean averting and mean reverting price behaviour in the stock market immediately following a dramatic rise in a share price.

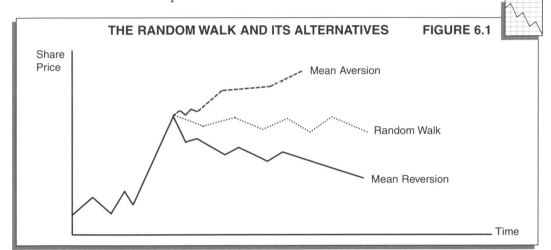

THE RANDOM WALK AND ITS ALTERNATIVES   FIGURE 6.1

Evidence for Mean Reversion

Three major research approaches have been used to evaluate the question of whether shares exhibit mean reversion.

1 The prediction of future returns from current dividend yields or price-earnings ratios

A number of academic studies have been carried out to predict whether long-horizon stock returns can be predicted from the dividend yield of the stock market or the price-earnings ratio of the market.[7] The argument goes that when dividend yields are high or price-earnings ratios are low, shares are relatively lowly priced and can be expected to show good returns in the future. This is because dividend yields and price-earnings can be expected to revert to their means over time. The converse also holds in that when dividend yields are low or price-earnings ratios are high, shares are highly priced and probably will not show good returns in the future. If the stock market does in fact follow a random walk, current dividend yields and price-earnings ratios would be of no use in predicting future stock returns.

The evidence from the studies is in favour of an element of mean reversion in stock market prices. There is a tendency for share returns to be related to their starting dividend yields or price-earnings ratios. Thus it is somewhat more advantageous, on average, to invest in the stock market when dividend yields are high and price-earnings ratios are low. This is not, however, a method which can be reliably used to make a quick profit. There is virtually no evidence that the method would be useful for investment periods of less than a year. Over longer periods, of around three or four years, the starting dividend yield or price-earnings ratio is a measure which is worth considering. Around a third of the total stock returns in the US market over these time periods have been predicted by the starting dividend yields or price-earnings ratios.[8] In effect, with respect to this predictor, the stock market acts more or less as a random walk in the short run but there is an element of mean reversion over fairly long periods. It must be remembered though that there are no absolute certainties on offer in the stock market. Even over the periods showing the greatest element of predictability, less than half the returns are predictable by this method.

 ## The prediction of good or bad market returns from the returns in previous years

The question of interest here is whether good years in the stock market tend to be followed by good years or bad years. Testing this proposition is really testing for mean reversion in its most basic form. If shares are mean reverting, good years will tend to be followed by bad years and bad years by good years. If shares follow a random walk it would make no difference to the returns in future years whether the returns in past years had been good or bad. Finally, if shares were mean averting good years would be followed by more good years and bad years by more bad years. McQueen and Thorley used what is known as Markov chain theory to investigate this question in the US market using data from the period 1947 to 1987.[9] Markov chain theory is a rather complicated area of mathematical theory which is based on the work of the mathematician A. A. Markov and is used to study how chains of events progress through time. There is no need for the reader to wrestle with the theory behind McQueen and Thorley's results. Their results are much more interesting than the way they obtained them. They found support for mean reversion. A good year in the market usually follows two bad years and a bad year usually follows two good years. Thus trends in the market tend to reverse after a couple of years. This has obvious practical applications. In other words, you might be wise to be a little more cautious than usual after a couple of good years and a little more optimistic after a couple of bad years.

3 The prediction of market returns from the correlation of returns with those in previous years

Before addressing the stock market issues directly in this case, it is worth introducing the statistical concept of **correlation**. Correlation concerns the strength of the relationship between two variables. If two variables tend to change in the same direction, they are positively correlated. For example, the distance driven and the amount of petrol consumed on a car journey are positively correlated. If two variables tend to change in the opposite direction, they are negatively correlated. For example, the rental of deck chairs at the seaside is negatively correlated to the rainfall at the time. The strength of the correlation between the variables can be quantified. This is achieved by calculating the **correlation coefficient**. The correlation coefficient varies between +1 and –1; with +1 representing perfect positive correlation and –1 representing perfect negative correlation. Figure 6.2 shows how the correlation coefficient scale works.

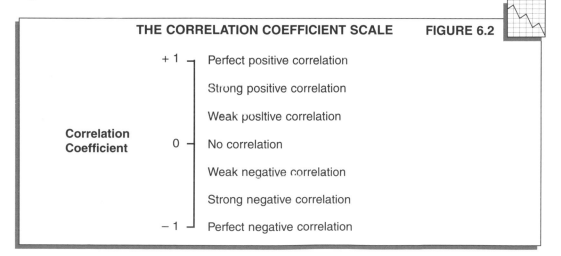

THE CORRELATION COEFFICIENT SCALE   FIGURE 6.2

+ 1	Perfect positive correlation
	Strong positive correlation
	Weak positive correlation
Correlation Coefficient 0	No correlation
	Weak negative correlation
	Strong negative correlation
– 1	Perfect negative correlation

Some examples can help to clarify the nature of correlation. An example of perfect positive correlation is the relationship between the diameter of a circle and its circumference. If one of these quantities is known, we can calculate what the other one will be. If the diameter increased by a certain percentage, the circumference would increase by exactly the same percentage. An example of positive but not perfect correlation would be the relationship between the height and weight of people. Taller people tend to be heavier, so the two variables are positively correlated. It is not possible, however, to exactly determine someone's weight from a knowledge only of their height. As we all know, some very tall people are very thin and some short people can be very heavy. This means that the correlation between the two variables is not perfect. An example of zero correlation would be the relationship between the scores on two dice which are thrown simultaneously. Knowing the score on one die would be of no help whatsoever in predicting the score on the other die.

Now that we have dealt with the general principles of correlation, we can now look at **share price correlations**. If share prices follow a random walk, returns will be uncorrelated through time and the return obtained in any particular period will be of no value in predicting the returns in any other period. If there is an element of mean reversion in share prices, returns will be negatively correlated at some lags. This is because, if share prices are mean reverting, high returns must be followed at some stage by low returns and low returns by high returns. If there is an element of mean aversion, then returns will be positively correlated at some lags. This is because, in the case of mean aversion, high returns must be followed by more high returns and low returns by more low returns. Thus it is possible to investigate the properties of stock price returns by examining the correlations in the series over different time lags.

Generally for all lags, from one day to a number of years, correlations between stock market returns are not large. In the UK, market correlations between daily returns for lags of up to five days have been calculated as less than + 0.1.[10] In the US, market correlations between annual real returns for lags of up to nine years have been calculated as being between 0 and − 0.21.[11] The small correlations observed are broadly consistent with the random walk model of the market. However, even small correlations are not incompatible with

NUTSHELL

The lag is simply the period of time over which the comparison is being made. So if we consider a lag of say, one year, we are comparing returns one year apart.

an amount of mean reversion which could form the basis of a profitable long term investment strategy.[12]

PRACTICAL CONCLUSIONS FROM THE RELATIONSHIPS BETWEEN RETURNS OVER TIME

After the above review of some of the main statistical approaches to assessing the randomness of the market, it may be useful to the reader to summarise the findings and to see what practical conclusions may be drawn. There are two main practical conclusions that can be reached:

! A large proportion of the price changes of shares is random movement. This means that no method can predict future price changes with any substantial degree of certainty. Investors should be very wary of any system or pundit that makes unqualified exact predictions. For example, when market strategists say they have a year end target of say 7,000 for the FTSE 100, this is a statement with not much more substance to it than someone predicting which number is going to come up when a die is thrown. The property of relatively random returns should not be taken to imply that no investment system can be better than any other but it does imply that there are limits to the success of any system. Even the best investment plans can be upset by unpredictable exogenous events which could not have been foreseen. To give some dramatic examples, an earthquake may affect the Japanese market, a crisis in the Middle East may affect the price of oil or the brilliant CEO of a company may die. To give some more routine examples, a company may suddenly announce that its earnings are not going to be as good as expected or that it is going to make an acquisition.

! There is some limited support for the view that markets revert to the mean in the long run and so investors should perhaps be more cautious after a period of very good share performance and more optimistic after a period of very bad performance.

However, in accordance with the previous conclusions, an investor should not be too sure that the trend will alter just when it is expected to. One may infer that the odds on something happening are getting longer but one cannot be certain that it won't happen. For example, at the time of writing (mid 1998) Wall Street has performed extremely well for a number of years and so the chances of it continuing to perform at an equally good rate in the future are decreasing but it can only be a matter of speculation as to when the next period of poor performance will start. The market has risen much further and for much longer than anyone expecting a fairly swift reversion to the mean would have anticipated. Anyone who switched out of the market when it first appeared to move too high based on historic notions of what was normal would have missed out on a considerable period of subsequent good performance.

THE STATISTICAL DISTRIBUTION OF EQUITY RETURNS

So far in this chapter we have dealt with the issue of how share price returns are related over time. An equally important issue is the size of the returns which are likely to be achieved or to use mathematical terminology, the **statistical distribution** of the returns.

The Normal Distribution

The best known statistical distribution is known as the normal distribution which was first recognised in the 17th century by the mathematician Abraham de Moivre. The main reason it is so well known is that it is so useful. A very large number of phenomena such as the height and weights of individuals, IQ scores, many measurement errors and most exam scores are normally distributed. The normal distribution has a characteristic bell shaped symmetrical curve as shown in Figure 6.3.

Now a particularly useful feature of the normal distribution is that if a phenomenon is normally distributed and we also know its average value (mean) and its standard deviation, it is possible to answer any question regarding the probability of future values of the phenomenon. (The standard deviation is a measure of the amount the phenomenon fluctuates from its average. For normally distributed phenomena, about 95% of the population will be within two standard deviations of the mean.) For example, if the heights of UK males are normally distributed with an average (mean) height of 69 inches and a standard deviation of 3 inches, it is possible to determine exactly the probability of a male being in any particular height range. The appropriate probability is the proportion of the total area under the normal curve which is in the height range of interest. So in Figure 6.3 the probability of a male being over 72 inches tall is the proportion which area A represents of the entire area under the normal curve. This area is in fact about 16% of the whole area, so the probability of a male being over 72 inches tall is about 16%.

NUTSHELL

The **probability** of an event occurring is the chance of it occurring measured on a scale from 0 to 1. Thus a probability of 0.1 of an event occurring is equivalent to a 1 in 10 (or 10%) chance of it occurring.

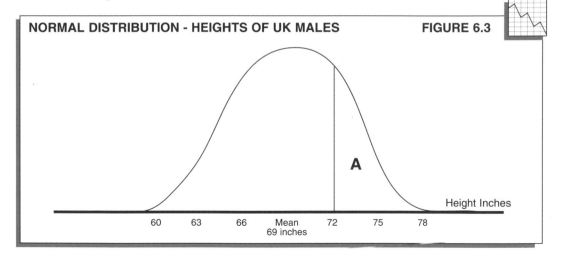

NORMAL DISTRIBUTION - HEIGHTS OF UK MALES   **FIGURE 6.3**

A

Height Inches

60   63   66   Mean   72   75   78
                        69 inches

The Stock Market and Normal Distribution

The relevance of the normal curve to stock market investment is that, like so many other phenomena, share price returns are reasonably close to being normally distributed. This means that we can estimate the probability of getting more or less than any given return over the next year in much the same way as we estimated the probability of a man being taller than a given height in the previous section. In fact the normal distribution is even more useful than this. Given the information about how share price returns are related over time, we can actually estimate the probability of getting more or less than any given return over any future period.

CLOSE-UP

Readers who are expert
in statistics might be
interested to note that a
lognormal distribution is
a more theoretically
appropriate distribution
to use for share price
returns. Table 6.1 has
been calculated on this
basis. For purposes of
exposition it was not felt
to be appropriate to
complicate matters for
the reader by explaining
the purpose of using a
lognormal instead of a
normal distribution.
Another feature of stock
market returns is that
very good or very bad
returns occur more
frequently than a normal
distribution would
suggest.

The appropriate calculations have been performed and a summary of the results is shown in Table 6.1. The calculations are based on the mean annual real returns and standard deviation of the UK stock market in the period from 1918 to 1996 which were 7.9% and 23.5% respectively.[13] The calculations have assumed that the market follows a random walk.[14]

| Table 6.1 | | |
| Distribution of real wealth over various periods from investment in equities based on a starting wealth of £100 | | |
Investment Period	Percentile	Ending Real Wealth (£)
1 Year	5	74
	25	92
	50	108
	75	127
	95	159
5 Years	5	63
	25	104
	50	148
	75	211
	95	352
10 Years	5	65
	25	134
	50	220
	75	363
	95	748
20 Years	5	86
	25	239
	50	485
	75	982
	95	2,735
30 Years	5	129
	25	449
	50	1,070
	75	2,534
	95	8,889

The table allows you to assess what an investment in equities is likely to produce in real terms over various investment periods. To use the table, you should find the investment period of interest in the first column. The second column shows the percentage of all possible returns which will fall below the amount of terminal real wealth shown in the third column. For example, if you are interested in an investment period of one year, you have a 5% chance of ending up with less than £74 in real terms if you invest £100. You have a 95% chance of ending up with less than £159. By subtraction, you can work out that you have a 5% chance of ending up with more than £159. After 30 years, you have a 50:50 chance of having more or less than £1,070 but there is a 5% chance that you will have more than £8,889.

The table is consistent with the figures in Chapter 1 which showed how equity investment has actually worked out in the past. Essentially, the equity returns that have been achieved over past time periods could be considered to represent actual outcomes from the set of possible outcomes shown in the table. If investors had been more or less fortunate, the returns they received in the past could have been higher or lower. Future equity returns will represent a different set of outcomes from the same statistical distribution. The returns actually achieved in the future will probably differ from those achieved in the past but the table indicates how large this difference is likely to be.

One measure of particular interest to the investor is the chance of him or her making a real loss over a particular investment period. Figure 6.4 shows this probability.

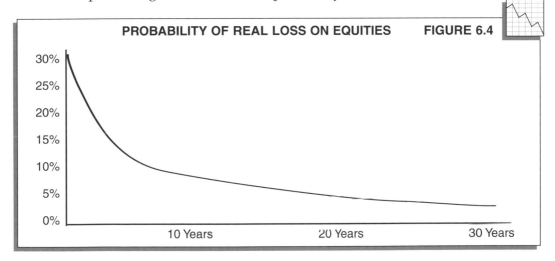

PROBABILITY OF REAL LOSS ON EQUITIES   FIGURE 6.4

It can be clearly seen that the risk of the investor losing money in real terms decreases substantially as the investment term increases. If this is the investor's main fear, he or she can take comfort in the fact that the longer his/her investment term the less risk he/she is taking, although as we shall see in Chapter 7 there are a number of other ways of looking at risk. The findings shown in the figure give statistical confirmation to the commonly quoted investment advice that shares are best looked on as a long term investment.

Table 6.1 and Figure 6.4 give an investor good rules of thumb on what sort of returns he/she can reasonably expect and how much of a risk he/she is taking. It is very valuable for the investor to reflect on this information when planning his/her overall strategy. It is much better to be realistic than to be overly optimistic or pessimistic.

CONCLUSIONS

The main benefit of using a statistical approach to stock market investment is of rationally quantifying risk and returns. Statistical methods can give you a level of insight and sophistication beyond what can be obtained from just 'eyeballing' past data. You can start to make more informed estimates of what may happen in the future.

LESSONS TO BE LEARNT

 Share price changes are largely random.

 Future share prices cannot be accurately predicted except by chance.

 There is some evidence to indicate that shares follow a mean reverting process, so you should be more cautious when returns have been very good and more optimistic after a very bad period.

 Statistical theory can provide a guide to the possible returns you may obtain over different time periods. You can assess what you may receive given varying degrees of good fortune.

 The risk of you losing money in real terms decreases as the investment term increases.

CHAPTER 7

Economics and Market Rationality

The popular view of the stock market is that it can be irrational and driven by sentiment. Many of the best known market sayings encapsulate this view; for example, 'a bull market is greed climbing a wall of fear'. There are many famous historic examples of what appear to be completely irrational episodes in markets which seem best explained by the 'madness of crowds'.[1] Chapter 3 described the Tulipmania episode in 17th Century Holland and the boom and bust in the prices of classic cars in the 1980s. Many commentators have claimed that irrational movements in the share prices of companies can be identified on a frequent basis. Graham and Dodd, the authors of *Security Analysis*, one of the most influential early works on the subject, argued that the market is not a 'weighing machine' that determines value exactly but a 'voting machine' in which countless people register their choices, which are the product partly of reason and partly of emotion.[2]

If markets really are so irrational, a level headed person could stand back and profit from this. He or she could simply buy shares when they were irrationally priced at less than their true worth and sell them again when their true value was recognised. As we shall see in later chapters, this is exactly what some of the most successful investment managers try to do. It is assumed by the majority of the general public and most investment managers that it is possible to 'outwit' the market in this way. However, a strong body of academic opinion disagrees with the idea that the market acts in an irrational way and also with the possibility of profitably predicting share prices in a consistent way.

THE ARGUMENT FOR RATIONALITY

Economics as a subject has traditionally assumed that individuals are rational and act in their own self interest. The classical economic theories of Adam Smith, David Ricardo and John Stuart Mill are founded on these assumptions. This approach has led to many important and influential results, not least the idea that free competitive markets are more likely to deliver optimal outcomes than any other economic system. The assumption that people behave in a rational way is very reasonable in many respects. People are intelligent and capable of deciding where their own best interests lie. They can also be expected to learn from experience and not to keep on making systematic errors. However, as we have seen, the assumption of rationality seems to go against the experiences of many individuals involved in stock market investment. There is, therefore, a potential conflict between the approach which is predominant amongst economists and the observations of many stock market practitioners.

Economists, of course, do not all agree on everything and Keynes, one of the greatest of them all, did not assume that people were always rational. It may be significant that Keynes was also a very successful stock market speculator. In his famous work, *The General Theory of Employment, Interest and Money*, he describes the stock market as 'a game of Snap, of Old Maid, of Musical Chairs - a pastime in which he is victor who says Snap neither too soon nor too late, who passes the Old Maid to his neighbor before the game is over, who secures a chair for himself when the music stops'.[3] However, the dominant paradigm in finance theory has been the assumption of rationality among market participants.

This chapter introduces and briefly describes the most fundamental ideas in finance theory. These ideas should not be lightly dismissed. It is fair to say that academic economists are amongst the brightest people around and they have no financial vested interests in biasing their results. Several of the main academic ideas regarding investment have been rewarded with Nobel prizes. In addition, the ideas have been subjected to a vast amount of rigorous empirical testing. The emphasis of the chapter is very strongly on making the ideas accessible and on discussing the practical insights to be gained from them and also their limitations.

EFFICIENT MARKETS

The efficient market hypothesis is based on the notion that share prices accurately reflect all available information about both the economy and all individual companies. If the market is efficient, the aggregate market view of a company, as reflected in its share price, is the best possible guide to the true underlying value of a company. If true, the hypothesis would have the most dramatic implications for investment management. The search for shares expected to perform well in the future would be essentially futile as no analyst would be better informed than the market itself. All the careful analysis of shares undertaken in the City and by countless individual investors would be a waste of time. Everything which could possibly be known about a share would already be incorporated in its price. No shares would be overvalued or undervalued due to excessive optimism or pessimism. Thus selecting any particular share in which to invest would just be a pure gamble that the share would be positively affected by unforeseeable future developments. In layman's terms, the efficient market theory means that 'the market is always right'.

The Rationale for Market Efficiency

There are good reasons for assuming that there will be a degree of efficiency in the markets. The stock market is extremely competitive. It is hard to beat the market because there are a lot of intelligent investors out there who are trying to do exactly the same thing. If it were easy to make large profits in the market, many new investors would be attracted by the rewards on offer and the increased competition would tend to cause the market to become more efficient. If a particular share selection method could make easy profits, a lot of other investors would rush to copy it and the opportunity would be arbitraged away. For example, if it became well known that the shares of companies with, say, high expenditure on research and development performed particularly well, many investors would buy companies of this nature and the price of these shares would be pushed up eliminating the future potential for excess profit. When new information appears which may affect share prices, competitive investors rush to use it as fast as possible so that easy opportunities to make money trading on new information are eliminated. It has been said that opportunities to make excess profits in the market are infrequent for much the same reason as finding a £50 note in the street is a rare event. Just as a lost £50 will soon be picked up by someone, an opportunity to make excess profits will soon be arbitraged away.

A Paradox

Efficient market theory appears to give rise to something of a 'chicken and egg' situation regarding stock market research. The market is supposedly efficient because many people are engaged in competitive research on company prices. If the market is efficient, however, it is not possible to earn excess returns by outperforming the market; so why would anyone do research as it would not be profitable? The theorists have, however, thought of a solution to this paradox within the rational economic framework. More and more people will do research until the excess returns generated by the research are equal to the cost of doing the research.[4] If only a very few people were doing research on companies, it would be a very profitable exercise. The large profits available would, however, attract more and more researchers until all the easy profits were gone.

Degrees of Market Efficiency

Academics often distinguish between three forms of the efficient markets hypothesis:[5]

1. **Weak Efficiency**: The weak form of the hypothesis assumes that the market is efficient in respect of past share prices, that is, current share prices incorporate all the information which can be obtained from past share prices. The implication of this is that it is not possible to make excess investment profits by trading on patterns which are revealed by looking at the history of share prices. Many practical investors do trade on past share price patterns. This process is known as technical analysis or chartism and is reviewed in Chapter 8 of this book.

2. **Semi-strong Efficiency**: The semi-strong form assumes that the market is efficient in respect of all published information about a share. In this case, it would not be possible to make excess investment profits from any amount of study or analysis of public information about a company, such as its report and accounts. This would mean that fundamental investment analysis, as reviewed in Chapter 10, is ineffective.

3. **Strong Efficiency**: The strong form assumes that the market is efficient in respect of all information about a share. In this case, it would not be possible to make investment profits, even from 'insider information' which is unknown to the public.

Tests for Market Efficiency

The statement that market prices fully reflect all available information is so general that it cannot be checked directly. The only way to proceed is to investigate different investment methods to see if they have produced returns which are too large and too persistent to be explained away as being the result of chance. When evaluating the method or system used, it is necessary to consider realistically the cost of operating the system. Some systems appear profitable until the costs of operating them are considered but when these costs are taken into account the profitability is illusory. In addition, the risk involved in operating the particular system should be evaluated. A very risky system may produce good results for a period but there is always a chance of a future investment 'disaster'. The results from systems with different levels of risk should not be compared without some adjustment for the levels of risk being accepted under each system.

CLOSE-UP

Academics like to make sure that the results they find are not simply due to chance. The convention that is normally used is that a result is accepted as being '**statistically significant**' if there is less than 1 chance in 20 that it was caused by pure luck.

Academics have been performing extensive tests of market efficiency since the 1960s. There are now small armies of researchers looking for what are termed 'anomalies' in the efficient market theory. This work forms by far the largest body of disinterested research on the behaviour of the stock market. It is worthwhile summarising the results of this research as many of the potential profit making systems in the market have been investigated. Investors can be prevented from 'reinventing the wheel' by being familiar with the findings of this research. It is convenient to consider the tests of the three forms of efficiency separately.

1. Weak Form Efficiency

Academics have used long records of stock market data to test technical trading rules which seek to predict future share price movements from patterns in past share prices. Some of the rules which have been investigated have been shown to be of value in predicting future share price movements.[6] However, none of the rules subjected to detailed academic study have been shown to be consistently profitable after allowing for the costs of trading.[7] Given that there is a potentially infinite number of technical trading systems and certainly many which have not been subjected to detailed statistical analysis, it is not possible to be too dogmatic about the uselessness of technical analysis. It is possible that profitable trading rules, which have not been evaluated by academics, may exist.

There is some, rather controversial, evidence that the stock market tends to overreact. De Bondt and Thaler found that the poorest performing stocks over periods of between two and five years subsequently performed very well over succeeding periods of the same length. Similarly the best performing stocks went on to perform badly.[8]

To summarise the evidence regarding the weak form efficiency of the stock market, there is no convincing evidence that the market is not weak form efficient.

2. Semi-strong Efficiency

The semi-strong efficiency of the market has been tested by determining whether superior investment returns could have been obtained by one of three main approaches, which are detailed below together with the main evidence regarding the effectiveness of each method.

i) Purchasing stocks to take advantage of new information
A number of studies, known as event studies, have been undertaken to determine whether investors could profit from taking advantage of new information about companies. One type of new information is the announcement of a company's earnings. If the earnings are good, this is naturally positive for the company's share price. It has been documented that if the earnings are better than the analysts of the company were expecting (a 'positive earnings surprise' in the terminology), the share price of the company tends not to fully react instantly but takes a number of days to complete the move upwards.[9] Similarly the share price takes some time to react to worse than expected results. Investors could potentially take advantage of this effect by trading on news of unexpected company results.

Tests have been performed to see whether company decisions, which may superficially appear to improve the position of the company but which in fact have no effect on the company's underlying value, can 'fool' the market. An example of this is an accounting change which has no effect on the company's cash flows. The evidence shows that the market can see through such tactics and it is not possible to make superior investment returns by exploiting this information.[10]

ii) Purchasing or selling stocks at advantageous times
A number of so called 'calendar effects' have been documented in the stock market. It has been found that movements in share prices can be partly predicted based on the time that they occur. The following anomalies are well known:

 The 'January effect' - In January prices tend to rise much more than the average monthly amount.

 The 'weekend effect' - Over the three days from Friday to Monday the average return is negative.

The 'holiday effect' - The returns on days preceding a public holiday are many times higher than the typical daily return.

The above effects were originally noted in the US but have since been confirmed in a number of other world stock markets, including the UK.[11] These effects are not generally large enough to allow them to be used for profitable trading in the light of transaction costs. However, they could be used to help with the timing of trades that were going to be made anyway. The existence of these anomalies is something of a puzzle. The January effect may be due to institutional investors rebalancing their portfolios at the end of a calendar year but the weekend effect and the holiday effect seem to lack convincing explanations.

iii) Purchasing stocks with particular characteristics

Stocks with particular characteristics have been found to perform differently from the market as a whole giving rise to potential investment opportunities. As described in Chapter 3, for a long period of time up to the 1990s, small company shares consistently outperformed those of large companies and this was often considered to be a market anomaly. Recently this effect appears to have disappeared (perhaps showing evidence of market efficiency) but in the past, investors could have beaten the market fairly convincingly by investing in smaller companies.

NUTSHELL

The **book value** of a company is the value of its assets as shown in the balance sheet.

A number of studies have found that stocks which offer what might be termed 'good value' have provided excellent returns. Fama and French found that when stocks are ranked by the ratio of their book value to their price, the high book-to-price ratio firms (value firms) tend to produce high rates of return and the low book-to-price ratio firms tend to produce low rates of return.[12] Haugen found that the shares of firms with low price to earnings ratios (value shares) are likely to outperform the shares of firms with high price to earnings ratios as the market tends to underestimate the speed at which the earnings growth of both fast and slow growing companies will revert to an average rate of growth.[13] A number of studies in both the UK and the US have shown that high yielding shares (value shares) have also tended to outperform low yielding shares.[14]

To summarise the evidence regarding the semi-strong efficiency of markets, it can be seen that quite a number of anomalies have been documented which seem to bring semi-strong efficiency into question.

3. Strong Efficiency

This is a rather extreme form of the hypothesis. If the market was strong form efficient, it would incorporate all private information about shares known only to company insiders, such as directors, managers and company advisors. In purely practical terms it is somewhat hard to see how the market can incorporate all private information. For example, if a company's sales director was the only person in a position to know how the products of the company were selling and he kept that information to himself, there would seem to be no mechanism by which the market could incorporate this private information. The private information of insiders can to some extent be deduced by observing whether they are buying or selling shares in their own company. A study by Seyhun did seem to confirm the idea that insiders can beat the market. Shares purchased by insiders earned positive abnormal returns and shares sold by insiders earned negative abnormal returns.[15] Some forms of insider dealing are, of course, illegal, such as third parties trading on news of a prospective takeover which is not available to the public. Given that it is illegal, it is rather difficult to conduct surveys on whether this form of dealing has proved to be profitable! However, extremely strong anecdotal evidence, some of it from court cases, would suggest that it can be extremely profitable. It is very easy to see why this is so. To give one example, consider the case where one company is about to make a takeover bid for another. When the bid is announced, the share price of the target company may be almost certain to rise substantially. A number of insiders will know that the bid will be about to happen before it is announced. These people will be able to make a large, almost risk free profit by buying shares in the target company.

To summarise the evidence on strong form efficiency, only the most zealous supporters of efficient market theory could even entertain the idea that the market is strong form efficient.

CLOSE-UP

On 22nd November 1990 it was reported in the *Financial Times* that Michael Milken, former head of the junk bond department at Drexel Burnham Lambert, had been sentenced to ten years' imprisonment, plus three years' probation, fined $200m and ordered to pay $400m in restitution after pleading guilty to six charges relating to securities law violation.

Can the Anomalies be Explained?

Believing in the efficient markets view has become something of an act of faith with many economists; it ties in so well with the paradigm of neo-classical economics that they seem to defend it at all costs. There is an enormous literature, far too large to go into here, which seeks to explain away the various anomalies in the theory. There are two main lines of attack which tend to be used against studies which find evidence of anomalies:

1. Allegations are made that the anomaly is the result of what are known as 'data mining' exercises. Data mining refers to the practice of trawling through the data until the researcher finds a positive result of some kind. The allegation is that if the researcher searches long enough in a large data set, he or she will be able to find what appear to be interesting results even though these are probably the product of pure chance.

2. The potential risk of the method is cited as an explanation for the anomaly. For example, if a particular type of shares has produced better returns, it will be argued that this is because the group is more risky. It is not necessary that there is any evidence for this. It can be said that grave risks did exist even though everything did work out all right in the end.

Some events like the 1987 Crash are very hard to reconcile with efficient markets. It is difficult to see how share prices could have been rational both before and after the crash, given that no important information seemed to have emerged which could account for the drop. Explanations within the efficient markets paradigm stretch credibility to the limit but many economists are prepared to make these arguments. Ultimately, one would have to question whether the efficient markets paradigm is open to falsification. It is always possible to construct a rational sounding explanation for any market movement and nobody can say with certainty that the explanation is wrong. On the other hand, in support of the efficient markets hypothesis, there is evidence that professional investors find it difficult to outperform the relevant market indices, although some do, as we will see below.

How do Fund Managers Perform?

The tests of efficiency which have been considered up to now have generally been tests of whether one particular system or feature of the market will enable an investor to achieve excess returns. In practice, most fund managers don't manage money using such simple systems. They use a complex and ever changing mix of rules and methods and often quite a bit of intuition as well. It is not easily possible to observe and measure their methods directly.

However, it is possible to observe their results. The overall results achieved by a fund manager provide a perfect summary of the success of whatever methods they have used. Academics have seized on the opportunity to assess the performance of fund managers. In an early and influential study of 115 funds, Michael Jensen found that mutual funds (the American equivalent of unit trusts) were unable to achieve a better return than could have been obtained by buying and holding a well-diversified portfolio of shares.[16] Later studies have largely confirmed the observation that it is not particularly easy for fund managers to earn positive abnormal returns. These findings have led to the emergence of index funds which are not actively managed by a fund manager but merely seek to match the performance of an appropriate index. The rationale behind these funds is the efficient market idea that the market price is 'correct' and so it is best to hold a portfolio which is a good proxy to the market as a whole. Academic purists would argue that fund managers can only beat the index by good luck or by taking high risks. To summarise the position regarding efficient markets and the performance of fund managers, it can be seen that there is some support for the academics' case that it is not a simple task to beat the market. Most fund managers do not beat the index. However, a substantial number of fund managers do succeed in outperforming the market so the case for efficient markets is by no means proven beyond doubt. Of course, the real test is whether specific fund managers are able to consistently outperform the market over a reasonable length of time. There is a relative absence of academic evidence on this point.

CLOSE-UP

Over the five years to 1st March 1998, about a third of UK Growth and Income unit trusts performed well enough to beat the FTSE All Share Index.[17]

Efficient Market Theory & Investment Gurus

Despite the difficulty of beating the market highlighted by some academics, many fortunes have undoubtedly been made on the stock market from Rothschild in Napoleonic times to George Soros of the present day. The later chapters of the book will review the fortunes amassed by some of the most famous historic and modern market participants and consider how their successes have been achieved. According to efficient market theory the market can only be beaten by luck. However, some of these investment experts have been so successful that it appears most implausible to believe their success is due to luck alone. It is certainly true that none of their fortunes has been based on the application of efficient market theory.

Warren Buffett, who has been one of the most successful investors of all time and beaten the market by a very considerable margin over many years, has had a number of disputes with the advocates of the efficient market hypothesis.[18] Given his fantastic success, his views are well worth noting. Regarding efficient markets, he commented, 'Observing correctly that the market was frequently efficient, [efficient market theory adherents] went on to conclude incorrectly that it was always efficient. The difference between these propositions is night and day'.[19]

If we return to the analogy of the lost £50 note, it might be commented that while it is a rare occurrence to find a £50 note in the street, it does sometimes happen.

Conclusions from Efficient Market Theory

In terms of its influence, the efficient market theory has been very important in the academic world (indeed totally dominant until recently). It has also had considerable influence in the 'real' world with the rise of index funds that do not even try to beat the market.

The theory raises some interesting practical problems for investors. Academic research has not really come to a definite indisputable conclusion about whether the market can be consistently beaten by investors. On the other hand, most investment gurus only comment on efficient markets to dismiss the idea. It is true to say, however, that academics have done enough work to show conclusively that beating the market is certainly not easy. It might seem rather disappointing that an individual can't just casually select a few stocks, using a foolproof system, sit back and make a fortune but such dreams of easy riches are really on a par with hopes of winning the jackpot on the National Lottery. Some investors, however, have beaten the market consistently and, in some cases, by very large margins and made vast fortunes by doing so. These very successful investors are in a minority but their existence does seem to prove that the market can be beaten.

The next few chapters will explain and assess the main non-academic approaches to investment management so that you can judge for yourself which, if any, of the approaches you would be prepared to put your faith (and your money!) in.

RISK & RETURN AND MODERN PORTFOLIO THEORY

Even the most inexperienced investors are usually aware that there is a trade off between risk and return in investment. They know that a very safe investment such as, say, a building society account is not going to produce a very high return. Naturally people will only put their money at risk if they are likely to get a higher return. The area of risk and return has been the subject of a great deal of academic research which is sometimes broadly described as Modern Portfolio Theory. This research has led to a number of conclusions which are very valuable to the investor.

Risk as Variability of Return

Risk is a concept which is familiar to everyone but not easy to define in a precise way. Harry Markowitz provided such a definition in a very influential article on portfolio selection.[20] He defined risk as the variability of the return that the investor may experience. The measure of variability of return which is used is the variance of return or its square root - the standard deviation. The variance of any particular security can be easily calculated from the variability of its past returns. A safe security such as a short dated gilt will tend to have a low variance of returns and a risky security such as a share in a company in a volatile industry will tend to have a high variance of returns.

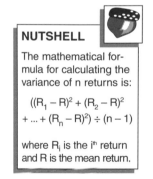

NUTSHELL

The mathematical formula for calculating the variance of n returns is:

$$((R_1 - R)^2 + (R_2 - R)^2 + ... + (R_n - R)^2) \div (n - 1)$$

where R_i is the ith return and R is the mean return.

The Risk of Different Portfolios

Having considered how to assess the risk of a single security, it is appropriate to move on to consider the risk of a portfolio of securities. Once again the measure of risk used is the variance of returns on the portfolio. The variance of returns on the whole portfolio depends not only on the variance of returns of the individual securities in the portfolio but also on the extent to which the returns of the securities move together. To measure the extent to which securities move together, we can use the concept of correlation which was described in the previous chapter. The mathematical formula to calculate the variance of a whole portfolio from the variance of the individual securities in it and their inter-correlations is complex, but the underlying principle of what is going on is fairly simple. Other things being equal, the less the returns of the securities in the portfolio are correlated, the lower the risk of the portfolio will be. Similar companies, for example companies in the same industry, are likely to give highly correlated returns. Thus a portfolio consisting of say, five different banks is likely to be more risky than a portfolio consisting of companies from five different sectors of the stock market. Thus mathematical analysis confirms the old advice not to 'put all your eggs in one basket'.

The Market Model and Beta

Calculating the correlations between the returns of a large number of securities proved to be a difficult and time consuming task even for professional investors. The practical difficulties of using quantitative portfolio selection techniques were considerably eased by William Sharpe who developed what is now generally known as the market model.[21] The market model assumes that the returns on shares are related to the return on the market as a whole. The measure of the relationship between the return on a particular share and that of the market is known as the share's beta coefficient. The beta coefficient is derived so that if the stock market as a whole moves by x% then a share moves by x% times its beta. Thus if a share has a beta of 2 and the market goes up by 10% the share should go up by 20%. Shares with a beta of greater than 1 will move by more than the market and are sometimes called aggressive shares. Aggressive shares are great when the market is going up and terrible when it is falling. Shares with a beta of less than 1 move by less than the market and are sometimes called defensive shares. Defensive shares will underperform a rising market but do better in a falling market. For example, if a share has a beta of 0.8 and the

POINTER

Betas for companies are quoted in the *Investors Chronicle* in the section on 'Company Results'.

market falls by 10%, this defensive share should only fall by 8%. Portfolios of shares, as well as individual shares, have beta coefficients and indeed the market itself has a beta of 1.

Systematic and Unsystematic Risk

If the stock market moved in a deterministic way and beta worked perfectly, investing would be a simple process indeed. The investor could just decide on how much risk he was prepared to take compared to the market and then pick a share with an appropriate beta. In fact things aren't by any means this straightforward. In practice, a particular share is unlikely to move relative to the market by exactly the amount its beta would suggest. The main reason for this is that each share has particular factors which may affect it but not the market as a whole. To give just a few examples, changes in management, new technology, changes in competition or alterations in consumer taste may affect a particular share, but not the market as a whole. Risk which affects a particular share, but not the market as a whole, is known as unsystematic risk. By contrast, systematic risk arises from developments which affect the market as a whole. Factors such as interest rate changes, inflation and the overall outlook for corporate profits give rise to systematic risk. Unsystematic risk can be eliminated by diversification whereas systematic risk cannot be reduced. This is because if you hold enough different shares and then one of them is affected by some particular factor, this will have very little effect on your whole portfolio. On the other hand, major developments which affect the whole market will still affect the portfolio in a big way.

Risk Reduction Through Diversification

For the investor, risk is not desirable unless it results in higher returns. It can be shown that by holding a diversified portfolio of shares, an investor can eliminate unsystematic risk without reducing his expected returns at all. This is a rare example of actually getting something for nothing and thus is a policy that is well worth following! It has been determined how unsystematic risk falls as the number of different shares in a portfolio increases.[22] The relationship between risk and the number of stocks in a portfolio is shown in Fig 7.1. As can be seen, risk drops very rapidly as the number of shares in a portfolio increases. However, once the portfolio gets above about fifteen shares or so, any further reductions in risk are very minimal.

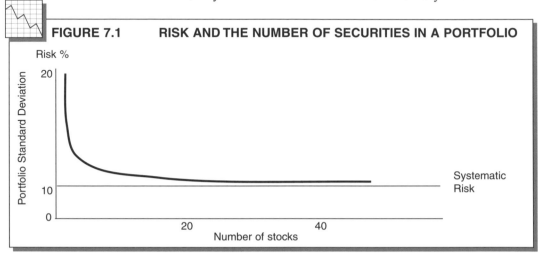

FIGURE 7.1   RISK AND THE NUMBER OF SECURITIES IN A PORTFOLIO

Capital Market Theory

Academics have taken the trade-off between risk and return to its logical conclusion. In theory, rational investors should hold only portfolios that offer the highest expected return for a given amount of risk or the least amount of risk for a given expected return. These portfolios are termed efficient portfolios (not to be confused with efficient markets which we have discussed at length above). For any group of securities, given their expected returns, their variances and the correlations between them, it is possible (although computationally complex) to calculate a set of efficient portfolios from which a rational investor should choose. The set of efficient portfolios is often depicted in a characteristic graph as shown in Fig 7.2.

The efficient frontier, shown on the graph, is the set of efficient portfolios which offer the best combinations of return and risk which are available. Different points on the line offer a different trade-off between risk and return. If an investor prefers to take less risk and accept a lower return, he/she will move along the line to a point to the left of his/her starting point. An inefficient portfolio, such as shown by point A on the graph, offers a combination of risk and return which is less attractive than that an efficient portfolio can provide. For example, a point on the efficient frontier directly above A can provide a greater return for the same risk.

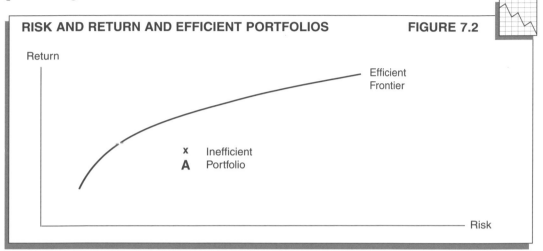

RISK AND RETURN AND EFFICIENT PORTFOLIOS   FIGURE 7.2

Return

Efficient
Frontier

x   Inefficient
A   Portfolio

Risk

Needless to say it is difficult for private investors to carry out the sort of calculations needed to arrive at a set of efficient portfolios. Thus the full implementation of this approach is left to academics and to the group of professional investors who are prepared to fully subscribe to the methodology. As detailed in the paragraph below, many practical investors are not fully convinced of the value of the approach.

Academics and the Real World

The findings of Markowitz and Sharpe have been highly influential with academics and to some extent with practitioners. Betas are commonly used within the professional investment community. Some large professional portfolio managers do calculate efficient portfolios according to the prescriptions of capital market theory. The theories, however, are certainly not without their critics. Many people are not happy with the idea that risk can be defined simply as the variance of returns. There are many views of risk, not all of which are necessarily compatible with this definition. For example, some individuals may consider risk to be the probability of their investments falling below a certain value; risk to some investment managers might be the chance of underperforming their peer group. Various criticisms of beta have been raised. Betas are necessarily derived from past share price movements. Some critics say that the future will not necessarily be like the past, so betas may not be stable over time. There is an element of truth in this but the advocates of beta claim that it is stable enough to be very useful. Some investors are inclined to the view that one should try to understand all aspects of a company in some detail from its products to its management to its finances. They think that trying to sum up all this detail and complexity with a single beta coefficient may be very over-simplistic. To investors who believe that there is a fundamental underlying value to a company which may differ from its market value, beta may appear quite perverse at times. If a share quickly halves in value, its beta will increase as it will have exhibited more past volatility. However, if one considers the value of the underlying business, by buying shares one is buying the same business for half the price it was a short time before. It is difficult to see how this is a riskier transaction despite the increase in beta.

Conclusions about Risk and Return

Whilst not all practitioners would fully agree with the academic analysis, there are undoubtedly some very useful insights to be gained from the approach to risk and return taken in modern portfolio theory:

 There is a trade off between risk and return in the markets. Generally the investments offering the best potential return are the most risky.

 A share's beta coefficient is an extremely useful item of information. As we have seen, it has its limitations but it is the best single measure of the risk of a share.

 Diversification of a portfolio offers one of the few examples in the field of financial markets where the investor really can get something for nothing. Through diversification the investor can get the same expected return for less risk or a better expected return for the same risk. When diversifying, it is best to hold a number of dissimilar shares. It is not necessary to hold an extremely large number of shares to considerably reduce risk.

COMPANY VALUATION BY DISCOUNTING FUTURE DIVIDENDS

The owner of a share in a company is entitled to any future dividends it may pay. In theory, the value of the share must be equal to the present value of these future dividends. This is a very important relationship which any investor would do well to keep in mind.

Discounting and Time Value of Money

An important concept for investors to be aware of is what is known as the time value of money. This is the idea that the value of a sum of money depends on when it is received. For example, if given the choice of receiving £100 now or £100 in a year, most people would opt to receive the money straight away. This can actually be shown to be the correct decision. Even if the money was not required for a year, the person receiving the £100 immediately could put it in the bank and withdraw it when it was required. After a year in the bank the money would have earned some interest and would have grown to more than £100. Thus there would be a definite gain by receiving the money earlier. If the interest rate was 10% p.a., the amount of money which would grow to £100 in a year's time would be £100 ÷ 1.1 (£90.91). Thus £100 payable in one year's time is equivalent in value to £90.91 payable now. This process is known as discounting, in this case the discounted value of £100 payable in one year is £90.91. This process can be generalised to different time periods and to different interest rates.

The discounted value of £1 receivable in n years time where the discount rate is k% is given by the formula:

$$\text{Discounted Value} = 1 / (1 + k)^n$$

To demonstrate this formula in action, Table 7.1 shows the value of £1 discounted at 10% p.a. over various time periods. We can see, for example, that £1 payable in 20 years time is worth just under 15 pence now.

Table 7.1 Discounted Value of £1 at 10% p.a. interest		
Discounting Period (years)	Formula	Present Value (£)
1	$1 / (1 + 0.1)^1$	0.9091
2	$1 / (1 + 0.1)^2$	0.8264
3	$1 / (1 + 0.1)^3$	0.7513
5	$1 / (1 + 0.1)^5$	0.6209
10	$1 / (1 + 0.1)^{10}$	0.3855
20	$1 / (1 + 0.1)^{20}$	0.1486

The Value of Future Dividends

The methodology of discounting future payments can be applied to find the present value of any future dividends a company may pay. Each dividend payable in the future can be discounted back to the present time. For example, using a 10% discount rate, if a company pays a dividend of £100 in 2 years' time, the present value of this dividend is £100 $\div (1 + 0.1)^2 = $ £82.64.

The Value of a Share

As mentioned above the value of a share can be defined to be equal to the present value of all the future dividends payable. This means that the investor needs to find the discounted value of all the future dividends payable. If P_0 is the value of a share at the present time and D_t is the dividend in year t then assuming a discount rate of k%:

$$P_0 = D_1 / (1+k) + D_2 / (1+k)^2 + D_3 / (1+k)^3 + \dots D_n / (1+k)^n + \dots \qquad (7.1)$$

This formula is straightforward enough except that it requires that all the dividends payable into the indefinite future are known. This information is not readily available. Only past dividends are known with certainty and analysts usually only make detailed dividend predictions for a couple of years into the future. One way around this problem is to assume that dividends grow at a constant rate for the indefinite future. This is a sensible approach as companies very often do try to grow their dividend at a fairly steady rate. If we assume that dividends grow at g% per annum then formula (7.1) collapses to a much more friendly looking formula :

$$P_0 = D_1 \,/\, (k - g) \qquad\qquad (7.2)$$

Equation (7.2) is known as the constant growth dividend discount model and is a very important and useful equation indeed.

Constant Growth Dividend Discount Model

The dividend discount model can be used to put a value on any share or on the market as a whole. For this purpose, the discount rate used should be the return required on the holding. As an example, consider a share paying a dividend of 2 pence. Furthermore, you expect the dividend to grow at 6% p.a. and require a return on the holding of 10% p.a. The value of the share is then $2 \div (0.1 - 0.06) = 50$ pence. This calculated value can be compared with the market price of the share. If you are confident about your expectations for the share and your calculated value for the share is greater than its market value, you might wish to consider purchasing it.

The difficulty with these calculations is deciding what assumptions to use in the formula. The calculated share price is very sensitive to these assumptions. If the required return on the holding had been 12% p.a. in the calculation above, the value of the share would have been 33.3 pence. If the expected rate of dividend growth had been 8% p.a. then the value of the share would have been £1. Some commentators are rather cynical about the discount model saying that it is easy to play around with the assumptions to get whatever result you require. This cynicism is well placed if the model is applied thoughtlessly. The process, at its worst, can easily become a case of 'rubbish in, rubbish out'. The consideration of the assumptions to use can, however, be a considerable aid to the better understanding of a company. When thinking about the dividend growth rate assumption, many pertinent questions arise: what rate has been achieved in the past? Will the company do better or worse in the future? How sure can we be of our judgements? These sorts of questions are deceptively simply but coming to satisfactory answers requires a lot of hard thinking and a good understanding of the company. Gaining this insight is a very worthwhile process in itself. Similar considerations arise when looking at the required return. The starting point for calculating the required return is the riskless yield on long-dated gilts plus a margin for the risk of the investment. The margin for risk does require a good deal of consideration: how risky do you believe the company to be? How large a return would you require to invest in it?

One of the most useful aspects of the dividend discount model is that it can give the investor an anchor on reality when market prices are fluctuating. When the price of a company falls or rises in the market, the investor can ask himself/herself whether the price changes really reflect correctly the discounted value of the future dividends the company can be expected to pay.

Conclusions about Company Valuation

 The value of a share can be defined as being equal to the present value of its future dividends.

 The dividend discount model can be used to value any share. Thinking about the right assumptions to use in the model is very useful in helping to understand a potential investment. The model gives a measure of value independent of market prices.

BLACK–SCHOLES AND ARBITRAGE FREE PRICING OF DERIVATIVES

As the final topic in this chapter, we will briefly discuss the Black-Scholes model for valuing derivatives, which probably represents the crowning achievement of financial economics. It is an academic idea that really has had a revolutionary effect on practitioners. It is paradoxical that the derivatives market, which has become so closely associated in the public mind with reckless and ill-judged speculation, is probably the one which has benefited the most from scientific analysis.

Chapter 4 introduced derivative securities such as futures and options. Options have a very long history; they existed early enough to play a big part in the Dutch tulip bubble of the seventeenth century. The peculiar thing about options was that although they had existed for so long, nobody had worked out how to value them in any rational way. Option valuation was a matter of educated guesswork. Some of the best brains in finance had worked on this problem and failed to come up with a solution. The puzzle was finally solved in the 1970s by Fischer Black, Myron Scholes and Robert C. Merton.[23] They derived a mathematical model which allows the prices of options to be calculated. As outlined in Chapter 4, the model calculates the value of an option as a function of the volatility of the underlying share, the current price of the share, the exercise price of the option, the remaining period before the option matures and the riskless rate of return. Although the formula looks complex, its derivation is based on a simple idea which is very firmly in the economic tradition of assuming that market participants are rational. In a market with rational participants, arbitrage opportunities will not exist. It is not possible to make returns in excess of the riskless rate of return except by accepting some risk. The Black-Scholes formula is based on the observation that it is possible to create a riskless portfolio from a combination of a position in the option and a position in the underlying share. As arbitrage opportunities will not exist, this riskless portfolio must earn the riskless rate of return. This deduction is used to set up the equations that are solved to provide the solution to the problem.

LESSONS TO BE LEARNT

 Most economists assume the stock market is rational. Many informed commentators do not fully agree with this.

 There is no strong evidence that the market can be beaten by trading on patterns in past share prices.

 There is some evidence that the market can be beaten by trading on public information about shares.

 It is very likely that the market can be beaten by people with insider information.

 Most fund managers do not find it easy to beat the market although some do by a large margin.

 There is a trade off between risk and return in the markets. Generally the investments offering the best potential returns are the most risky.

 A share's beta coefficient is the best single measure of its risk.

 Through diversification the investor can get the same expected return for less risk or a better expected return for the same risk.

 When diversifying it is best to hold a number of dissimilar shares.

 It is not necessary to hold an extremely large number of shares to considerably reduce risk.

 The value of a share can be defined as being equal to the present value of its future dividends.

 The dividend discount model provides a simple formula to value shares. Applying this formula can help an investor to ask the right questions about an investment and can give him a way of thinking about value independently of market movements.

 The academic approach has revolutionised the derivatives markets.

PART FOUR

CLASSICAL APPROACHES

TO

INVESTMENT

CHAPTER 8

Market Traders
and
Technical Analysis

Having visited the wisdom of the academics on the operation of equity markets, we will now look at what investment practitioners actually get up to and what techniques they bring to the market. From the outset, we need to be clear that the majority do not accept the academic belief that markets are fully efficient. In contrast, they take the view that careful study can lead to superior investment decisions. Over the next few chapters, we will explore some of the techniques used by investors to try to achieve superior returns. In this chapter, we will start by looking at who actually trades in the markets and how the advent of computers has radically changed the world in which they live. For the informed private investor, computer technology also makes available some interesting quantitative techniques, and we will use this chapter to introduce some simple tools of 'Technical Analysis'.

IMAGE IS EVERYTHING

When it comes to understanding the operation of financial markets, most people never get past the smoke-screen of image. The markets are seen as confined to those who walk the corridors of gleaming glass towers in the City of London. After all, most people who have a vested interest in the value of shares do not trade in equities for themselves. Most investors will operate through a multi-layered, institutional system that keeps them at more than arm's length from the markets. Individual investors, whilst making their own investment decisions, will use the services of a broker to buy and sell their shares. Brokers, in turn, may be part of a major banking operation with its own treasury and market trading functions. Many more investors hand over their money to savings institutions, such as pension schemes and life assurance companies, who will invest the money collectively on behalf of their members or policy holders. The individual investor never really gets to see what is going on. The closest we come to seeing the markets in operation are the background shots of dealing rooms used to spice up the financial stories on the evening news; or perhaps back in 1989 you were one of those who avidly tuned-in to watch the weekly drama unfold at Shane-Longman in Thames Television's 'Capital City'. The image we remember is one of row after row of open-plan trading desks with young, pressurised dealers staring with desperation into dozens of computer screens and yelling into three phones at once. We recognise the image, but, for most people, what traders do is still a mystery.

Reaganomics and Thatcherism instilled in the popular culture of the 1980s the right to pursue wealth. Although the Lawson boom was a relatively short lived affair, the image of the 80s remains one of consumerism and prosperity. Against the backdrop of large privatisation issues and economic boom, the Stock Exchange underwent the 'Big Bang' of 1986. The transformation of the stock market's image from that of gentleman's club to hi-tech, high adrenalin drama did the public image of the market trader few favours. Greed and the markets seemed to become synonymous in the 80s. Probably the most common image associated with the market, even today, is that of the yuppie trader - under thirty, Porsche, red braces, greedy, stressed and with not enough free time to spend his five figure bonus.

Since the 1980s, the world's best known real-life traders have been those whose activities have been either grandiose or downright illegal. Frequently when traders hit the news, it is usually in the context of scandal or calamity, as when Nick Leeson brought down Barings Bank in 1995. Failure and collapse make good copy for the newspapers. As a result, it tends to be the case that the financial community shies away from the public eye. They willingly hide away in the shadow of incomprehension, and investment firms are wealthy enough to arm themselves with powerful press relations departments to defend themselves against media intrusion.

SO WHAT DO TRADERS ACTUALLY DO?

A trade is simply a transaction between a buyer and a seller. Of course, for a trade to take place, somebody has to want to sell and somebody has to want to buy, at the agreed price. Trading is the mechanism in the market for bringing these parties together. Potential buyers and sellers of securities may be separated by vast distances around the globe and operate in different time zones, but through the 'bridge' of the market trader, they can find each other, agree a mutually acceptable price and complete their transaction within seconds. Without the traders, potential sellers wouldn't know that there were potential buyers out there.

Say an investor decides that they want to change their portfolio of shares; they decide to sell ICI shares in order to buy some Marks and Spencer shares. If the investor had to personally seek out someone wishing to purchase their ICI shares and agree a price with them, the whole process of investing would be extremely slow indeed. Fortunately, market traders build the bridge between the seller and someone who is wanting to buy ICI at the current price. It is the market trader who creates liquidity in the market, making it easy to get rid of or obtain shares very quickly.

It is through trading that the market operates 'price discovery' and it is the activity of market trading which collectively determines the price of a lot of what we see around us each day.[1] Prices in the world commodity markets determine what we pay for our petrol, coffee, orange juice or bread. Prices on the foreign exchange markets determine the price we pay for our imported cars. Prices of fixed rate money on the swaps market determine the price we pay for our mortgages.

Traders operate in different types of exchanges and in different markets. If you've ever seen the film 'Trading Places', you will have seen how traders call bids and offers in 'open outcry' in the trading pits of a commodities futures exchange. Many other types of exchange have now replaced open outcry with telephone based trading. Dealers don't negotiate

CLOSE-UP

Price discovery is the process by which the acceptable price of any tradeable instrument is agreed between two parties. The price emerges as demand and supply fluctuate in the market. One trader bids to buy so many of a particular instrument, another sells and they agree on a fair price. This process is repeated by many traders in many securities around the globe, around the clock.

NUTSHELL

A **'Swap'** is another type of traded financial derivative. It is a contractual agreement to swap or exchange either a stream of cash payments over a period of time or the price of foreign currency.

face-to-face in a pit but voice-to-voice over the telephone. Nowadays it is even possible for traders to programme their computers to deal inside some electronic exchanges.

BUY! BUY! BUY!

Traders tend to fall into two broad categories. They either work as a 'buy-side' trader or a 'sell-side' trader. A buy-side trader might be working for a portfolio manager of a big investment institution. The portfolio manager may decide that they wish to hold more ICI shares. The buy-side trader is commissioned with the task of obtaining the shares at the best possible price. The trader will seek out who is offering ICI for sale and at what price and negotiate between their sources to strike an equitable price for the number of shares they need. They seek out and select from all the alternatives in the market. Sell-side traders can operate in two different ways. Firstly, they are there to meet the demand from the buy-side. They negotiate the other half of the transaction, becoming the bridge between buyer and seller. Secondly, they can act as what are known as 'proprietary traders'; they trade with their own firm's money. They may either arbitrage between markets or stake a position in a market, managing their risk exposure and hoping to make huge rewards if the market moves their way.

The growth of institutional investment in equities has led to a more favourable position for the buy-side trader. As more and more money has flowed into savings institutions, so buy-side trading volumes have increased and the buy-side has become a stronger competitive force in the market. The big institutional players move huge blocks of shares in and out of their portfolios. Historically, buy-side traders have been paid a lot less than their risk-taking, sell-side cousins, but now they are catching up in the income and the kudos stakes.[2]

SERIOUS MONEY

It is stating the obvious, but there is big money to be made in the markets. In a single year $300 trillion is traded on the world's currency markets and some $16 trillion worth of shares change hands (or at least electronic accounts) on the world's stock exchanges. The sheer scale is daunting. With the press of a single computer key, a trader can transfer millions of pounds from one country to the next. If you are a trader holding tens of millions of pounds of investments, each small change in price means your holding is changing its value every second by huge amounts of money. This means that for the trader, speed is everything. There's not a second to waste. Any new piece of information can have an impact on the price of the shares a trader is holding, so the impact of each piece of news needs to be evaluated and the decision made as to how to adjust their position. The art of trading is to react - and react correctly. Traders in New York can make $1 million a year including bonuses; those who work in London don't quite get up to that level. Contrary to their Yuppie image, most traders are experienced professionals, interpreting world events and making continuous judgements about the price of the securities they trade. Far from courting risk, they manage it with great care. Traders will not normally expose themselves to overly large risks which may break them if the market moves in an unfavourable direction.

Traders operate in an extremely dynamic working environment and tend to be those people who seem to thrive on the chaos of continuous change. They constantly need to keep their eye on the ball as they juggle trades in multiple markets around the globe. Almost without exception, traders will have a passion for their work and the belief that they can achieve what they set out to do. To take a position in the market requires self-confidence. Traders must handle stress as a necessary part of the job. Yet their methods and trading styles can be quite diverse. Some work on a logical 'programme' basis, responding mathematically to the numbers on their screens; others have their own analysis and decision rules which they keep to unshakeably; still others seem to fly the market by the seat of their pants, going with their instincts. Some traders operate by arbitraging between markets simultaneously, others predict the future direction of the market. Developing a winning system or style, however, is not enough. It takes courage to stick with a system in the face of changing circumstances. Much of the difficulty about trading lies in the need for the trader to master his or her own fears and emotions. Traders cannot control the market, but they can seek to control their own responses. Many of the most important trading principles run against human nature. For example, it is important to run with profits when they are being made but to cut losses quickly. Most people would tend to do the reverse. Successful trading systems frequently depend on making a few very profitable trades which will more than offset many unsuccessful ones. Balancing losses against potential gains and limiting the risks are part of the art of trading. Occasionally, if a trader's overconfidence in their market position goes unchecked and the risk exposure grows too large, the consequences can be disastrous.

THE LONE GUNMAN

ORIGINS

Founded in 1762, Barings was the oldest merchant bank in London. In 1803, it financed the 'Louisiana State Purchase', effectively doubling the size of the US. Well respected in the City, the bank was one of the main managers of HM The Queen's assets. Barings was sold in 1995 to the Dutch banking group, IMG, for the token sum of £1.

NUTSHELL

Traders '**go long**' when they purchase a security and hold it as an asset. The position gains if the price rises and loses if it falls. A '**short**' position is created by selling securities you don't yet hold. The position gains if the price falls, but loses from a price rise.

On February 26th 1995, Barings Bank was driven into insolvency by the actions of one lone trader sitting behind a desk in Singapore. Ironically, Barings Futures Singapore was a firm that was meant to operate with little risk. Its job was to arbitrage the level of prices between Singapore and Japan. It would take advantage of any small price differences in the two markets, buying in one and selling in the other, causing the prices in the two markets to come back into step and picking up a small profit on each transaction along the way. Nick Leeson was a 28-year-old trader for Barings Futures in Singapore who decided that there was money to be made by taking a view on the future direction of the Japanese market. Although he was not authorised by the bank to do so, he took a long position in futures on the Nikkei. When the Nikkei moved against his position he hid the losses he was making in a back office account. To square off these losses Leeson sold options, taking the view that the Nikkei would stay above the 18500 level. As the losses mounted, Leeson required funds to pay for the margin calls. At the end of each trading day, the Singapore International Money Exchange (SIMEX) would require the extra collateral. Barings in London kept sending him the money he needed. On January 23rd 1995, the Japanese market fell to 17800. Instead of realising his losses, Leeson bought more and more futures. Rumours began to spread around the Far East markets of an amassed position. By 17th February, other merchant banks started to consider Barings as risky. When Leeson walked away from Barings on 23rd February, his position held 60,000 futures contracts. Upon its collapse, Barings' losses amounted to £927 million.[3]

THE RISE OF THE ELECTRONIC MARKET

The impact of the computer on our age is perhaps far greater than we imagine. It is the use of computers and telecommunications which has revolutionised the world's financial markets. The sheer scale and speed of operation of the global markets affects the state of economies and the world around us. It is scarcely believable that things have changed so quickly. The introduction of telephone direct dialling in 1967 revolutionised international securities trading. Back in the 50s and early 60s, securities prices had been passed between the world's capitals by cable or telex. Huge computers used for back office accounting began to be developed in the mid-1960s. The New York Stock Exchange introduced an automated system for trading large blocks of stocks in the late 60s. In 1971 the NASDAQ over-the-counter exchange allowed dealers to trade based on prices quoted on computer screens. The development of options contracts in the 1970s was the 'mother of invention' of more computational tools for use in the markets. The late 1970s saw the development of software, such as VisiCalc, which made complicated financial calculations that much easier to handle. IBM introduced its first PC only as far back as 1981. As PCs have become more sophisticated so they have become more and more empowering to the market trader.

In 1986, Big Bang changed the face of the City of London forever. Big Bang marked the end of open outcry on the floor of the London Stock Exchange with its old blackboard lists of prices. Traders moved to remote dealing desks, spread out across the city. They saw what was going on in the market through an electronic billboard system known as SEAQ. The various prices bid and offered by market makers for shares are all quoted on a computer screen. Most London traders today still collect all the information they need from their screens but then actually transact business over the telephone. When the trader sees a favourable price on the screen, they phone the party who placed the quote and begin the negotiation for the trade. This type of trading is known as a 'quote-driven' system. Today, however, computers can also exercise trades automatically.

The introduction of the Stock Exchange Electronic Trading Service (SETS) in 1997 may not have had the same glare of publicity as Big Bang, but its impact on the market could be

CLOSE-UP

An over-the-counter (OTC) market exists when a security can be traded between parties by telephone or computer screen even though it is not listed on a formal organised exchange. **NASDAQ** is a screen based quotation system which allows dealers to trade both OTC and listed securities in the USA.

NUTSHELL

Market makers are effectively wholesalers who always make both bid and offer prices for particular securities. This means that anyone coming to the market can always find someone who is willing to buy or sell that security.

as great. SETS is an 'order-driven' system. A seller inserts the number and price of the shares they are willing to sell; buyers insert the price and volume they are willing to buy. When orders match up, the trade is executed automatically and anonymously inside the computer system. In general, SETS should have the benefit of narrowing spreads and lowering dealing costs. At the moment market makers quote an average spread of something like 0.6% in London, whereas in continental European markets, where similar order book systems are used, spreads can be as low as 0.15%.[4]

The use of computerised order matching has even led to the establishment of a competitor for the London Stock Exchange. 'Tradepoint' is an example of a new kind of exchange altogether; one which is completely automated. Buy-side institutional investors can reduce their dealing costs by using these automated systems.

QUANTITATIVE TRADING

Using computers to provide information about share prices and even to execute trades is one thing, getting computers to decide when and what to trade is quite another. Computers now enable the use of sophisticated mathematical models to help traders generate returns using quantitative techniques. Computers can monitor the prices of securities in hundreds of markets simultaneously, 24 hours a day, and automatically arbitrage if the prices drift out of step. Some traders even use chaos theory and artificial intelligence programs to predict where prices are moving next. Neural nets are used to identify patterns in share price movements. Other models respond to changes in the volumes of shares being traded on the market. Programs are even developed to seek out undervalued companies based on the trader's particular criteria.

The growth in the use of PCs also opens the way for quantitative techniques to be used by the private investor. We may not want to go to the extreme of developing artificial intelligence programs, but some simple computational techniques can be a handy weapon in the investor's arsenal. The internet now provides a wide range of information on companies and share prices, while PC software packages can help in the analysis of companies and markets.

TECHNICAL ANALYSIS

Technical analysis, also called Chartism, is the practice of forecasting future price movements from the past history of the price and trading volumes. The analysis relies on the study of the price history itself rather than any underlying economic factors. Technical analysis is, therefore, frequently contrasted with fundamental analysis which, in the case of shares, would seek to identify the intrinsic value of the share by looking at the underlying company itself.

Technical analysis is probably the oldest form of investment analysis and can be traced back to the 19th century. It is still widely used in the markets today. Indeed, it has been determined that in the foreign exchange markets, 90% of chief foreign exchange dealers use some chartist input in forming their exchange rate expectations.

As we saw in Chapter 7, the academic evidence in favour of the efficacy of technical analysis is not very strong but given that it is so widely used by investment professionals, we should familiarise ourselves with some of its techniques. The rules that technical analysts use in deciding when to buy or sell shares are either in the form of 'patterns' or 'computations'. Buy or sell signals are picked up from the pattern being formed by the shape of the share price graph over time. Alternatively, they are triggered by the value of a calculated monitoring figure.

Dow Theory

Dow theory suggests that share price graphs move in identifiable trends. The reason that the movement in the price of a share graph looks a lot more chaotic than merely following a simple trend, is that there are actually three levels of trending going on all at the same time. The primary trend, as the name suggests, is the most influential. This is the 'big-picture' upwards or downwards trend which the price is following when you look over a period of, say, one year. As long as the upwards trend is in force the investor will profit from holding the share. The trick is to spot the point at which the share has peaked and a primary downwards trend has begun. That would be a good time to sell. Dow Theory tries to help us spot these turning points.[5]

ORIGINS

Every day, reporters around the world quote the Dow Jones Industrial Average. This index was launched in 1896 by Charles Dow, co-founder of the *Wall Street Journal*. Charles was one of the founding fathers of what has come to be known as 'Dow Theory' which underpins many of the technical analysis tools.

Within the primary movement exist intermediary trends, which will be observed as being in force for a few weeks or a few months before being reversed. So inside a given primary trend upwards, for example, you will see some 'up' intermediary trends building up the move and some 'down' intermediaries holding it back. Finally, there also exist tertiary trends, inside the intermediary trends, which last for only a few days to a week. Of course, it is only a matter of judgement as to what represents an intermediary trend and what represents only a tertiary movement.

Figure 8.1 shows how the movement on a share price works in terms of these trends. An upwards primary trend is considered as continuing up as long as each successive intermediary downward step ends higher than the last. The primary upwards movement of the share price is said to be over once one of the intermediary downwards steps is seen to drive lower than the last and the next intermediate upwards rally fails to achieve the level of the last.

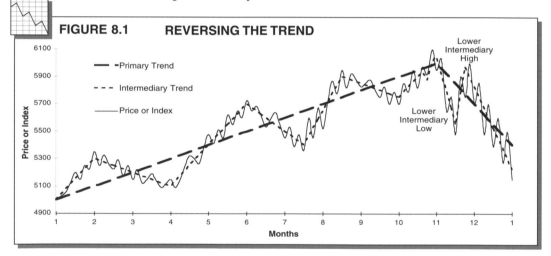

FIGURE 8.1   **REVERSING THE TREND**

The Head and Shoulders

The principle that Dow Theory lays down is that certain patterns in the share price can indicate the point of a reversal in price movement. The most famous reversal pattern is probably the 'Head and Shoulders' pattern, which is so-called because it is meant to be similar to the silhouette of someone shrugging their shoulders. Figure 8.2 gives you an idea of what the pattern looks like. A Head and Shoulders at a peak announces that a significant price drop is in the offing. Conversely, if you get the pattern after a period of declining share price, then you could be in for a large price rise. If Head and Shoulders patterns occur, they do so at the turn of a significant upward or downward trend. It is not surprising, therefore, that they form infrequently. Furthermore, it should be emphasised that we are dealing with the turn in a trend of an individual company share. Head and Shoulders patterns are not renowned for providing useful information about the whole market.

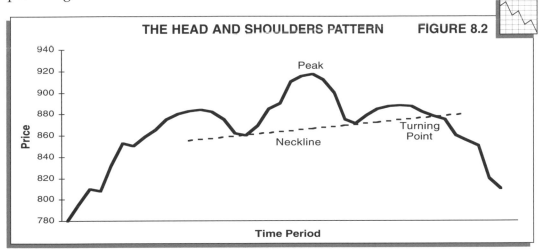

THE HEAD AND SHOULDERS PATTERN   FIGURE 8.2

When the share price has been on a rising trend and is approaching a peak, some investors will think the rally has been sustained long enough and will take their profits, causing the share price to fall back a little. This causes the track of the share price to form the left shoulder. The price level that the share falls back to is called the 'neckline'. Typically the volume of shares traded is heavy as the left shoulder starts to take shape and slackens off as the price falls back to the neckline. With the reduced price and the expectation that the rally will actually continue, new investors buy into the share and the price rises to form the top of the head; but this is as high as the price goes. The price then falls back, often virtually to the neckline. More buying then takes place, bringing the price up a little but with much lower volumes. This causes the small right shoulder to form. As the price comes over the top of the right shoulder the traded volumes are high as the price slips away toward and through the neckline. At this stage the Head and Shoulders pattern is complete and recognisable. In the view of the technical analysts, if the price track carries on down below the neckline by, say, three percent, a large drop is expected to follow and now is the time to get out. The scale of the drop is sometimes computed as being to a point as far below the neckline as the top of the head was above it. It is important to wait for the drop below the neckline to confirm that a true reversal has occurred.

Again, it is a question of judgement as to when a Head and Shoulders pattern has actually formed. The investor needs to construct a set of rules which will flag up the fact that a desired pattern has been spotted. Schwartz reports that once a Head and Shoulders peak is recognised, there is strong evidence that there is no money to be made by continuing to hold the shares.[6]

Deviation

Technical analysis not only uses shapes to monitor possible future price movements but also a host of numerical calculations. One simple monitoring tool used to try and spot a turning market is the deviation of current prices from their average value over the last year. The theory goes that if the current value is getting too far above the average for the year, then the market is getting overvalued and it is more likely to turn downwards in the near future. Conversely if the current value is low relative to the average for the whole of the last year, then it may be a good time to get into the market.

By looking back through time, chartists can see what level deviation is associated with the index continuing its trend and what level of deviation signals a change in direction for the index. If the ratio stays in the range of 1 to 1.1, say, then it may be that the market appears neither over nor under priced. If the deviation starts to be significantly above 1.1, some technical analysts would claim that, historically speaking, the market is ready to turn down. Conversely, if the index is less than 1, then historically the market looks cheap and it is more likely to move ahead rapidly in the months to come.

Volatility

A further trick up the sleeve of the technical analyst is to keep a watchful eye on the volatility of the market. On the evening news we may hear that the FTSE 100 rose 40 points on the day. However, during the trading day the index may have gradually eked its way up those 40 points bit by bit. Alternatively, it may have been up 70 points one

CLOSE-UP

One measure of the average value of the FTSE 100 index for the year to 1st January 1998 can be calculated by taking the average of the 12 previous monthly figures. This gives an average level of 4716.6 for the year. The current value of the index was 5435.5 at that date. The ratio of the current value to the 12 month average was therefore 1.088.

NUTSHELL

Volatility is a measure of how much the market is oscillating up and down above and below its primary trend.

hour and down 20 the next and then back up and down again, before finishing the day where it did. Similarly over a longer period, a rising market may be rising smoothly, gradually and consistently or it might be up and down frequently as it makes its headway.

Volatility can be calculated in terms of percentage movement. For example, on day 1 the market may have been up 1.5%, on day 2 it might be down 0.8%, then on day 3 it might be up 2% and so on. The total of all these daily values over a full year, irrespective of whether they were up or down, gives us a measure of the total amount of movement undergone by the index. In a given year, for example, let's say this summation came to 140 percentage points. If, over the course of the same year, the index itself had actually risen or fallen by 20%, then this measure of annual volatility would work out as 120.

Interestingly, periods when annual volatility is particularly high or particularly low tend to precede a rising market. Periods of typical volatility by this measure (say, 100 to 150) tend to precede periods where prices do less well.[7]

Relative Strength

A variation on the volatility theme is the use of a Relative Strength index. This is a tool used to give the investor a feel for how well the market is pushing ahead, or otherwise. Its trick is to separate out the days on which the market has risen and see if the sum of these rises represent a high proportion of the total movement on the index. Take, for example, a fourteen day Relative Strength measure of the FTSE 100. Let's say that in the last fourteen trading days, the FTSE 100 had had ten good days where it had been up on the day by so many points, and just four bad days where it had closed down. Let's say that the sum of these ten individual daily gains came to 150 points and the sum of the four individual daily falls came to 80 points. The net movement on the index over the fourteen days would have been a gain of some 70 points, but the index (just going by end of day figures) would have 'travelled' 230 points to reach its current level. The Relative Strength measure would be calculated as:

$$\frac{150 \text{ (the sum of the total gains)}}{230 \text{ (the sum of the total market movement)}} \times 100$$

So in this case, the relative strength is approximately 65. The measure can be calculated on a rolling basis each day. Chartists claim that if this measure drifts outside the range 30 to 70, then it is time to take action.[8] High values of Relative Strength precede a price fall; low values precede a price rise.

Daily Advance Line

A further variation on how to measure whether the market is pushing forward is a simple daily advance line. The daily advance measure is simply the ratio of the number of rising shares to the total number of shares listed within the index of your choice. For example, 150 rising shares out of a total of 865 would give a ratio of 17%. Although the figure on any given day is not very informative, Schwartz reports that the use of a rolling average of this figure over, say, fifty days can be very helpful.[9] If the average daily advance figure gets above 20% then the market may be approaching a turning point; a bull market could be reaching its peak or a bear market may be about to turn upwards.

CONCLUSIONS

The sheer scale of the financial markets means that they influence economies around the globe. It is the role of the trader to make the markets work smoothly and effectively, bridging the gap between sellers and buyers. The development of computers and telecommunications has changed the way traders and stock exchanges do business; increasing the speed at which information is passed around the world and increasing the complexity of financial instruments. It has also led to the development of sophisticated quantitative trading techniques which can aid traders in their analysis of the markets. Some simple technical trading rules can also add another dimension to the strategies of the private investor.

LESSONS TO BE LEARNT

 Investment practitioners tend not to believe that markets are fully efficient, but rather that careful analysis can lead to superior investment decisions.

 Traders operate in a variety of markets and on different types of exchanges. They connect the buyer and the seller and 'discover' the market price.

 Without the proper controls, an individual trader can establish a sufficiently large position in the market as to topple entire banks.

 Developments in computer technology have promoted a move from higher cost 'quote-driven' trading to lower cost, automated 'order-driven' exchanges.

 Technical Analysis, or Chartism, deals with the forecasting of future securities prices from the history of the price itself rather than any underlying economic factors.

Some simple technical analysis tools can be used by the private investor to monitor the market.

CHAPTER 9

Top Down Investment

When planning their investments, investors who use a top down strategy are concerned with the 'big picture'. They look for large social, economic or political trends and invest to take advantage of them. The detailed analysis of particular companies is a secondary matter to these investors. For example, a top down investor may decide that oil prices are going to rise and so the oil industry will be a good investment. The decision to buy into oil companies would be more important to them than a detailed examination of which particular oil company was the best investment.

This investment style can be contrasted with the bottom up approach to investment. As the name suggests, investors who use a bottom up strategy work in the opposite direction to top down investors. Bottom up investors look for the best companies and are relatively little concerned about how they fit into some greater pattern. They take the view that if the individual investments are right, the whole portfolio will look after itself.

An aspect closely related to top down investment is the issue of 'market timing'. This is the attempt to anticipate future movements in the level of the whole stock market. The potential rewards of doing this are obvious. Predicting movements in the market frequently involves addressing the major economic, social and political issues familiar to top down investors. Thus it is appropriate to deal with market timing in the same chapter as top down investment.

THE DEVELOPMENT OF INVESTMENT IDEAS

The variety of ideas which can potentially be used to develop a top down investment strategy is limited only by the imagination of the investor. Some ideas come 'out of the blue' but it is worthwhile to always try to be alert to the possible investment implications of things you encounter in everyday life. Newspaper and television stories, conversations with friends and situations you may encounter at work or in your leisure time can all be good sources of new ideas. Rather than taking up a lot of space trying to instruct you how to think imaginatively and creatively about new investment ideas, it is probably much more constructive to offer a number of examples of the type of top down ideas that have been used and still are being used. The list cannot be exhaustive as countless ideas have been used. It is difficult to definitively categorise such a wide range of ideas but, as far as possible, they have been grouped into similar themes. The examples are designed to get you thinking. You might like to reflect on which of the ideas you can believe in and which you think are implausible. Most importantly, the list might inspire some of your own ideas. The ideas with the greatest potential are likely to be completely original ones.

GEOGRAPHICAL ALLOCATION

An important and constantly recurring theme in top down investment is the idea that it is advantageous to allocate some assets to particular overseas equity markets. In general, it is a good policy to place some assets overseas to gain the advantages of diversification. However, some markets have, at different times, been considered to have particularly attractive features and to be worthy of special attention. Below we have given brief accounts of some of these episodes.

Post-war Japan

Directly after the Second World War, Japan was literally in ruins and surely appeared one of the least promising places in the world to invest. By the late 1980s, the

Japanese economy was the second largest in the world. Japanese cars and consumer goods were flooding global markets and Japanese industrial methods were constantly being held up as examples of best practice. Investors who recognised, at a fairly early stage, how fast Japan was changing and progressing could have participated in one of the greatest and most sustained bull markets in all history, just on the strength of that one single idea.

Japan in the 1990s

In the end, the Japanese economic miracle went badly wrong. Naturally there has been much debate over the causes of the problems. Many observers feel that the high level of government interference in the economy and the emphasis of companies on growth rather than an adequate return on capital eventually became counterproductive. There was certainly a remarkable bubble in asset prices. The price of land, property and shares seemed completely out of touch with reality in the late 1980s. In any event, the stock market and economy have been depressed throughout the 1990s. The Nikkei index reached over 40000 at the start of the 1990s but is now well under half that level eight years later. Over the same period most other world markets have multiplied in value. There have been numerous false predictions of a sustained recovery in the Japanese market often based on little more than the idea that what has gone down must come up again. The latest top down concept is that economic deregulation and a more free market approach to the Japanese economy will finally cause a recovery. The jury is still out on whether this idea is going to be a money making one.

The Tiger Economies

The post-war growth in the Japanese stock market was so profitable that a very promising idea for investors was to try to invest in countries where a similar pattern of development might be repeated. The obvious places to look were a number of Far Eastern countries such as Korea, Malaysia, Singapore, Indonesia and Thailand. The story was that these nations were very underdeveloped with lots of scope to grow fast, had industrious populations and had the Japanese economic model to follow. Simplistic though it may have been, this idea certainly produced the goods for a long time. The Tiger economies, as they became known, did achieve extremely high rates of economic growth throughout the 1980s and most of the 1990s. Stock market growth was equally impressive; the people who caught on to this concept early made a great deal of money. The party ended in late 1997 when the deficiencies of the region's economies came to light and a very serious economic and financial crisis ensued; as in Japan, it seems that a good thing can't go on forever. The stock markets of some of these countries suffered catastrophic losses. The question now is whether the crisis is going to be short lived with an early resumption of rapid economic growth or whether severe, lasting damage has been done to the Tiger economies.

Emerging Markets

Having initially succeeded so well in Japan and the Tiger economies, the idea of investing in underdeveloped economies that are potentially capable of rapid economic progress has been pushed to its logical conclusion. Emerging market investors now target the stock markets of just about every developing nation. Particular favourites are South America, the countries of Eastern Europe and China. These emerging economies form a much less homogeneous group than the Tiger economies. The main thing they have in common is the fact they are underdeveloped. The question is whether this top down investment approach is going to work again. Perhaps these economies will be the dynamic growth regions of the next 20 years, or maybe they are underdeveloped because of fundamentally intractable problems.

Europe and EMU

A currently fashionable theme in top down investment is the idea of investing to benefit from the increasing integration of European economies. There are a number of rationales for this. One idea is that the emergence of a single European market will allow industry groups to consolidate. Companies in the same industry in different countries will merge and thus realise considerable economies of scale to the benefit of shareholders. The whole European market is fairly comparable in size to that of the US and American companies in most sectors do tend to be much larger than their European equivalents. Another argument used in favour of European investment is the prospective advent of the single currency. There are, of course, many potential ramifications of this but the bull story is that the lack of currency risk will encourage investment in equities across European borders. In addition, the convergence in European interest rates will mean that interest rates can be reduced in countries which previously had soft currencies causing a re-rating of equities in these markets. Yet another strand of the argument favouring European investment is the idea that European companies are becoming more shareholder oriented. That is, they are putting a much higher priority on increasing returns to their shareholders rather than pleasing a wider range of stakeholders such as their employees and the community in general.

GENERAL ECONOMIC ANALYSIS

The state of the general economy has a big effect on the stock market. Company profits ultimately depend on the buoyancy of the economy. Individual companies are affected by economic variables in different ways. For example, if the pound is high, exporters find it difficult to sell their products abroad; while if interest rates go up, companies with a high level of borrowings will suffer. If the economy is in recession, most companies will suffer to some extent but some do much worse than others. Cyclical companies, such as construction or engineering businesses, are particularly badly affected by downturns in the business cycle; other companies such as, say, supermarkets or brewers are much less affected. Some top down investors try to take advantage of anticipated economic trends. For example, they sell exporters if they expect the pound to rise or sell cyclical companies if they anticipate a recession.

The 'Goldilocks' Economy & New Paradigm

Some top down investors think on a more grand scale about the economy than merely trying to anticipate minutiae, such as when the next interest rate movement will occur. In recent years, some investors have anticipated and made a great deal of money on the back of what has been termed the 'Goldilocks' economy in the US. The reference to Goldilocks is because of the fact that the US economy has neither been growing too quickly or too slowly but 'just right'. A fast growing economy is generally good for company profits and shares but in the past, fast growth has often led fairly quickly to inflationary pressures. Central bankers have usually had to raise interest rates to control inflation and this has tended to cause recession. Usually a booming economy has been followed fairly quickly and predictably by a bust, leading to a pronounced business cycle. In the 1990s, the US economy has been able to grow fast for an unusually long period without generating inflationary pressure, much to the consternation of many economists who have consistently predicted the emergence of such pressures. Some observers have described this as a 'new paradigm' economy based on technology and globalisation and they anticipate continued steady high growth. The traditionalists simply think we are observing a somewhat extended business cycle. So far the believers in the new paradigm have made all the money and, if their predictions are correct, they will make a lot more but it remains to be seen if the traditionalists will have the last laugh.

SOCIAL TRENDS

Some of the current social and demographic trends which provide possible investment ideas are now briefly explained.

Baby boomers

The 'baby boomer' generation is the large generation of people who were born in the baby boom after the Second World War. The term was coined in the US but the UK also experienced a post-war baby boom. These people have now reached the age where they are becoming seriously interested in saving for their retirement. The top down investment idea is that the baby boomers will direct a wall of savings indiscriminately at the equity market. This will result in a fantastic bull market for equities. The flip side of this idea is the danger of a nasty bear market in ten years or so when the same generation starts to retire and sells their equities.

The Ageing Population

Another investment idea is to try to take advantage of the fact that the population is ageing quite quickly in most developed countries. To an extent, this idea is related to the baby boomer idea described above in that an ageing population may be more inclined to direct money into the equity markets in order to save for retirement. This is particularly the case in many European countries where there is a strong body of opinion that the State will no longer be able to afford to support pensioners with the same generosity as in the past. It may also be possible to take advantage of an ageing population by investing in companies which produce products or services which cater to the needs of older people. Obvious examples of these are health care and pharmaceutical companies and nursing homes.

The Increased Spending on Leisure

A very long established trend in Western economies is for people to become generally more wealthy. As people's basic sustenance requirements are relatively fixed, a disproportionately large amount of the increase in wealth goes on leisure spending. Thus industries catering for leisure activities should be able to take advantage of a very positive long term trend.

Mass Consumerism and Brands

CLOSE-UP

In 1889, the recipe for Coca-Cola was sold for $2,003. In May 1998, the Coca-Cola Company had a market capitalisation of almost $200 billion.

One of the most successful business trends of the twentieth century has been the move towards mass consumerism based on international brand recognition. For example, McDonald's and Coca-Cola are well-known worldwide. Some observers believe that given the population and increasing wealth of developing countries, there is still scope for massive growth in companies with strong international brands.

POLITICAL TRENDS

At times political factors can be important in investment. In the UK there is no strong evidence that the stock market in general has performed better under either of the two main political parties after the effects of random fluctuations have been taken into account.[1] However, in some specific situations taking account of the political element has been important. Most of the privatisation shares sold in the 1980s and 1990s subsequently performed very well indeed. Given that the government of the day had a professed policy of widening share ownership in the UK, it is not really surprising that these particular issues were not overpriced at issue. Some investors hope now to take advantage of a similar privatisation policy being undertaken in various other countries. On a rather grander scale, the world-wide collapse of communism may be a good opportunity to take advantage of investing in countries where regimes in favour of private enterprise are in power for the first time in decades.

CLOSE-UP

Technological innovation can have very big rewards. Henry Ford, the pioneer of the production line, became a billionaire. Bill Gates of Microsoft is currently the world's richest man.

TECHNOLOGY

Nobody could fail to be aware of the fact that technology has had a major influence on our lifestyles and the business world and will almost certainly carry on doing so for the foreseeable future. Obviously there may be some very good investment opportunities here. Below we briefly review some of the most exciting areas of technology for investors.

Information Technology

To see the potential rewards of investing in the right information technology company, investors need look no further than Microsoft. This famous software company which developed the now ubiquitous operating systems for personal computers has probably been the greatest stock market success story of the latter half of the twentieth century. In less than 25 years, it has grown from nothing to become one of the four largest companies in the world. It has become a cliché to say that technology investors are searching for the next Microsoft. The trouble is that information technology companies are difficult for the non-expert to understand. Many small and apparently promising information technology companies fail either because of business mismanagement or technological failure. Even some very large 'blue chip' information technology companies, such as IBM and Apple, have gone through difficult times due to unexpected technology shifts.

Biotechnology

Biotechnology companies apply modern technology to developing new drugs. The potential rewards of this is are enormous. One can hardly imagine how much a miracle cure for heart disease or cancer would be worth. The problem with these companies is that the potential rewards are matched by dramatic risks. It is very difficult to get new drugs approved. It is quite possible to spend years of time and many million of pounds on developing a new drug only for it to be rejected as useless at the last hurdle. Picking the right stock is incredibly risky for the amateur investor.

Communications

Satellite and cable technology, the internet and many other developments are transforming the media and communications industries. There will be large rewards for investors who can pick the companies which will best be able to cash in on this revolution.

CONCLUSIONS ABOUT TOP DOWN INVESTMENT

The idea of top down investment is seductively attractive and has certainly been used very successfully by some investors in the past as we will see in Chapter 12. The method is very feasible for small investors, who may even have an advantage over many professionals in that they are not as constrained to take a conventional approach to asset allocation. However, there are pitfalls; many of the concepts, whilst initially brilliantly successful, are eventually massively overdone resulting in asset price bubbles and crashes such as the boom and busts in Japanese stocks in the 1980s and Tiger economy stocks in the mid 1990s to name just a couple. Many of the concepts are being used mainly as marketing tools to sell investments by the time casual investors hear about them. As a rule of thumb, by the time everyone is talking about a particular investment idea it is much too late to get on the band wagon. The investor would be well advised to do a lot of his own thinking rather than taking up the latest investment fashion. Another danger of the top down approach is to fall in love with one's own ideas about the future and forget to apply the necessary touch of realism. It is wise to temper one's enthusiasm with a substantial dose of scepticism. It is not sensible to invest just on the strength of an idea (although many people do). It is essential to dig out the hard facts and do some analysis to confirm the merit of the idea. If you can't find any hard facts or the numbers don't add up, maybe it is not such a good idea after all.

MARKET TIMING

There are probably more articles published about market timing than any other topic in investment. It is fairly hard to read any financial magazine or the financial pages of any newspaper without coming across some predictions about what the market is going to do next. People seem to have an insatiable desire to read predictions. As we have seen in the chapters on the academic approach to investment, the element of randomness in share price movements means that specific predictions of market levels in the future can only be correct with the aid of a great deal of luck. If you don't believe this, get hold of some back issues of investment magazines and marvel at how badly the predictions of future market levels have turned out.

Despite the negative comments in the paragraph above about the accuracy of specific predictions, it is worthwhile to have a general idea of whether the market is high or low. There are many measures of market value and they don't always give the same message, so it is wise not to rely on just one indicator. The most important measures of which every investor should be aware are set out below:

Dividend Yield
The higher the dividend yield on shares, the better value the market offers. The long term average dividend yield has been around 5%.

 Price-Earnings Ratio
The lower the price-earnings ratio, the better value the market offers. The long term average price-earnings ratio has been around 11.

 Gilt Yield/Dividend Yield
This ratio compares the value of equities with that of the principal alternative long term investment - UK government gilt-edged securities. The lower the value of the ratio, the more attractive equities are compared to gilts. Out of the three ratios, this is probably the most reliable as it takes account of general investment conditions. If long term interest rates are low, as reflected by gilt yields, it is reasonable to accept a lower dividend yield on equities. The long term average of this ratio has been around 2.3.

At the time of writing (June 1998), the dividend yield was 2.79%, the PE was 22.37 and the ratio of gilt yields to dividend yields was about 2.1. Thus the market was very highly valued on the first two measures but around average on the third. The above methods of market valuation are somewhat mechanistic although they have the considerable benefit of being objective. Some investors have a feel for the sentiment in the market and have managed to judge when to get out or buy back in on this basis. We return to this topic in Chapter 12.

CONCLUSIONS ABOUT MARKET TIMING

No matter how sophisticated the methods used, market timing can never be an exact science. However, it is possible to get an insight into whether the market is high or low. The problem is that the market might not fall until it is much too high, e.g. Japan in the late 1980s and the US may be a present example. However, being cautious when the market is high is a good discipline for preserving money.

LESSONS TO BE LEARNT

 Top down investment can be very successful.

 The ideas that can be used are limited only by your imagination.

 Don't get carried away by concepts that have already been overdone.

 Confirm top down ideas with hard facts.

 Market timing is difficult but it is wise to have some idea of whether the market is high or low.

CHAPTER 10

Fundamental Analysis

So far in this part we have considered trading and technical analysis in Chapter 8 and top down investment in Chapter 9. These have been characterised, respectively, as understanding the mood of markets and the impact of big ideas on share prices. Here we consider fundamental analysis which traditionally was defined as understanding the basic business and financial characteristics of companies and sectors. In this traditional sense, it is a straightforward application of the CORE approach to the analysis of companies and sectors that we presented in Chapter 5. As we will see, however, the term has been used increasingly to cover several approaches to investing in shares and this may reflect partly the fact that a number of modern investment gurus tend to be pragmatic in their use of a variety of investment techniques. To avoid confusion we start by considering the best defined of the techniques.

VALUE INVESTMENT

At the simplest of levels, value investment is concerned with applying quantitative techniques to identify underpriced shares. The application of given financial measures and ratios to the most recent accounts of companies is supposed to reveal which are undervalued by the market. To the strict value investor, the merits of the company and future cash flow generation are seemingly irrelevant. It must be admitted, we take a different view. To illustrate the concept of value investment we turn to the father of the approach Benjamin Graham, whose ideas on the subject are to be found in the classic 1944 book *Security Analysis*.[1] This text explains the essential financial characteristics of each sector and how to spot underpriced shares. Whilst many of Graham's measures are still in use today, it must be accepted that sectors and companies have changed in their basic operating characteristics - the context is no longer the same. Imagine how the modern retailer compares to the retailer of 1944!

Possibly the best known aspect of Graham's approach is his 'bargain issues technique'. Here the key measure is the market capitalisation of a company as a percentage of net current assets (that is, current assets minus current liabilities minus all other claims on the business). If the shares in total are selling at a price less than two-thirds of the net current asset value, then they are a safe investment and a potentially good bargain. Note this approach is ultra conservative because it ignores any fixed asset values and it considers shares only worth buying if they are less than two-thirds of their net current asset value. Thus, even if the company is liquidated, you should get back most of your investment. In the event that the share price rises, the share should be sold once the price equals the net current asset value. Graham added other ratios which you might consider if you are looking for value in companies. First the debt to equity ratio (gearing) should be low (less than 100%), as should be the PE ratio. Of course, as we stated in Chapter 5, what should be classed as low all depends on the situation of the company, the sector, the economy and the market. None the less, pure value investors would stick by a given level for the PE until it is shown not to be working. A further criterion of Graham's was that value companies should have a high dividend yield (dividend per share divided by price per share). These last two measures form part of the double 7 rule (a PE less than 7 and a dividend yield greater than 7) we discussed in Chapter 3.

There are two basic problems with Graham's highly quantitative approach to investing. First, it can easily be programmed as a search routine and, therefore, anybody with access to a personal computer and a database of company accounts can run the analysis. Therefore, the 'easy pickings' are increasingly likely to be competed away as computing power becomes more widespread. In fact at the moment it is very hard to find shares that meet Graham's criteria. In contrast, Graham was writing in the aftermath of the Wall Street Crash when share prices had been driven to extremely low levels. Second, there is a need to adjust Graham's measures to reflect the facts of modern business. Indeed, the *Investors Chronicle* has been building value portfolios based on adjusted Graham principles since 1992. One interesting feature of these portfolios is that Graham's principles have been adjusted on a number of occasions since 1992. In 1992, the selection process only subtracted long term debt from current assets and included shares selling up to 130% of net current assets as compared to Graham's original 66% (2/3). In 1998, the *Investors Chronicle* had changed this to shares selling up to 200% of their net current assets. The 21st November 1997 issue of the magazine reviewed the performance of their 1996 'value portfolio'; it had gained 23% across the year as compared to the 18% achieved by the FTSE All Share-Index. In evaluating these returns, you should be aware of the risks involved. The value portfolio included shares which varied from plus 105% to minus 50% of opening values. It should be noted, however, that the *Investors Chronicle* does not strictly adhere to Graham's purely quantitative approach. It builds its final portfolio by excluding technicals (those companies with low bargain ratios because of their type of business), 'hopeless habituals' and those companies deemed to have little chance of escaping from their lowly valuations.

In summary, value investing has the benefit of being quantitative, reasonably objective and ideally suited to the increasing availability of computer power and on-line data facilities for company accounts. Don't expect, however, to be the only investor using this approach to stock selection and be prepared to show some flexibility in assembling your final portfolio.

GROWTH INVESTMENT

In contrast to value investment which involves using quantitative techniques to search through company accounts to identify currently underpriced shares, traditionally defined growth investment is concerned with identifying those companies with potential earnings growth above that of the general market. Such companies should display a long term rising share price on the back of the continued growth in earnings. Sadly, the term 'growth investing' has been diluted to include any companies that have potentially rising share prices. Thus, no distinction would be made between share prices rising on the back of market sentiment as compared to real earnings growth. We will stick here to the traditional concept of growth investment.

Now that we understand what is meant by growth investment, we need to consider how to find and select growth stocks. Here we are helped by some of the ideas covered in earlier chapters. One obvious place to start to look for growth stocks is to first find growth sectors and the methods of top down investment can be applied here. The use of STEP analysis might help you understand how sociological, technological, economic and political forces will come together to give growth impetus to certain types of activity. For example, the growth in financial services is a reflection on an ageing population with more money to invest and better customer service via advances in technology. However, as we argued in Chapter 5, via our discussion of the CORE approach, it is dangerous to invest on the basis of half-hearted analysis. Picking hot sectors and hot stocks without a full appreciation of the detail of a sector is like betting on cards without seeing their face values.

So, the first issue to consider, once you have identified a growth sector, is do you understand it sufficiently to warrant making an investment? While there is always going to be a tendency to rush into a growth sector to try to pick up the easy pickings that occur in the early phases of growth, remember that not all firms in a growth sector will exhibit growth! A variety of factors, including competition, may well limit growth to a select group of companies or no companies at all. The profitless expansion of US airlines is a good case in point. So it is just as important to understand the context of a growth sector as any other.

In understanding growth stocks, we need to be clear about the different types. First, there is the true growth stock that progresses earnings for decades and seems able to ride out business cycle after business cycle. There are a few examples of this type of stock, such as Coca-Cola. They have a product that has a 'unique' appeal and continues to be successfully marketed. These are rare. A more common type of growth stock is one which shows a long period of growth, often on the back of a technological breakthrough, but where the growth eventually comes to an end. The effect of the motor car on railroads and aeroplanes on passenger shipping springs to mind here. Similarly, the development of the micro-processor in the 1970s led to a whole array of growth stocks. How many of us could have foreseen the consequences of over-capacity in the 1990s and the 'dumping' of electronic products? In addition to technological developments, growth stocks may also be built on the back of process development and new ways of delivering a service. Consider the innovation of Direct Line in providing insurance services. Although this provided a healthy stream of earnings growth for many years, it has come under attack from competitors who have attempted to copy Direct Line's approach to service. Furthermore, there is now the threat of the internet providing an even more cost-effective and efficient service than the telephone.

The above types of 'real' growth stock can be added to by two further types. These are cyclicals and turnarounds (recovering stocks). Cyclicals are stocks which show strong growth and decline across the up and down phases of the cycle respectively. Examples are chemicals and building. Turnarounds are companies which have almost gone to the wall but have the potential for substantial growth through recovery. These different types of growth stock have clearly different characteristics and this has implications for the way they should be invested in. The real growth stock, such as Coca-Cola, can be bought at almost any time as it will provide good returns across the long term. There is almost never a wrong time or a wrong price at which to buy these rare beasts of the stock investment world. It should be recognised, however, that the *Financial Times* has stated on a couple of occasions that Coca-Cola may be over-valued on a PE of 40 plus!

The more common growth stock which is eventually overtaken by events needs more care. Here you need to be in as early as you can to pick up the high growth pickings before the stock matures. You need to watch the price you pay because the stocks can be over-hyped and you need to watch for the right time to exit! Clearly, cyclicals need a great deal of care in timing both the entry and exit. You will find that the market also anticipates the gains to be made from riding the up-cycle and prices often start to rise before the downs cycle has finished. Turnarounds are just plain risky and while a few gurus make a career out of such investments, most tend to stay well clear.

A further aspect you need to consider is how will the growth in earnings be achieved? In general, it seems fair to say that the market is far more understanding and forgiving of organic growth than growth through acquisition. Possibly because of the difficulties involved in merging cultures/operations and with understanding the fine detail of acquisition accounting, acquisitive companies attract suspicion at the best of times. The market needs to be kept sweet and it will want to see some evidence of synergies and the potential for consolidation. History tells us that growth by acquisition is a risky business - just look at Hanson. Credibility is all with this type of growth strategy and, once it is lost, it is rarely recovered. Beware!

So far we have not given you too much detail on how to spot individual growth stocks because a number of stock selection techniques will be tackled when we look at the gurus of fundamental analysis in Chapter 13. However, it seems appropriate to offer a few tips here and now. The founding father of growth investment, T. Rowe Price, offers a clear picture of growth investment characteristics:[2]

 a company with progressively higher earnings, acceptable margins and above average earnings growth.

 good management, a market differentiator such as a patent or a 'unique' product, strong research and development.

Thus, while you might use past company accounts and corporate news to identify strong earnings growth in the past, the essence of the approach is to look to the future.

Does the stock reflect a company able to create wealth out of a patent or franchise, a change in technology, the changing interaction of sociological, economic and political influences, by riding the business cycle or turning itself around? Not an easy call to make, and this leads us on to the final part of this section: how has growth investment performed as compared to value investment?

As usual, the above question is not as simple as it seems. The first issue to confront is what exactly do we mean by value and growth stocks? For example, should recovery stocks be placed under a value or a growth heading? Clearly, the adopted definitions will affect the conclusions. A second issue is what time frame should form the basis of comparison. A number of US and UK studies, including James O'Shaughnessy's *What Works on Wall Street?*, have shown that over several decades stocks offering high fundamental value (allowing for the definitional problems) have out-performed growth portfolios significantly.[3] However, in very recent years the growth portfolios have performed remarkably. It may, however, be the case that growth prospects are becoming increasingly overpriced and the time is ripe for a reversal of fortunes. As for so much of the topic of stock investment, it is difficult to reach an unequivocal conclusion on value versus growth and it is perhaps for this reason that a number of the more modern gurus have adopted a mixed approach to the subject.

A MIXED APPROACH TO STOCK INVESTMENT – VALUE AND GROWTH INVESTMENT

We have described value investment as using quantitative techniques on current company accounts to identify underpriced (good value) shares, whereas, growth investment has been described as looking into the future and selecting shares with above average earnings growth (good business). Not surprisingly, there is much to be said for an investment strategy that combines an understanding of the future with that of the present and is sensible in its application of qualitative and quantitative techniques. Essentially, what is wrong with searching for good businesses that are currently good value? Nothing!

In fact, this reflective, pragmatic, quantitative and careful approach to investment is at the heart of Warren Buffett's amazing success. As the most successful investor of the modern age, there is much to learn from Warren Buffett. While Chapter 13 details Buffett's approach to stock investment, we outline here the basic value/growth approach to stock investment.

In one sense, we have already covered the value/growth approach to investing when we discussed the CORE approach to company analysis in Chapter 5. Remember that this approach first emphasised the importance of understanding the external and internal context of a company. Here there is a need to understand the dynamics of the sector and the likely position of the company within it. Similarly, we emphasised the need to review the internal operations, management and culture of the company - the internal context. What we were stressing here is do you understand the business and its environment sufficiently to come to the conclusion that it is good business with prospects? This is similar in emphasis to growth investment. We pointed out, however, that this is not the whole story. There is much information to be gained from overviewing and analysing the accounts of a company compared to its competitors. It is this quantitative analysis that allows you to harden up your qualitative contextual judgements. Furthermore, it is the bringing together of the context overview and ratios/analysis of a business that enables its future net cash generation to be formulated and evaluated. It is only when the future net cash generation of a business is compared to its current share price that true value can be assessed. As Warren Buffett correctly noted, the distinction between growth and value is nonsensical. You need to understand growth to correctly calculate the future net cash generation of a business, the value of the business. In other words, value cannot be assessed without growth!

A share may look underpriced according to a number of current accounting ratios but whether it is truly underpriced cannot be assessed without forming a judgement as to its future prospects.

Now that we have outlined why a value/growth approach might be a good investment strategy (allowing for the time and costs involved with carrying out the analysis), let's start to add a bit of detail. You should begin by considering sectors that you understand or know. It is pointless investing in a sector that you know little about. It is for this reason that you should not invest in a sector just because it is 'hot'; this is too risky. However, a little 'tail-wind' from a successful sector is not to be scoffed at. Our view here is that although investment should not be based on chasing hot sectors, it is best to avoid stagnant sectors. Some sectors, such as paper and packaging and textiles, seem to earn poor returns on capital year after year.

Once you have found a couple of sectors you understand, and we doubt whether it can be more than a couple, then it is time to try and find businesses with good prospects. Here Buffett refers to the idea of franchise businesses. Essentially, it is some form of power in the market place that will not be competed away. It may be a TV or a radio franchise, it may be a well-established brand (Coca Cola), it may be a location (the well sited public house in a student area), it may be a patent, etc. All in all, the business has something that is unique in its appeal to the market place and which can be protected against competition. Such a position will lead to the business having a high share of the market and good margins. It will also be able to leverage its position to maintain earnings growth year after year. Here you need to consider the sustainability of the barriers to entry. You need to isolate the exact cause of the competitive advantage - be it brand, control of distribution channels, service quality, geography, technology, physical assets, etc. and assess how far it can be replicated. Normally, a 'good business' has a high market share and a difficult to replicate barrier to entry.

The above test of a 'good business' can be hardened by considering the status of the cash and profit generation of the business. The first line financial test is the ability of a business to generate cash. Second, the business should also produce a high rate of return on equity capital in the long term. Both of these tests rule out the types of businesses that constantly need new investment if they are to be competitive; for example, capital intensive industries such as chemicals. Third, the cash and profit streams should show signs of stability. 'Good businesses' should largely avoid the pressures of competition and business cycles. A good business is able to inflation link its revenues and profit margins but keep its capital spending under control.

A third aspect of a 'good business' but one that is difficult for a private investor to judge, is the quality of the management and the overall culture of the organisation. As we discuss this issue in Chapter 13, we will merely leave you with a question that is worth reflecting on - what has enabled Marks and Spencer to maintain its high street dominance for so long? It can't be the location!

Once a 'good business' has been identified, the remaining issue is to assess whether it is good value. Here the future net cash generation of the business should be discounted back to the present (see Chapter 7) and compared to the current share price. If the discounted net cash flow figure is substantially above the current share price, then the company is good value as well as being a good business. What more could you want? Of course, this leaves two questions to be answered; how to estimate future cash flows and what discount rate to apply?

TECHNIQUES OF VALUE/GROWTH INVESTMENT

NUTSHELL

Business strategy is about businesses 'winning' in a competitive environment. The future growth generation of a business depends on how well its products compete. This in turn depends on how well its products meet the needs of customers.

In this chapter we have offered a number of tips for spotting growth businesses - the idea of barriers to entry, a strong brand, etc. You will have noticed, however, that the tips have not been discussed in a systematic manner. This is a reflection of two factors. First, the provision of tips was not the primary purpose of the prior sections and second, future growth generation is, by nature, not just a simple set of rules to be applied but a highly complex subject. If this latter point was not the case, how could we explain the high salaries of business consultants and the mountains of words devoted to the subject? We couldn't. Given the complexity involved in analysing the key determinants of business growth and the limited space available, we have decided to provide you with a set of 'strategy analysis' templates.

 Ansoff's Product-Market Leadership - with this approach you need to compare the product of a company with its market (both demand and supply).[4] Is the product a radical leader, superior or merely the same as the rest of the market? Are the demands for the product well defined and can you characterise future demand trends? Is the market characterised by barriers to entry and high demand to capacity ratios? Therefore, from this perspective, growth is explained by having a competitive product that can be protected - this is similar to Buffett's notion of a 'franchise' business.

Porter's Generic Strategies - from this perspective, business success is a function of a company understanding the balance of competitive forces within its industry and choosing a generic strategy accordingly.[5] Here a company must decide to be a cost leader, the provider of a truly differentiated product or a niche player. It must choose one of these strategies and be clear in its role within the industry. To try to follow more than one generic strategy leads to poor performance. Therefore, with this framework, a successful company is one that understands the competitive nature of its industry and has adopted a clearly defined position within it.

> **CLOSE-UP**
>
> Management guru Michael Porter identified 5 competitive forces: rivalry between competitors, potential for new entrants, buyer power, supplier power and the availability of substitute products. How strong is each force facing the company?

Porter's Value Chain Analysis - this adds detail to his earlier generic view of strategy. Here 'value' refers to the idea that each part of the chain - from raw materials to the eventual transfer of the product to the customer - adds characteristics to the product that are valued by the eventual customer.[6] Does the company fully understand where in the value chain - from the suppliers of inputs to the final customer - are the factors that might give rise to product differentiation or to cost leadership. For example, if speed of delivery is seen as a critical differentiator of the product, is this more a function of inbound logistics, internal operations or customer supply? From this viewpoint, one might identify future success by the efforts/investment a company is making in different aspects of its value chain. Of course, world class companies seem to understand and invest in the whole value chain. Consider the supply to customer value chain of Marks and Spencer.

Hamel and Prahalad's 'Competing for the Future' - here we move from the emphasis so far on the external competitive environment, to one which brings in the importance of management and culture.[7] To Hamel and Prahalad success comes from a company having well defined and shared ambitions. The whole company must understand what needs to be done to win the competitive war. The whole company is driven towards delivering the future needs of customers and it is committed to constantly improving its core competencies. For example, Honda is about making the best engines in the world. The whole company understands that it must build on and protect this ability to make outstanding engines. There is a continuous investment by everyone to be the best at its chosen endeavour. Here a successful company may be recognised by its stream of innovative products or by its emphasis on a particular aspect of service. The key feature of this notion of success is that the company understands, knows and leads what the customer wants and it builds an internal emphasis/culture that is difficult to replicate. In this respect, you might like to consider the factors that have led to McDonalds' global domination of the fast food market. Is this merely a product phenomenon or is it more a reflection of the management's dedication to winning the game?

NUTSHELL

When firms talk about **core competencies**, they mean the combination of productive skills and technology which they have cultivated in order to pursue their competitive ambitions.

 Kaplan and Norton's Balanced Scorecard - this moves us on to the last of the 'assessment' frameworks. It is the one we favour because it incorporates a lot of the earlier thinking; it balances the internal with the external and builds on the CORE analysis of companies. It is simple but powerful. The successful company understands that real wealth creation comes from balancing the demands of the four quadrants shown in Figure 10.1 and ensuring that they support and feed one another.[8] Let's start with the management and staff quadrant (also depicted as the learning and innovation quadrant). Real value creation comes from having well trained/motivated staff and management. The successful company invests in creating an environment where its employees enhance and unleash their capacity for inventiveness, enterprise and good business. Without this basic building block in place, the rest is a waste of time.

FIGURE 10.1

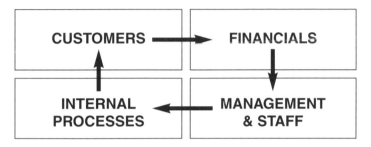

Moving on to internal processes, the employees are supported in their aspirations and ambitions by the development of efficient and effective internal procedures. There is no point in having well trained and ambitious staff if they are constantly undermined by poor processes. Of course, part of the secret here is to let employees identify and highlight weaknesses with internal processes. Once these internal quadrants have been invested in, they can be turned to satisfying the customer quadrant. Here the successful company knows and understands its customers, and leads its competitors in meeting the demands of customers. Finally, if these first three quadrants are fully aligned, then the financials of the company can be defined, targeted and fulfilled. The financial rewards are then either reinvested in the business or distributed to shareholders. The 'good business' understands the need to balance both the demands of the shareholders and the business, and the overall importance of sustaining its value creation cycle. In other words, the 'good business' knows that if future success is to be achieved it has to continuously invest in both the external and internal dimensions of its activities, and balance the aspirations and ambitions of its various stakeholders. This is easier said than done and this is why there are so few really 'world class' businesses. Also, it takes quite a lot of background research for the investor to identify these companies. None the less, Buffett's accumulated billions suggest that the effort may well be worthwhile.

Finally, we left two questions unanswered at the end of the previous section - how to estimate future cash flows and what discount rate to apply to these cashflows? The material presented in this section should start to help you think through the cash flow generation potential of a business. You need to consider how a business generates cash inflows through understanding how it competes in the market place. This then needs to be offset by the cash outflow of the business - the money it spends on operations and investments. The discount rate is usually calculated to reflect the cost of capital (the cost of equity and debt finance) of the business and this will include some allowance for the risk of the business. However, Buffett uses the riskless rate of interest, as he argues that the identification of a 'good business' rules out any risk. If only we all could be so confident! Once the cash flow potential of a business has been calculated on a per share basis (and the dividend policy of a company is a good starting point in this regard), you merely need to compare it to the present share price to ascertain if it is good value.

CONCLUSIONS

This chapter has considered investment strategies that are based on understanding the fundamentals of the business. In this regard, they are not for the investor with little time to spare. None the less, the various approaches discussed in this chapter do differ in the time and effort required. As noted, the value investment approach with which we started the chapter is open to mechanisation via computer programs and on-line data facilities. In contrast, the growth approach to investment is not open to mechanisation but rather involves understanding the potential of companies and their relevant sectors. Here you can avoid the detailed calculations of the value investment approach but you cannot avoid fully understanding a sector and its constituent companies. In other words, neither value nor growth are 'back of the envelope' investment strategies. However, a number of gurus have shown the gains to be made from adopting value or growth investment strategies. In fact, Buffett has shown the wealth to be made from using the approaches together. Let the growth approach identify the good businesses and let variants of the value approach select stocks that are good value; a good business at a good price, the stocks to fulfil every investor's dream! In discovering the value and growth approach, we reviewed briefly a number of 'strategy templates' that should help you to identify the cash flow generation potential of companies. The cash flows can then be discounted and compared to the current share price to indicate whether they are good value. We will add more detail to this discussion when we review the gurus who use fundamental analysis as a part of their investment strategy.

LESSONS TO BE LEARNT

 Value investing is concerned with using quantitative techniques on the most recent accounts to identify underpriced shares. The *Investors Chronicle* has used an adjusted version of this approach to reasonable effect since 1992.

 Growth investment is concerned with spotting those companies with real future potential.

 A number of gurus have mixed the value and growth appoaches to invest in companies that are both good value and good businesses.

 There are a variety of techniques that can be used to identify growth companies (good business) and we added the idea of using 'strategy templates'.

 Each strategy template gives a different emphasis as to the factors that lead to corporate success.

PART FIVE

INVESTMENT GURUS

AND

AUTHORS

CHAPTER 11

Technical Investors
and
Traders

As we have seen throughout Part Four, there is no single, correct method for selecting which shares to hold or for timing your investments. There's no 'Holy Grail' to stock market investment. It all comes down to choosing an approach (or a combination of approaches) that works for you personally. In this next section, we will endeavour to spy on some of the approaches which have demonstrably worked for those people who are regarded as experts in the investment field.

We will see that a whole variety of investment styles have proved successful in the marketplace. Some professionals have made exceptional returns by buying small companies, while others have focused on blue chip shares. Some investors look to diversify into currency markets and derivatives, others focus on picking exactly the right set of company shares. Some will invest in far flung markets across the globe, while others will spend most of their working week visiting and talking with the companies they own. Professional investors develop a style which is very much their own. Having discovered the method that suits, they tend to stick with it in a disciplined fashion.

By considering the styles that the professionals use, you should be able to spot some of the characteristic elements which will suit you as you develop your own investment approach. In this chapter, we will begin by looking at those investment experts who make some use of the more technical and quantitative approaches. Not all of their

CLOSE-UP

The success of the professionals is not simply based on the profit they make in absolute terms. Rather, their performance is judged on the extent by which they have outperformed the market, or how much better they have done than their rivals. Not every investor will set out to beat the market in this way. For example, some 20% of UK pension fund money is invested in tracker funds which seek to match the performance of the market rather than beat it.

techniques are able to be applied directly in the field of private equity investing but each will provide insight into how the mind of the professional works.

BRITISH RESERVE

Perhaps the first point to note about the technical approach in professional investment, described in Chapter 8, is that it is rarely used in isolation. When it comes to equity investment, most professionals like to be well versed about the companies they are buying as well as their share price activity. It is not surprising, then, that where investment gurus are happy to use technical analysis, they do so as a supplement or 'checking system' on top of other forms of company analysis.

One highly respected British investment guru who is happy to use a lot of technical analysis to supplement his investment approach is Anthony Bolton. Although frequently described as a quiet and placid individual, Bolton's approach to investment could perhaps be best labelled as 'systematic fanaticism'.[1] His investment style involves a high degree of commitment and of focused activity. This in turn necessitates a rigorous and orderly system of information management. Bolton's style also emphasises the importance of maintaining contact with the companies you are investing in. As a matter of routine, his investment approach means meeting and talking with several companies each day. As a shareholder, regular communication with a company can help you assess the quality and consistency of its management. This can be particularly helpful when investing in smaller companies. Taking a more active, dynamic style to investment also means processing a large amount of information and paperwork. Bolton emphasises the need to have a systematic and orderly approach to collating information about the companies you hold or are potentially interested in.

Unlike some of the investors we shall meet in later chapters, Bolton does not 'buy and hold' shares for long periods. Some 70% of his portfolio might be turned over in a given year, as he sells out of shares when they appear to be fully valued by the market. Don't be afraid of exploring and investigating smaller companies or even companies that have looked 'down and out' for a while. One of Bolton's specialities are those companies which are in so called 'special situations'. Here he is looking to pick out those companies where there is soon to be a turnaround in their fortunes; firms where things are about to change for the better. For example, the company may have a change in its senior management which will spark a new move towards profitability, or it may be a potential target for a take-over bid. A company may be out of favour with the market because things have gone wrong in the past, but it may now be in the process of correcting its mistakes and have the potential to grow in the future Bolton's watchword is straightforward. To have an investment performance which is different from the market, you need to be holding something other than the market. To beat the market, you have to dare to be different.

On top of identifying a company's fundamental prospects, Bolton also uses technical analysis and share price charts. Technical analysis can be used as an additional filter that will cause you to ask helpful questions about your investment decisions. Furthermore, it can provide a feel for the collective view of market investors as a whole. Bolton, for example, does not over-emphasise the use of price charts but, unlike many top-class investors, he is open minded as to how they can help. Interpreting the movement of a company's share price from a chart can cause you to go back and check you have the fundamentals right.

Technical analysis may be of more use when considering investing in larger, well known, heavily traded companies. The bigger the company, the more useful the charts. Some leading shares which are traded in large volumes every day can swing in and out of favour with the market. This element of sentiment in the market is reflected in the share's price movements even if there is no underlying fundamental change to the company's profitability. In his book, *Money Makers*, author Jonathan Davis quotes Bolton's attitude to charts:

> *"The reason why charts do have some value is that they give important clues about the current balance of advantage between buyers and sellers: they are the footprints which investors have left behind them."* [2]

In the same way that technical analysis is of varying assistance for companies of different sizes, it may also be more applicable to some markets than to others. John Carrington is another highly respected figure in the UK fund management business. Funds under Carrington's management have made exceptional returns above the level of the FTSE All Share index over the last decade. Carrington, like Bolton, will use charts, not as a starting point but as an extra check before going into a trade. He gives short shrift to the academic idea of efficient markets, labelling it 'absolute nonsense'. He takes the view that charts may be more of a help when dealing with some markets than others. Carrington, for example, emphasises the application of charts when buying in the Japanese stock market.[3] Technical approaches are even more commonplace in other investment arenas such as the world's commodities markets.

CHARTING THE MIND

It's easy to see how US commodities trader, Al Weiss, developed his reputation: between 1982 and 1992 he averaged returns of 52% annually! Weiss is a technical trader using technical analysis and charts of past prices to indicate the current state and direction of the markets.[4] When using charts, Weiss insists that the longer the period considered the better. As a commodities broker, he takes some commodity price charts back over 100 years. When taking a technical approach, it is important to obtain as long a run of data as possible. The motivation behind such a long term view is the belief that markets behave differently at different points in an economic cycle. For example, a chart pattern which indicates a given trading signal during a period of low inflation need not be interpreted as giving the same signal if it appears during a highly inflationary period. You can't always interpret a pattern the same way every time that it appears because you need to simultaneously consider how the price is moving relative to economic factors. Furthermore, Weiss would put less emphasis on reacting to individual patterns, such as spotting a Head and Shoulders pattern as described in Chapter 8. He would be more concerned with sequences and combinations of trend-indicating patterns. He argues that multi-pattern combinations provide much better signals. Even so, Weiss would admit that most chart patterns only give an accurate trading signal 50% of the time.

Having found the investment strategy to suit your personality, most investment gurus would advise you to stick with that system. Even the best technical traders, however, don't follow their systems blindly on one hundred percent of occasions. Sometimes they will overrule the message from the charts on the basis of their intuitive interpretation of how traders will react in the market.

Weiss' commitment to a technical trading approach flows from the conviction that financial markets are driven more by psychological effects than by factors affecting underlying fundamental values. On a short term basis, prices can swing with the sentiment of the market. Fundamentals give investors a solid grounding over the longer term, but over the short term the market is more temperamental. It should be remembered that market prices are discovered through the interaction of traders; ultimately they are determined by human psychology. Taking this viewpoint, charting market prices is actually the equivalent of charting the psychological perspectives and opinions which are operating in the market, some of which will repeat over time.

MUSIC PRACTICE

Linda Raschke is one successful trader who believes that price swings can be predicted - but only in the short term.[5] She holds a particular respect for the principles of Chaos Theory. You can't predict the market very far forward because some small unexpected event will occur which may have a very large impact on the way prices move. Trying to make a profit from short term price movements makes for 'on the hoof' trading. Raschke will work on the basis of expecting to hold some securities for only two or three days.

She says that even for the time periods where price moves are predictable, it is only the direction which is known, not the size of the move. You can't predict the amount by which the price will move in the new direction before it turns again. There may only be an opportunity to make a small profit at each change in price direction. In terms of Dow Theory, you can't predict the separation of tertiary highs and lows.

NUTSHELL

Chaos Theory deals with systems - like the weather or possibly the financial markets - which never settle down into some static equilibrium but which are constantly progressing in a manner which is very sensitive to small changes in variables.

In an interview with Jack Schwager for his book *The New Market Wizards*, Raschke offers this advice:

"Some of the best trades come when the market is panicky. The crowd can often act very stupidly in the markets." [6]

Price patterns are driven by aspects of human behaviour. If you are setting out to turn a short term gain, it is not a good idea to be following the crowd. For example, Raschke observes that the market lingers in its opinions. A price rally may have been moving ahead a few days before it looks exciting enough to draw in large numbers of buyers in earnest. Conversely, a falling market may make the market in general sluggishly overcautious.

The choice of trading signals used needs to be part of the individual trader's style. Investors who are taking a technical approach will need to learn over time which signals they are confident in interpreting. Some people will have more of an ability to recognise patterns than others. Linda Raschke contributes at least some of her excellence as a trader down to her years of musical training. In the same way that music compositions are constructed from repeating patterns and variations on themes, so too are the movements of the financial markets. Developing skills in pattern recognition can take years of practice, but as every musician knows, it takes dedicated practice to make perfect.

PLAYING BY NUMBERS

PROFILE

William Eckhardt is a mathematician who has had outstanding success at developing analytical systems-based trading. He argues that the human mind is overly willing to see patterns and will spot patterns that aren't truly there.

Within the world of technical and quantitative traders there is a debate as to the usefulness of visual charts as opposed to computational indicators. With the development of computer technology, sophisticated computations can be carried out on the market's price and volume data which can then be used as trading signals. Some traders argue that the intuitive nature of the human brain makes it the most useful instrument to interpret market indicators and that the brain can summarise information better in chart form. William Eckhardt would disagree. He contests that the alternative is to test the data in the chart using mathematical algorithms and determine if a mathematical pattern exists.[7]

Financial markets around the world are constantly on the move. For the trader, getting an optimum investment strategy is like hitting a moving target. Traders need to be constantly processing market information and realigning their position. In today's computer age, mathematical techniques are being applied to market data in an attempt to predict the direction of securities prices, to pick out individual undervalued stocks and to arbitrage between different markets.

Norman Packard and Doyne Farmer are two US physicists who have developed software which uses mathematical models of Chaos Theory to try to predict the direction of market prices and provide traders with signals about when to trade.[8] American researchers have even developed artificial intelligence programs to mimic how human traders behave in the markets and which will trade by themselves. David Shaw, who has a doctorate in computer science, is one of the new breed of market players who uses mathematical models to identify the relationships between securities' prices in various markets and to arbitrage between them.[9] Additionally, by monitoring the correlation between different shares, his computer models can suggest favourable prices for 'basket trades' - where a trader may make a bid on a single basket of, say, a hundred different shares. These gurus of quantitative trading may be at the cutting edge of computer science; yet their endeavours may have a real impact on the individual private investor as Internet trading makes the world's financial markets more accessible.[10]

CONCLUSIONS

Where successful professional equity investors use charts and technical analysis, they usually do so to supplement other forms of company research. Technical approaches to investment in general tend focus the mind on the next short term movement in prices. As a result, technical approaches are usually associated with a more active style of investing. These types of investors only hold securities for short periods of time and trade frequently. If a high level of activity and the pursuit of short term gains suit your personality, then it may be worth considering an approach enhanced by technical analysis.

LESSONS TO BE LEARNT

 There is no single correct way to identify investments. Professional investors develop their own unique investment style.

 Technical analysis is frequently used as an additional check on top of fundamental analysis rather than as a starting point.

 Technical approaches tend to generate an active trading style.

 Technical charts are more useful for larger, well known, well investigated, highly traded companies.

 When using technical analysis, obtain as long a run of data as possible.

 Some traders believe the markets are driven more by sentiment and psychological effects than by changes in underlying fundamentals.

 Select those trading signals which you feel most confident about interpreting.

 Some technical traders don't like visual charts but trust to mathematical algorithms to spot a pattern.

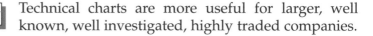 Advances in computer technology have generated sophisticated computational models to identify trading opportunities.

CHAPTER 12

Top Down Investment Gurus

In this chapter we focus on some of the investment gurus who have achieved success using a top down approach to investment. As we will see, some of the most famous and successful investors have benefited from this investment approach. Top down investment involves flexible and conceptual thinking and, as a consequence, the gurus operating this way are not easy to pigeonhole. None the less, as an aid to the reader, we have broadly classified the gurus according to the ideas with which they are most strongly associated. Some investors have made their names as a result of their approach to the geographical allocation of assets. In this category we examine the approaches of John Templeton and Nils Taube. To gain some insight into using economic analysis as a basis for investment, we look at the methods of the fabulously successful (and famous) George Soros. To see how a whole range of top down investment insights can be used, we cover the approach of Jim Rogers and very briefly examine some useful comments from other investors. Finally we cover the subject of market timing. Even top investors are divided on the efficacy of market timing. We consider some insightful comments by Jim Slater on this subject. Finally we offer conclusions regarding the lessons to be drawn from the experiences of the different gurus.

GEOGRAPHICAL ALLOCATION

John Templeton

PROFILE

Sir John Templeton is generally regarded as one of the great investors of the twentieth century. He came from a poor background in Tennessee. He worked his way through Yale and then won a Rhodes Scholarship to Oxford. After returning to the US he achieved a great stock market coup when he borrowed money to buy shares in 1939, reasoning correctly that war would pull America out of its economic depression.

Templeton's lasting claim to fame is that he was one of the main pioneers of international investment in the post-war years. In particular, he was one of the first western investors to realise the superb opportunities available in Japan. His investors certainly reaped the rewards of his insight. The Templeton Growth Fund was the top performer of all funds over the twenty years ending on 31st December 1978. Although Templeton is now retired in the Bahamas, and the idea of international investment is commonplace, the underlying principles of his methods are by no means out of date. The clarity and logic of Templeton's approach make it well worth examining.[1]

In a sense, Templeton was a value investor in that he searched for companies selling for the smallest fraction of their true worth. He was very familiar with the full range of techniques of fundamental analysis necessary to value companies. Where Templeton differed from many other value investors was that he had the vision to look for value around the world, not just in his home market. In the early 1960s he became interested in Japan. At that time the leading Japanese companies were fantastic bargains compared to their western equivalents. The Japanese economy was in a phase of rapid economic development which allowed company profits to grow at a very fast pace. Despite their much superior growth potential, Japanese companies were rated very lowly compared to their western equivalents, often selling for only a third of the multiples of comparable US companies. Templeton saw that it was quite legitimate to compare companies in the same industry across national borders. For example, Nissan and Toyota can be compared to Ford and General Motors or Japanese supermarkets to US ones.

It was many years before most investors started to catch on to the bargains to be found in Japan, which in the 1960s was generally thought of as a producer of cheap and substandard copies of western goods. In due course investment in Japan became all too popular leading to a share price bubble in the late 1980s and a collapse in the 1990s. Templeton had largely sold his investments in Japan long before the market entered its manic phase as he perceived much better value elsewhere in the world. Knowing when to sell is just as important as knowing when to buy. As we mentioned in Chapter 9, it is vital to subject any top down investment concepts to an analysis of the hard facts underlying the situation. Templeton was able to do this in Japan as he combined the vision to see the initial opportunity with the hard analytical techniques necessary to realistically assess the value of what he was buying and to decide when to start to sell.

Nils Taube

Nils Taube is not as famous as some of the other investors in this chapter but his investment track record has been exceptional. He has been in the City for around fifty years and has produced spectacular returns for the investors in the funds he has managed.[2] Although here we are emphasising some of his more qualitative ideas, it is important not to lose sight of the fact that the initial ideas are confirmed by hard and realistic analysis.

Taube has originated a deceptively simple but extremely useful investment concept that he calls 'international plagiarism'. This is the idea that if a business has worked somewhere in the world, there is a good chance that it will work over here too. It is a little like seeing the future and knowing it works. Many good business ideas have crossed the Atlantic from the US to the UK. Taube was able to spot and take advantage of one of the most spectacularly successful of these ideas. In the 1950s supermarkets were a proven success in the US but were only just beginning to appear here. Taube was correct in being sure that the idea would work in the UK and was able to buy into Tesco at a very early stage in its development.

Taube's plagiarism concept can be applied to ideas and market trends as well as to businesses. For example, he became familiar with the ideas of an American investor called Shelby Cullom Davis who had developed a new approach to analysing life insurance companies which gave a much better idea of the true value of the companies than the traditional methods. Taube simply applied the new analytical approach to German and English insurance companies and was able to make very attractive profits.

Another example of looking across international

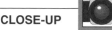

boundaries is to consider whether market trends exhibited in particular countries might be repeated elsewhere. As an example of this Taube noted the tremendous rise in bank shares in the UK and the US after the end of the recession of the early 1990s. The European banks, by contrast, have not yet experienced a similar re-rating and Taube calculates that they offer much better value to investors.

ECONOMIC ANALYSIS

George Soros

PROFILE

Soros moved to England from Hungary after the war and, after attending the London School of Economics, started a career in the City. He moved to the United States in the 1950s and continued his financial career. In 1969 he started the Quantum Fund which has undoubtedly had one of the very best investment records of any fund since then. Having made a huge fortune, he has turned to philanthropy in recent years, donating hundreds of millions of pounds to charitable causes in Eastern Europe.

George Soros is possibly the best known investor or speculator in the world.[3] He became famous in the UK when it was reported that he had made over $1 billion by speculating against the pound on 16th September 1992, which has become known as 'Black Wednesday'. More recently, in 1997, he was at the centre of the controversy about the causes of the currency crises in the Far East.

Soros' methods are highly complex and individual. He is well known for simultaneously taking large and risky positions in a number of different financial markets. He is very interested in theories of market behaviour and has gone so far as to develop his own theory which he has named the 'theory of reflexivity'. In the simplest of terms, reflexivity is strongly related to the notion of 'feedback', whereby economic processes can become self reinforcing. Soros has, in fact, written a book explaining his methods and theories - *The Alchemy of Finance* - which is well known for being impenetrable.

Obviously, it is understating the case to say that it is not possible to do Soros full justice in the space available here. However, we can use his investment approach to illustrate how economic analysis can be used to make investment decisions. Many of Soros' biggest investment decisions are based on a view of the overall economic picture. He is prepared to take a view on how currencies, commodities, interest rates or general share prices are likely to move. For example, in 1992 he correctly perceived that the economic recession in the UK would force sterling to be devalued and leave the ERM. In 1985, he made a great deal of money after the Plaza meeting of finance ministers and central bankers, when he correctly predicted the yen would rise against the US dollar. In many cases, Soros uses derivatives to leverage his positions so that his fund will benefit disproportionately from the moves he predicts correctly. Soros is careful to manage the level of risk he is prepared to assume, which is vital in such a high risk operation. He is also highly flexible and will change tack immediately if he appears to have made a mistake. In trading it does not matter too much how often you are right and how often you are wrong, as long as the maximum profits are extracted from the correct decisions and the effect of incorrect decisions is minimised.

Soros is a master of the art of speculation and it is too difficult and too risky for the average reader to try to emulate him. However, some useful insights can be gained from his methods. It is possible to invest on the basis of economic predictions but it is more or less impossible to get all your predictions right. If you are thinking of adopting this approach, you need to prepared to be flexible and to admit when you are wrong. Success depends as much on the ability to run profits and cut losses as on accurate prediction.

> **CLOSE-UP**
>
> Leverage, of course, also means that mistakes are costly. Predictions of this nature are difficult to get right and even Soros makes a lot of mistakes. In accordance with his reflexivity theory, he believes that accurate prediction is difficult partly because market movements have an influence on the events that they anticipate. He made a famous blunder in 1987, just before the crash, when he stated in interviews that the Japanese market was overvalued, and that he had shorted Japanese stocks. In the event, Soros lost heavily when Wall Street plunged much further than the Japanese market.

GENERAL TOP DOWN INVESTMENT

Jim Rogers

Jim Rogers is a investor with a whole range of top down investment ideas.[4] He formed an investment team with George Soros and, from 31st December 1969 to 31st December 1980, they achieved an average return of almost 38% p.a. with no down years. Over the same period of eleven years, the Standard and Poor's composite index only rose about 47% or approximately 3.5% p.a. Within the team, Rogers particularly specialised in research whereas Soros' speciality was in trading. Rogers is noted for his ability to foresee how broad social, economic and political trends can be used to make specific and successful investment decisions.

When developing his investment concepts, Rogers is particularly interested in the idea of anticipating major fundamental changes, not just fluctuations due to the business cycle. A good example of the sort of change he hopes to catch would be the success of the oil industry in the 1970s. Shares in oil companies did very well because of the oil crisis, even though most of the economy was really suffering. In looking at the big picture, Rogers is quite prepared to buy every stock available in an industry he anticipates will do well rather than getting into the detailed selection of individual stocks.

One of Rogers' simplest but most useful ideas is that it is very useful to compare supply and demand in an industry. For example, if we again look at the example of the oil industry in the 1970s, the oil price and the price of oil shares initially soared as demand exceeded supply after the OPEC oil embargo but when the price became sufficiently high, there was a massive increase in energy conservation and in oil exploration. As a result of this, the balance between supply and demand reversed and the price of oil and oil shares collapsed.

Rogers has formulated some particular types of change to look out for:

❗ Company and industry disasters. These can give rise to great opportunities. If an industry is in great crisis it is often a very good time to invest. For example, Rogers made a lot money investing in the US motor industry when all the major companies were losing money. However, it is necessary to be careful applying this method. There must be a reason to expect a fundamental change for the better.

❗ Changes for the worst. Rogers is very concerned when an industry is particularly popular, especially when its leading companies are mainly owned by investment institutions. In these cases, the shares in the industry are often overvalued in the market.

❗ New trends. It is very advantageous to take advantage of major new trends. For example, in the 1970s there was a trend for women to put on less make-up. Rogers realised that this development was going to be very negative for Avon. New trends are, of course, happening all the time. The difficult thing is to be fairly early in recognising them. Rogers is a voracious reader of newspapers, periodicals and trade journals; always on the look out for a new investment idea.

Government spending. Rogers has realised that when governments want to act on a problem, they have the resources to throw money at it. This is often very much to the profit of particular sections of industry.

Rogers has had a number of successes investing in countries which he believes offer promising investment opportunities. He was one of the pioneers of investing in what are now known as emerging markets. In some cases, he was one of the very first foreigners to invest in the emerging country's stock market. In recent years, the emerging markets investment theme has become a very familiar one and many unit and investment trusts are being marketed on the basis of this idea. Rogers developed ideas of what to look for in a developing country and some of these are well worth reflecting on. Rogers thought that:

1. The country must be becoming more prosperous.

2. It must be more prosperous than generally realised.

3. Its currency must be convertible.

4. There must be liquidity, allowing shares to be sold.

Rogers always liked to see a reason why the perception of a country will change for the better. There is no point in buying into a cheap market if it is going to stay cheap.

MISCELLANEOUS TOP–DOWN ADVICE

Here we cover briefly some ideas from other top investors:

Anticipate how the public will react to new concepts. New products and consumer concepts are constantly being launched. Some will succeed brilliantly, some will fail; it is really public reaction which decides. As examples of successes, consider the Body Shop chain or the mid 1990s boom in shops retailing sports clothing. As an example of failure, consider the ill-fated Sinclair C5. Brave investors can invest on the basis of whether they believe concepts are going to work. Robert Wilson was one of the richest US stock market operators in the 1970s. He primarily worked with images or concepts when investing, rather than the underlying financial realities of a company. He considered what will focus interest on a company.[5] He bought companies that were doing something new or doing something in a different way. This can be a very successful way of investing but it is also risky. Anyone doing this needs an instinct for knowing how the public will react to new innovations. If you haven't got the popular touch, this is a recipe for disaster.

Wilson also offered the useful advice that it is not a good idea to write off an established company too quickly because it has started to face competition. It is best to wait and see what really happens. McDonalds continued to do very well after Burger King started to compete with it.

The successful fund manager Ralph Wanger has offered the insight that when an industry is being transformed, the most money is made outside the core business.[6] For example, the semi-conductor industry has probably not made much money on balance but the broadcasting and computer industries have made fortunes out of the advances in semi-conductors. In turn, computing advances are vastly improving the profitability of many areas of industry. Similarly, in 19th century, railway companies didn't make much money but the world economy was transformed by better transport.

CLOSE-UP

One of the most celebrated examples of good market timing was when Sir James Goldsmith, who had been one of the highest profile investors in the 1980s bull market, reduced his shareholdings in time to escape the effects of the 1987 stock market crash.

GURUS AND MARKET TIMING

Finally, we cover the subject of market timing, which is basically the attempt to profit from anticipated market movements. An investor might, for example, sell his shares if he is expecting the market to fall. Even the most successful investors are divided about the wisdom of market timing. Some top investors think this is worthwhile and have had good results, others think it is futile and that investors trying to do this will probably just out-smart themselves.

In the chapters on the academic approach to investment we have already seen the difficulties of successful market timing. In Chapter 9, we developed some objective means of determining whether the market is high or low. We now consider some more subjective measures. Jim Slater, the well known British investment guru, has developed some worthwhile rules of thumb for catching the top of bull markets and the bottom of bear markets.[7] Each market cycle is different, so don't expect history to repeat itself exactly. However, the following indicators have been helpful in the past:

 Institutional cash holdings tend to be very low at the top of a bull market and very high at the bottom of a bear market.

 Value as measured by PE ratios, dividend yields and premium to book value is very difficult to find at the top of a bull market. In contrast, value is very easy to find at the bottom of a bear market.

 Interest rates are usually rising or about to rise at the top of a bull market. At the bottom of a bear market, rates are usually falling or about to fall.

 The money supply is usually contracting at the top of a bull market and increasing at the bottom of a bear market.

 Investment advisors tend to be bullish at the top of a bull market and bearish at the bottom of a bear market.

 New issues tend to be very common towards the top of a bull market but rare at the bottom of a bear market.

 Good news often causes little positive market reaction near the top of a bull market. At the bottom of a bear market, bad news tends to cause little negative movement in share prices as lots of bad news will already have been discounted.

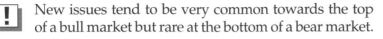 At the peak of a bull market, the stock market will feature strongly in the media. At the bottom of a bear market, media interest will be very weak.

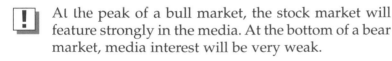

CONCLUSIONS

There are a number of ways to develop and use top down investment concepts as shown by the varying approaches of the investors covered in this chapter. Many of the broad approaches are essentially timeless. The challenge is to use them to find specific investment opportunities. This task is helped by having an inquiring, flexible mind and trying to cultivate a wide range of interests. It is, however, important to be realistic and do enough analysis and research to check whether the opportunities you find are sensible and practical investments.

LESSONS TO BE LEARNT

 There will always be investment opportunities to be found by comparing market values across national borders.

 'Plagiarism' can be an extremely useful way of getting investment ideas.

 Economic analysis can be used to make investment decisions, but is one of the most difficult and risky ways to make money in the markets.

 Try to anticipate fundamental changes in industries and the economy.

 The professionals don't invest on hunches. If they think they have a good idea, they will do enough research and analysis to make sure that it is a realistic investment proposition. You should do the same.

 There are a number of ways to get a feel for the state of the market and it is useful to keep an eye on these.

CHAPTER 13

Fundamental Analysis Gurus

This is the final chapter on investment methods and investment gurus. As we have described the basics of the different approaches to fundamental analysis in Chapter 10, the purpose of this chapter is to offer a bit more insight into how gurus have used the techniques to achieve their success. To make the chapter manageable in terms of length, we have decided to focus only on the principal proponents of each of the techniques. For value investment we concentrate on Benjamin Graham, for growth investment we discuss the approach of T. Rowe Price, for value/growth investment we consider Warren Buffett, Jim Slater and Jayesh Manek. While it is a bit premature to include Manek in the same company as Graham and Buffett, it seems worthwhile reviewing his approach to investment given the amount of press coverage he has received in recent times.

BENJAMIN GRAHAM – THE GREAT VALUE INVESTOR

It is difficult to over-emphasise Graham's influence on investment thinking. His careful and quantitative approach to the analysis of company accounts moved investment from a largely hit and miss affair to one that was based upon discipline. Although his *Security Analysis* book is often quoted as the classic text on the subject, *The Intelligent*

Investor is the book that has guided investors to search for reality when buying and selling shares.[1]

He brought a new rigour to investment analysis and it is perhaps this characteristic that defines his approach more than any other. If a company did not pass the criteria he had carefully distilled from the lengthy analysis of many companies, then it was not considered. Graham's strength was to develop a system and then stick to it. His insistence on companies being heavily underpriced did, however, lead to him missing out on the great bull market which began in 1950.

While Graham's approach continued to be quantitative throughout his life, he realised that the ever increasing number of professional analysts using his method meant that it was more difficult for the private investor to identify underpriced shares. In fact, in the last couple of years of his life, in the mid 1970s, he suggested a highly simplified approach to identifying 'bargain issues', believing this to be the only meaningful option open to private investors. While we have touched on this in Chapter 10, it is worth re-iterating how it works.

 The purchase of common stocks at less than two-thirds of their net current asset value (giving no weight to plant and other fixed assets, and deducting all liabilities in full from the current assets) and their sale at 100% of net current assets.

 Buying groups of stocks at less than their 'intrinsic value'. One could use a PE of less than 7 or a dividend yield of above 7%.

 Selling after your stock has increased by 50%, or selling after two years, whichever comes first. Selling if the dividend is omitted.

However, as we have stated before, competitive pressure within the investment market is likely to erode any potential gains from rule based investment approaches. If a 'mechanical system' is seen to be making excess returns, then competitive imitation will drive down the returns to normal levels.

As an example of the success that can be achieved by the application of value principles, we can turn to Tweedy,

Browne and Co. of New York. This company has applied Graham's 'bargain issues' approach since the 1920s. It has managed a portfolio of up to $850 million with investments in up to 1,000 companies. It has tended to hold stock for about three years, and it has achieved an average yearly return of approximately 15%. Interestingly, it has found no set of rules to be superior to Graham's net current asset technique. What more can we say?

T. ROWE PRICE – THE GROWTH INVESTOR

If Benjamin Graham is the most eminent investor of this century, then T. Rowe Price comes a close second. His 'growth' approach to investment has underpinned a whole school of thinking on the subject and many billions of dollars of investment funds. The approach is relatively simple in that investors should buy shares in companies with potential and hold them for long periods of time. Of course, it needs to be recognised that greater growth can be achieved in the early phases of a company's life than in the later stages of maturity.

For the private investor, there is much to commend Rowe Price's approach. It seems likely that the private investor will be better served by searching out exceptional companies and holding them for the long term, rather than trying to buy and sell a whole range of companies. For a start he would not have to keep track of a lot of different sectors and make difficult decisions on a frequent basis. To select such stocks, the investor needs some experience of social, political, economic and technological forces, as well as the particulars of a couple of sectors. The Rowe Price approach needs common sense and some basic understanding of the forces in operation in an economy. In contrast, Graham's approach needs a good and solid understanding of financial statements.

Rowe Price argued that growth stocks could be isolated by first identifying promising sectors and then picking the good companies within these sectors. Good companies have such characteristics as:

PROFILE

Rowe Price was just as disciplined as Benjamin Graham. He arose early in the morning with a strict agenda for the day that he worked through methodically. He adopted a similarly disciplined stance with his investments. If he had decided to sell a stock at 60, then this is what he would do. If he decided to buy more of a stock at 25, then so he would.

- superior management

- patents

- a favourable location

- strong finances

- leading research

Rowe Price did not, however, believe that a company's performance could be firmly predicted, there are just too many events that might take place. None the less, in his early writings, Rowe Price suggested that good returns could be achieved by correctly predicting the up-cycles of cyclical stocks.

In terms of buying shares, Rowe Price emphasised a price-earnings (PE) approach to valuation. The following factors should lead to a willingness to pay a higher PE for a share:

- a good record of earnings growth

- the stock is currently in fashion

- the stock is a blue-chip

- stable earnings

With these factors in mind, Rowe Price would establish the high and low PEs over the past few market cycles and pay a maximum of 33% over the lowest PE.

In terms of selling, he suggested the following:

 Watch out for a decline in the return on the invested capital as this may be a sign of a maturing company.

 If there is a bull market, Rowe Price would wait until a stock had risen 30% over its upper buying price limit, then he would sell 10% of his holding of the stock and then sell 10% more for every 10% increase in the price.

 If the bull market peaked, or if there was bad news from the company, then he would sell his entire holding.

By the mid 1970s, however, Rowe Price had become alarmed by the number of analysts adopting simple rules of growth stock investment and the tendency to chase growth fads. He seemed to be suggesting that you really need to understand the causes of growth if you are to follow a growth investment strategy. Here you need common sense, realism and flexibility if you are to follow the changing fortunes of companies within a market economy. The true growth investor cannot live by rules but only by a deep understanding of the forces that drive economies, sectors and companies forward. Not an easy approach to investing but a potentially very interesting one.

WARREN BUFFETT – THE GREATEST INVESTOR OF ALL

It should be evident that we, as well as many others, hold Warren Buffet in the highest regard. Although we have not analysed in detail the reasons for this level of admiration, it seems to be a reflection of his 'common sense' view of investing and, possibly, his undeniable level of success. Before we look into his investment approach, let's consider a brief sketch of his background.

It seems that from an early age, Buffett was intrigued by the stock market. He developed his own indices and measures of technical analysis but as he did not understand what they told him, he abandoned this as a means of investing. His boyhood business activities of reconditioning pinball machines, retrieving and reselling golf balls and running several paper routes for the *Washington Post* are a better indicator of his later investment methods - simple businesses that can be understood. This is evidenced by the fact that while still at college, Buffett had recognised that Ben Graham was a director of GEICO which sold automobile insurance direct by mail, bypassing the brokers. He liked the idea and went to the offices of GEICO and talked to a senior executive for many hours! Buffett bought some stock on the back of this approach of selling insurance direct and the fact that it was making 20% on its underwriting activities against a normal margin of 5%. It is worth noting that Buffett recognised both the soundness of the business proposition and the quality of the financial results being produced.

However, Buffett's approach to investing was also influenced by Benjamin Graham. Upon leaving Columbia University, Buffett decided his 'education' could be best continued by working for the most successful stock

PROFILE

From his background of a down-home guy from the mid-west, Buffett has developed the reputation as being the 'Oracle of Omaha'. He is the second richest man in America after Bill Gates. His investment statistics speak for themselves; if you had invested $10,000 in his investment vehicle, Berkshire Hathaway, in 1956 and reinvested the profits, you would now hold shares worth $80 million. Over the years he has usually outperformed the index by a large margin.

investor of the time - Benjamin Graham. Although Buffett offered his services for free, Graham declined and Buffett went to work for his father's stockbroking firm in Omaha. However, Buffett and Graham kept in touch and eventually in 1954 Buffett went to work for the Graham-Newman Corporation in New York. In the two years he worked for Graham, he used Graham's quantitative techniques to analyse hundreds of companies.

After this intense training at the temple of quantitative investment, Buffett returned to Omaha. As for many individuals from farming and industrial areas, Buffett seems to have inherited an inbuilt appreciation for the quality of assets and what makes a business work. It is understood that business is about sustainable cash generation and fancy notions of 'accounting profit' are given little truck. Business is essentially simple and this is recognised for what it is by people who are descended from the generations that worked at the core of the wealth creation process. In essence, his background has enabled him to understand how businesses work and his time with Benjamin Graham gave him the skills to analyse/see through company reports. Not a bad starting point if you want to make serious money from investing.

Buffett's wealth and performance have been built on the back of a well grounded faith in well managed companies with solid earnings. He tries to find companies that he thinks he understands, where he rates the management and where the price is sensible. Invest in value, look for high earnings, hold for the long term..... those are the cardinal virtues of intelligent investing.

Of course, even Buffett admits the difficulty in spotting the real value creators and he has stumbled occasionally, buying less than exciting stocks such as US Airways and Salomon Brothers. None the less, in general his approach has worked. His identification of companies with a strong competitive advantage (thereby avoiding commodity businesses such as paper), some form of consumer monopoly (either a branded product or service - for example, Gillette razors, regional TV companies and local newspaper companies), an attraction to retailers (Disney videos, Coca Cola, etc.) has allowed him to benefit from strong business profits. Once a company has been identified with some or all of these characteristics, he then concentrates on buying it at the right price, and here his work with Graham comes into play. Do you understand the future value potential of the business as compared to its current price? We provide below a complete checklist of the characteristics that Buffett associates with good businesses.

! The best businesses take a royalty from the growth of others. For example, top international advertising and insurance agencies prosper when their clients prosper. The benefit of these businesses is that they do not require a lot of capital.

! There is a high return on total stocks plus plant. This emphasises whether the basic assets of the business are being well managed.

! The earnings are predictable (for example, do not invest in cyclicals or hi-tech companies if you do not understand where the profits come from).

! The industry is not a target for regulation (for example, utilities).

! The firm requires low inventories and little replacement of capital. Some industries require almost constant renewal of the physical assets.

! Are the management aligned to the shareholders (more of this later)?

! Does the company have a good franchise and, therefore, flexibility to adjust prices (some form of consumer monopoly). Of course, all franchises are open to some competition, just look at Filofax!

! They shouldn't need exceptional management to run them because there may be problems of succession etc.

! They generate cash, have a good return on capital and can be understood.

The above is quite a long list of characteristics that need to be considered and the obvious question is whether the average private investor can sensibly use the approach. Here, Buffett highlights six features that he sees as being essential if you are to be a successful investor.

1. You must want to make money and be fascinated by the investment process. There is a balance to be struck between the action driven by 'greed' and the reflection needed to understand the company.

2. You must be patient. The stock market will go up and down but if you have bought a good company, then the share price will follow.

3. Don't be swayed by public opinion. Form your own judgement and stick to it.

4. You should only invest what you feel comfortable with. If not, you won't have the patience to see the real returns.

5. Be aware of your own limitations. This will allow you to recognise the exact depth of your understanding.

6. Be focused.

The above is quite a tough set of requirements to meet but we do know personally of a couple of private investors who have adopted the Buffett regime to investing and they too have been successful; although neither has yet managed to emulate the master himself - but then, who has? Of course, there are professional investors in the UK that adopt a Buffett-like stance and it is to these that we now turn.

JIM SLATER

The best known of the UK investment 'gurus' is Jim Slater. Most individuals with at least a passing interest in business and financial matters will have come across his name. But who exactly is Jim Slater?

In the late 1960s and the early 1970s he was a charismatic, and then a notorious, investor. In 1964, Jim Slater, an accountant, and Peter Walker, an MP, formed Slater Walker Securities (SWS) but Walker did not stay long. From its inception, SWS concentrated on investment dealing and management and on buying controlling stakes in badly performing industrial groups. This strategy was successful and on its back SWS became an 'investment bank' with an empire of British and foreign satellite companies. It both held stakes in these companies and lent them money, much of it to purchase property assets. However, the property boom collapsed, as did the Slater Walker empire. SWS had to be rescued by the Bank of England in the 1973-74 bear market. Given the ensuing DTI investigation and the threat of his extradition to Singapore, it is perhaps not surprising that many are still wary of the Slater name.

None the less, Slater has managed to re-invent himself as the UK investment guru. The basis of the 'new Jim Slater' was his development of the 'Company Refs' system. This is designed to pick out stocks with strong earnings growth potential and healthy cash flows. Although Slater's approach to stock picking seems to have evolved, we describe below our understanding of his current approach.

In one way, Slater is very much like Graham in that he works from the general to the specific. His system considers 2,000 stocks and works its way down to just a few. He manages to achieve this by working with a CD Rom database of company data. CD REFS gives private investors access to the Hemmington Scott database of UK quoted companies. From this pool of 2,000 companies he devises screens (tests) to gradually focus down to a 'select' group of 'winners'. The screens used by Slater seem to be as follows:

> [!] A Price-Earning Growth (PEG) Factor - this is the foundation stone of Slater's approach and it eliminates most companies. If a company is to be awarded a PEG factor, it must achieve a continuous growth in normalised earnings per share (EPS) for four consecutive periods including current forecasts. This screen identifies real growth companies and only about one-fifth of the initial 2,000 companies get through.

> [!] Earnings growth - having identified growth companies in general, the second test imposes a stricter growth condition of companies needing to achieve earnings growth of 20%. This seems to reduce the sample by another three-quarters and leaves only approximately 100 companies in the game.

> [!] These super growth companies are further reduced by demanding a ratio of price/earnings to future growth rate of less than 70%. In other words, the

market's expectation of the future (the PE ratio) must be substantially exceeded by the forecast earnings growth of a company. The PEG is, therefore, in theory, a measure of how far the market has underpriced a share vis-à-vis the expected growth in earnings. This sieve reduces the sample to approximately 70 companies.

 The cash flow of a business should exceed its earnings by at least 30%. This drastically reduces the set of companies by approximately two-thirds and, therefore, there are about 30 companies left.

 Positive relative strength - this tests whether the share price of a company is keeping up with the market. It should exceed the market for the previous 12 months.

 A rising margin trend - indicates the market strength of a company.

 A low level of gearing.

The above criteria would reduce the initial 2,000 companies down to a handful of expected winners. With these, Slater would then check the status of management shareholdings and the volatility of shares. Eventually, you might focus down on to 2 or 3 companies and these are the ones to invest in. As you can see, Slater is a true mixture of value and growth, with a real emphasis on the quantitative. Slater is not, however, without his critics. One particular concern is the dependence of his approach on brokers' forecasts of earnings growth and there is always doubt as to how far these capture future realities. The real question to ask here is whether there might be a better way to identify a pool of likely growth shares? Buffett uses the more qualitative approach of understanding sectors and companies, and then isolating those with a history of growth and the potential for more. We leave it up to you to decide which you prefer.

JAYESH MANEK – A NEW INVESTMENT GURU?

While this chapter has concentrated on describing just a few of the established greats of the investment world, this section looks at a new name on the block - Jayesh Manek, the Ruislip pharmacist who seems to be also a bit of a wizard with stocks and shares. He is the man who has received lots of press coverage because he won the *Sunday Times* Fantasy Fund Manager Competition in both 1994 and 1995. This success, the associated media attention and the support of veteran investor Sir John Templeton, has allowed Manek to develop a £50 million plus unit trust. Although it is too early to tell whether his competition success will translate into real investment performance, it is worth reviewing his stated approach to investment.

In basic outline, he is a growth/value investor. His investment criteria include above average earnings growth, high return on capital employed, good business franchise, simple business, proven management, healthy cash flow, etc. His original approach to diversification has now been adjusted to take into account the risk and return preferences of the smaller shareholders who have invested in his unit trust. While still attempting to remain focused, the unit trust is said to contain about 35 stocks. This portfolio is not rebalanced on a regular basis with companies only being dropped once their lack of performance indicates real problems. Thus Manek invests in good businesses and these are held until they have shown themselves no longer to be part of this category.

Interestingly, Manek also takes account of the stock market when buying shares. He claims that one of his most successful strategies is to buy stocks when they have moved through previous market highs. The reasoning behind this is as follows:

> **CLOSE-UP**
>
> Manek could be seen as a UK clone of Warren Buffett with a few minor variations. Originally, Manek was very similar to Buffett, holding large positions in just a few stocks; although unlike Buffett he did tend to rebalance the portfolio on a regular basis.

"It's tempting to buy when stocks are falling but the problem is that they often carry on falling. And when the stock tries to go up, each time it matches someone's break-even, they will sell because they've been waiting 16 months and psychologically it feels good to break-even... Instead, if the fundamentals are right, I like to go into a stock when it clears the previous high, because then nobody's losing money!" [2]

He does not see, however, this as market timing, rather as just trying to take benefit from understanding the psychology of the market. His approach is firmly based on investing in companies with potential (and here he is more growth than value in outlook) but he is still acutely aware of the financials. What we take from Manek is similar to that of Buffett and to a lesser degree, Slater - find good companies but don't ignore the accounts. Or in other words, look to the future but don't ignore the past. We will have to wait and see, however, whether Manek's ability to pick winners and avoid losers even gets close to that of Buffett's.

GOOD COMPANIES AND MODERN TECHNIQUES

A lot of this chapter has been concerned with describing gurus who invest on the basis of identifying good companies. While we have reviewed a variety of techniques for identifying good companies, there are a few more ideas that should be covered before we conclude this chapter and our discussion of different approaches to investment.

World Class Companies

One obvious place to start to learn about what makes great companies is to analyse existing world class companies. A word of caution is, however, needed here. There is no guarantee that a world class company today will be a world class company in the future. Of the top 12 companies in the world in 1912, only three remain within this category now - General Electric, Royal Dutch Shell and Exxon. Interestingly, the 'demise' of the rest is at least partly explained by a shift in sectoral emphasis. The emphasis on steel, textiles, railcars and cigarettes in 1912 has been replaced by pharmaceuticals, brands and computers in the 1990s.

In trying to learn from world class companies, we are helped by the fact that Walter Goldsmith and David Clutterbuck have updated their best selling book, *The Winning Streak, a Study of Top Performing Firms*.[3] Although it is difficult to do justice to the book, in essence, real corporate success is seen coming from an ability to balance a set of operational and strategic tensions. These balances are captured under a series of bullet points:

Control versus Autonomy - top performing companies are constantly struggling to achieve a balance between giving individuals and business units sufficient freedom to allow them to achieve enterprise, innovation and unit efficiency, and yet offering enough control to gain the benefits of a common direction and efficient internal transactions for the whole organisation.

The Long Term versus the Short Term - good companies realise the benefit of longer term strategic thinking. It provides a road map for the organisation and individuals. With this in place as an integral part of the culture, there is less need for short term fire-fighting. Good long term 'planning' provides the time for effective short term actions.

Evolution versus Revolution - following on from the previous point, high performing companies are constantly searching for improvements. It is part of the culture for every individual to identify weaknesses and suggest improvements. Only when this process of evolution does not offer sufficient pace of change do top performing companies embrace the need for revolution.

Pride versus Complacency - good companies have a culture of pride, yet this has to be 'checked' to avoid it becoming complacent arrogance. This is achieved by the development of a learning culture; this provides the necessary internal humility.

Focus versus Breadth - we all know it is important for companies to focus on their core activities, yet good companies also know they have to develop. The trick here is judging the pace and timing of change.

Values versus Rules - high performance is underpinned by a well articulated and understood set of corporate values. If these do not offer sufficient guidance in certain circumstances, then there are established rules and procedures. These are not meant to constrain action but rather avoid confusion.

Customer Care versus Customer Count - there is recognition of the need to balance growing the customer base of the company against offering existing customers high quality service. This is never easy to achieve.

 Challenging People versus Nurturing People - part of achieving success is to stretch the organisation and the individuals within it. However, if this stretch is to be obtained, then the company has to offer the necessary support and understanding.

 Leading versus Managing - good companies are led as well as managed.

 Gentle versus Abrupt Succession - top businesses achieve a careful, almost seamless succession of its management. This provides the necessary stability and continuity of the underlying value structures.

It is true that it is more difficult for the investor to gain information on the management of companies than other aspects; for example, the nature of their brands, the past growth rates, etc., but what the above suggests is that although brands, sectors, etc. are important, it is the quality of management that builds and sustains competitive performance and for this reason it cannot be ignored. Therefore, when you buy a share it might be worth asking the question, how much do I know about the management of this company?

Director Shareholdings

While it is often difficult to obtain information on the detailed management of a company (although it is often possible to form a reasonable impression from a fair amount of homework), one readily available indicator is the directors' shareholdings in the company. The simple idea is that you want the directors to behave like owners of the business and this can be achieved through them holding substantial blocks of shares. A similar argument might be made for employees as well. The holding of shares is supposed to align the financial interests of directors and employees to those of outside shareholders.

As a test of the potential worth of this indicator for private investors, the *Investors Chronicle* looked at the share performance of companies where directors spent a minimum of £150,000 on shares in their own company within a 30 day period between January 1993 and June 1995. They identified 252 cases and the results were disappointing with the returns only being 7% ahead of the FT All Share Index; not a great margin given the room for error and the increased risks. However, further analysis revealed an interesting fact. Changes in directors' shareholdings seem to offer a reliable indicator of large returns when a company is coming out of the doldrums. In other words, directors are able to forecast recovery and they buy shares accordingly.

You might also want to consider the following questions if you are intending to use director shareholdings as part of your investment strategy.

? What is the purchase worth relative to the directors' existing holdings? It needs to be substantial.

? What is the overall balance of director buys and sells in the company?

? What are the key executives (chief executive, chairman, finance and sales directors) doing in terms of buying and selling?

? Are the purchases taking place just before the start of a close period (that is, when directors cannot trade in the shares of the company - generally a period of 2 months immediately preceding the announcement of the company's results) running up to a results announcement?

Finally, remember that there is a substantial difference between directors buying shares with their own hard cash and them owning share options granted by the company!

Measures of Value

Of course, it could be argued (and many have done so) that it is not the actions of management that are important but the consequences. Therefore, we should not care about the culture of an organisation, etc., but only whether these lead to the appropriate responses from customers and the generation of positive net cash flows. It is this perspective that has underpinned two recent valuation trends, Economic Value Added and Market Value Added. We consider each of these in turn.

 Economic Value Added - this takes a company's after tax operating profit and deducts the company's cost of capital. The cost of capital includes the cost of equity (what shareholders have an expectation of receiving through capital gains and dividends) as well as the cost of bonds and loans. The cost of capital can vary across companies because some are more risky (hence, needing a higher cost of capital) and because they differ in their mix of sources of capital, with equity being more expensive than debt. EVA™ (although this is now the term in most use, it is actually a trademark of Stern Stewart & Co. and a number of authors have remained faithful to the generic terms of 'economic profit' or 'residual income') has received increasing emphasis because it measures whether the management of the company is adding value (profits) over and above the cost of capital. More conventional measures such as earnings per share do not take into account the cost of capital and, therefore, it is not possible to tell whether value is being created or destroyed.

Market Value Added - is a similar but not identical concept to EVA™. In line with EVA™, it attempts to determine whether a company has added or destroyed value for its shareholders. It takes the total capital entrusted to a company (share issues + retained earnings + borrowings) as the book measure of the money that has been invested in a company and compares it to the market value of the company's shares and debt. If the market value exceeds the book value, then value has been created.

Therefore, MVA takes the market's assessment of the company and compares it to the money invested in the business; whereas, EVA™ takes the profits generated by the business and compares it to the money invested. Both approaches have strengths and weaknesses. The strength of

MVA and EVA™ is that they attempt to assess whether management is really adding value without the seeming need to go through the laborious process of working out the discounted cash flows of the business. However, EVA™ is dependent upon the published profit figures of the business and these can be 'created' by management and be a poor approximation of future cash generation. The weakness of MVA is that it uses the market's assessment of a company and, as we know, this can be the subject of sentiment. Therefore, although both of the measures are currently in vogue, it is worth being aware of their limitations.

In summary, there seems to be no such thing as a free lunch when it comes to investment. There seems to be no sensible alternative to understanding the management and taking a view on the cash generation of the business. The real issue raised in this section, however, is how much weight should you place upon the difficult to define, but important, management component as compared to the achieved growth rate, past cash generation, sector, etc. Our view is that the quality of management should not be ignored but Peter Lynch who ran Fidelity's Magellan Fund (the world's biggest unit trust) had a very different perspective; namely,

> *"I choose a company which can be run by an idiot because you can be sure that one day it will be!"* [4]

CONCLUSIONS

The first general conclusion is that investing is hard work. No matter what approach you adopt, there is a fair amount of background work to be gone through if you are to be successful. Second, although it may not have been obvious from our descriptions, the gurus invest for substantial gains. There is little point in 'nickel and diming' because the trading costs plus the effort required soon negate any gains. Third, with the exception of Graham, none of the other gurus rely on numbers alone; there has to be an element of judgement and understanding. You need to combine an appreciation of the financials with the other key characteristics of business success.

LESSONS TO BE LEARNT

This chapter offers the following broad principles of investment:

 Know what you know.

 Target great businesses - although Graham would not mind buying a 'bad business' if it was cheap enough.

 Compare future value with current value.

 Go for real gain - given the work involved, you need substantial returns.

Each of these principles can only be operated in a meaningful way with a lot of effort and persistence. Finally, bear in mind that any rigid system of stock selection is likely to run out of steam. The trick is to balance flexibility with rigour and discipline.

PART SIX

INVESTMENT GUIDELINES

CHAPTER 14

Personal Financial Planning

We have now comprehensively covered all the basic building blocks that you will need to understand in order to begin investing in equities. We've considered the theory of investing and we've seen how investment professionals go about the task in practice. From here on, the remainder of the book is designed to help **you** get 'up and running' as an equity investor. It will take you through some of the implications and the day-to-day practicalities of holding shares. In this chapter, we will consider some general guidelines and questions that you will need to ask yourself as you decide when and how to invest. Chapter 15 will offer some more specific advice about putting your investment in shares. In Chapter 16 we will talk you through the practicalities of dealing with a stockbroker, complemented by real-life examples from a modern service provider.

In deciding how you might use the lessons from this book, it is important that you are fully aware of your own circumstances and characteristics; your financial commitments, your (and your family's) attitude(s) towards risk, the time you have to spend on investing in the stock market, your contacts, etc. For example, it is pointless trying to pursue a high risk investment policy of investing in, say, bio-technology shares, if your natural attitude towards risk is to wear a parachute and crash helmet when travelling on a local British Airways' flight!

In essence, you need to take a long, hard look at each of the factors mentioned above and then try to decide how various investing methods might best fit your overall situation. You will clearly not get this correct immediately; you will only truly learn about your attitudes towards investing in shares through the actual process itself, but you can lessen the pain of choosing investment models that do not suit your innate character. It pays to spend some time at the outset reflecting on the various factors.

HOW MUCH SHOULD I INVEST IN SHARES?

The first thing to be fully aware of are your financial commitments. You should only really invest money in the stock market that you and your family can do without. For although the evidence suggests that extreme losses are not very common, they do exist in small numbers and the possibility shouldn't be ignored. Furthermore, if the money you invest in the market is largely surplus in nature, you can enjoy trying out and following a range of investment models. You then know that although, on average, you should make money, if the worst comes to the worst, all is not lost. Thus, we would suggest that you take careful stock of your financial commitments before investing in the stock market.

Taking stock of your financial commitments gives rise to deciding what period of time you should consider as your budgeting horizon. Well, this is not an easy question to answer, because individuals have different types of planning horizons, but we would suggest that a calendar year is a sensible choice. With this type of period you can take account of your weekly and monthly expenditures and also those one-off purchases and bills that you are likely to make or be faced with. In terms of the latter, don't forget that the roof might need serious repair or the washing machine might have to be replaced. It is not a good policy to believe that you can meet such 'one-offs' by the sale of some of your shares; it might be the worst time to sell! Instead, you might keep a 'buffer' of short term, liquid savings in, say, a bank deposit account to cover such unforeseen events. At the same time, you also need to plan for your long term future and your (and your family's) financial security. Understanding and taking account of your financial commitments will give you the peace of mind and freedom to make full use of the stock market for personal gain and satisfaction - not a bad deal!

Making Budgets

It tends to be the case that in any given week or month, most people will spend a significant proportion of their time earning money and spending money, but little time on actually managing it. If you are to embark on a regular programme of investment, you will first of all need to work out what funds you have available. A good place to start is to work out a simple monthly, quarterly and annual budget of your income and expenditure. Figure 14.1 provides a basic template for you to think about.[1] A range of budget headings has been included as food for thought. You will need to adjust the categories to suit your own personal circumstances, but make sure you put down all your significant expenditure items.

To find out how much of a monthly surplus you have available for regular investment and saving, many books on financial planning suggest that you work out all your annual outgoings and then divide by twelve to get an average monthly expenditure figure. This approach, however, causes you to lose sight of your actual cash flows during the course of the year. Remember that some bills have to be paid only once every three months (for example, your telephone bill) or even once a year (for example, your car's MOT test). Furthermore, most people these days will use credit or store cards to defer payments for purchases. When working out your monthly outgoings, it is important not to lose track of your spending on credit. The balance on your credit card statements one month (for example, balance 'B' in Figure 14.1) influences how much you will need to pay out the following month (payment 'P' in Figure 14.1).[2]

Once you have compiled your own version of Figure 14.1, you will be able to compare your monthly income to your expenditure. This will give you a good feel for how much you have available on a regular monthly basis for savings and investments. It will also give you the opportunity to review your current outgoings and see if you can transform some of your spending into increased savings.

FIGURE 14.1 REGULAR INCOME AND EXPENDITURE BUDGET

HOUSEHOLD INCOME AFTER INCOME TAX:

	Jan	Feb	Mar	....	Dec	Total
Take-home Pay(s)						
Bonus(es)						
Child/Other Benefits						
Maintenance						
Pension Income(s)						
Interest and Dividends						
Other Income(s)						
Total Income						

REGULAR SPENDING BY DIRECT DEBIT:

	Jan	Feb	Mar	....	Dec	Total
Mortgage or Rent						
Car Loan Repayments						
Student Loan Payments						
Council Tax						
Property Insurance						
Health Insurance etc.						
Electricity/Gas/Water						
Car Insurance						
Motoring Organisation						
Other						

SPENDING BY:

	CASH, CHEQUE, DEBIT CARD:						CREDIT CARDS:					
	Jan	Feb	Mar	....	Dec	Total	Jan	Feb	Mar	....	Dec	Total
Balance on Card (Start)							A	B	C	....	L	
Food and Household												
Chemist / Hair Dresser												
Clothes												
Dry Cleaning / Laundry												
Telephone Bills												
TV Licence												
Childminder Costs												
Petrol												
Road Tax												
MOT & Car Servicing												
Likely Car Repairs												
Parking												
Public Transport												
Cinema/Theatre/Meals												
Presents / Cards												
CDs, Tapes and Videos												
Drinks and Cigarettes												
Newspapers/Magazines												
Subscriptions/Charities												
School Fees												
Holiday Expenses												
Others												
Credit Card Payments	O	P	Q	....	Z		(O)	(P)	(Q)	....	(Z)	
Balance on Card (End)							B	C	D	....	M	
Total Outgoings												
Income Less Outgoings												

A Quick Wealth Check-Up

Having established what portion of your regular income can be directed towards savings and investments, you should also take stock of your current financial holdings and liabilities. This is equivalent to building your own household 'balance sheet' similar to that shown for a company in Chapter 5. Figure 14.2 shows a basic template for your current net wealth. Having drawn up a statement of your assets and liabilities, you will be able to see more clearly whether you have any surplus liquid funds which can be invested for a better potential return.

FIGURE 14.2 FINANCIAL ASSETS AND LIABILITIES

Assets at Present or Most Recently Reported Market Value	£	Liabilities	£
House		Mortgage	
Car / Motorcycle		Other Secured Loans	
Caravan		Car Loan	
Household Furnishings		Student Loan	
Electrical Appliances & Equipment		Other Unsecured Loans	
Computer		Store Credit Arrangements	
Jewellery		Store Cards	
Cash		Credit Cards	
Bank Account		Bank Overdraft	
Building Society Deposit Accounts		Personal Debts	
TESSA		Unpaid Bills Currently Due	
PEP		Unpaid Tax Liability	
Unit Trusts		Other Liabilities	
Ordinary Shares			
Individual Savings Account (from 1999)			
Pension Plan			
Cash Value of Life Insurance			
Other Assets			
Total Assets		Total Liabilities	
Total Net Assets / (Liabilities)			

Consider Your Financial Targets

Now you have established the funds you have available for regular saving and investment, you should take some time thinking about your financial targets.[3] What are the broad targets of your investment goals? The investment strategy which will be most suitable for you will depend on what outcomes best suit your current and future circumstances. You may decide that you need to aim at building a lump sum 'nest egg' for some point in the future. Again you should try and identify roughly how much you will need and how far into the future. You will need to ask yourself over what timescale you need to have your savings available; for example, are you saving for a family wedding that you hope to see happen in the next five years, or are you saving for your retirement? Alternatively, you may decide that you are less concerned with a nest egg than building up an improved regular income. Once you have a good idea of the various destinations you want to achieve with your finances, you will need to build a long term route map of financial plans to get you there.

Dividing Your Investments

As you build up your financial route map for the future, you should make sure that you have covered some key elements. Most personal financial planning texts would identify certain cornerstones to financial security which you will need to have in place. These will probably include:

 Adequate insurance cover, including life assurance that will meet the needs of your dependants.

 Adequate pension provision for your retirement years.

 Short to medium term funds in 'safe havens' such as savings products, available for rainy days.

 Regular savings and investment for your medium and long term future.

Once you have decided how much to save, how soon you will need access to your savings, and what level of returns you are seeking, you will begin to have an idea of where you need to place your investments. As we have already mentioned, it is generally a good idea to hold a buffer of accessible savings for those unforeseen items of expenditure which crop up from time to time. Chapter One outlined the potential benefits of equity investing compared to other forms of saving and introduced the idea of investment returns being related to some extent to risk. Figure 14.3 shows how the various places that you might put your investments compare on a risk/return scale.[4]

FIGURE 14.3 COMPARING RISKS AND RETURNS

	Low Risk/ Lower Potential Returns ⟷		High Risk/ Higher Potential Returns
Non-Equity Investments	Bank Deposit Accounts Building Society Deposits Gilts National Savings Individual Savings Account (Cash Element) Fixed Interest Assets		Currency Futures Options Venture Capital Trusts
Equity Based Investments	Guaranteed Equity Bonds Protected Unit Trusts	Ordinary Shares Tracker Funds Broad Based Funds Individual Savings Account (Share Element) With Profit Endowments	Small Company Shares Specialist Funds Emerging Markets Warrants

Safe havens for some part of your savings will include bank and building society accounts, National Savings or gilts. In selecting a bank or building society deposit account, you will need to consider both the rate of interest paid and the accessibility of your funds. Most newspapers frequently carry tables of current interest rates on offer. You will also need to be aware of your tax position and try to minimise your overall tax bill. Certain National Savings' products enable you to invest tax free. Fixed Interest Savings Certificates, for example, are one way to invest a lump sum for a fixed period at a guaranteed interest rate. As there is no tax to pay on the interest, these types of products may be of particular interest to higher rate tax payers. Another example would be Indexed-Linked Savings Certificates which are designed to keep pace with inflation; for example, a certificate may pay 'inflation plus 2.5%'. Chapter 4 also discussed the option of investing in government gilts. Gilts offer security of both income and capital (if held to maturity) so they can be particularly useful to people who know in advance when they are going to be spending their investments; such as those making provision for school fees. Any capital gain on selling gilts is tax-free, but the coupon income you receive is taxable, so it is important to be aware of your overall tax position. Similar products issued by building societies are called Permanent Interest Bearing Shares (PIBS) which, again, are liable to income tax but not capital gains tax.

Individual Savings Accounts (ISAs) are the new replacement for Personal Equity Plans (PEPs) and Tax Exempt Special Savings Accounts (TESSAs). They come into operation from April 1999 and will offer investment free of income tax and capital gains tax. ISAs will have three components: cash, stocks and shares, and life insurance. As with PEPs and TESSAs there will be a limit to the level of annual contribution into the scheme. This limit will initially be set at £5,000 per year, of which £1,000 can go into cash and £1,000 into life insurance (although for the first year only of the scheme, the limit is expanded to £7,000 of which £3,000 can be cash). The cash component will cover such items as bank and building society deposits, cash funds and taxable National Savings products. The life insurance component is expected to cover a range of single premium policies. The stocks and shares component will include such investment instruments as ordinary shares, unit trusts, investment trusts, preference shares and convertibles. There will also be a tax credit given on the dividends from UK equities within the scheme for the first five years of the scheme's operation. Chapter 15 will cover the practicalities of putting your investment in shares.

Advice

When dealing with investments it is helpful to know where to get professional financial advice. The Financial Services Act, which is designed to protect investors, divides all financial advisors dealing with investment products into two categories; tied agents and independent

ORIGINS

Personal Equity Plans were introduced in January 1987 as a tax free incentive for investing in shares. Since then 10 million general PEPs have been taken out and more than one million single company PEPs. General PEPs can be a collection of individual shares, or a pooled fund like a unit trust. Single-company PEPs can only invest in the shares of a single company.
Tax Exempt Special Savings Accounts were introduced in 1991 as tax free deposits with banks and building societies. On the whole they failed to increase the general level of savings as the majority of funds were transferred from existing accounts.

financial advisors (IFAs). Tied agents or company representatives are tied to a particular company and sell only that company's products. IFAs are not tied to any particular company. They look at a whole range of investment products and will advise the customer which one suits best. Remember, however, that many IFAs are paid commission for the products they sell and so have at least some degree of incentive to sell particular products. Some financial planners charge their customers fees rather than taking commission. Advisers can either be specialists in particular areas (for example, pensions) or general practitioners who advise on a broader range of financial products. Financial advisors can also assist with income and capital gains tax planning and with estate planning, including inheritance tax and making wills. Chartered accountants and solicitors are very active in financial planning as it is a natural extension of their core legal and tax services.

RISK ATTITUDES TOWARDS EQUITY INVESTING

We mentioned earlier the importance of being as aware as possible of your (and your family's) attitude(s) towards taking on board risk. We are not going to pretend that this is an easy, nor a necessarily accurate process, but it is better to give some effort to understanding your risk attitudes than blindly misapplying a given investment approach. One or two books go so far as developing detailed risk questionnaires to help their readers in this regard. As we believe such 'precision' to be false, given the difficulties inherent in measuring the risk attitudes of an individual (never mind his/her family) and then matching these to specific investment models, we take a far more general approach. Furthermore, attitude towards risk is just one element to consider when considering what investment approach to adopt.

To aid you in your assessment of your attitudes towards risk you might like to consider the following:

Part A

 Do you buy extended warranties when buying household consumer durables?

 Do you buy the full package of assistance from motoring organisations, such as the RAC or AA?

 Do you always make sure you carry a torch and jump leads in your car?

 When going on holiday, do you take a comprehensive first aid or medical kit?

 When you last took an exam, did you take a spare battery for your calculator?

 Do you unplug most electrical appliances when leaving the house?

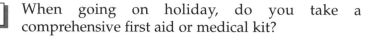 In light of the recent CJD scare, did you stop eating British beef?

Part B

 Do you gamble on the horses, or other sports, on a frequent basis?

 Do you undertake any dangerous sports (hang-gliding, pot-holing, rock climbing, etc.)?

 Do you ignore taking out travel insurance when going on holiday?

 Have you ever considered giving up a safe job to start your own business?

 When playing cards, do you normally play for relatively high cash stakes?

 Do you keep large amounts of cash in the house or carry large amounts of cash on your person?

 Have you intentionally gone through a red light when driving?

If you answered yes to the majority of questions in Part A and no to the majority of questions in Part B, then you definitely do not enjoy taking risks. You will need a method of stock market investment that emphasises the minimisation of risk.

If you answered no to the majority of questions in Part A and yes to the majority of questions in Part B then you enjoy taking risks and you are the kind of person who would enjoy the thrill of investing in an emerging market or a newly listed bio-technology stock.

If you answered yes and no in almost equal number in both Parts A and B, then you are approaching risk neutrality - you neither enjoy taking risks nor do you necessarily avoid them.

If you answered yes to almost all of the questions or no to almost all of the questions, then you are one of those 'schizoid' individuals who are risk averse in certain parts of their lives but risk taking in other parts. You will need secure elements in your investment portfolio but you also might need to include some risky shares to keep you interested in the game. Of course, the risk of an investment portfolio should be gauged in its entirety and this is not merely the summation of the risk of the individual elements because of possible compensation between the individual elements. For example, while gas and oil shares may be individually risky, holding them both reduces the risk as they are substitutes in the way people heat their homes.

Now, as we said earlier, the above questions were merely intended to give you a feel about your attitudes towards risk. Don't forget to consider how far your own attitudes reflect those of your family! Of course, such attitudes (both yours and your family's) will become a lot clearer once your investments have undergone the usual run of gains and losses. Finally, once you have a feel for your capacity to live with risk, you need to develop/apply an appropriate investment method.

TIME AVAILABILITY

You will also need to think through the time and effort that you will be able to spend on following the stock market. The different investment approaches described and discussed so far in this book require varying amounts of time commitment. For example, it is not a quick and easy process to complete an in-depth fundamental analysis of a given company.

Now, as is the case for financial commitments, you can avoid a lot of potential problems if you give careful prior consideration to how much real time you will be able to commit to your investment portfolio. Will you be able to spend 1 hour a day assessing your portfolio, or will it be more like 1 hour a week? The actual time you have available is relatively unimportant, the key issue is being realistic in your assessment - it is pointless following an active trading approach if you don't even have the time to open the financial pages. Remember, there is an investment strategy to suit your time availability.

CONTACTS

While you should always be sceptical of tips from others, it is likely that you will have some specialist knowledge of an industry or a sector. Use it. Such knowledge always helps to put other information sources into context. There is no better benchmark than personal knowledge of a business. Such knowledge and business contacts are likely to increase with age but a number of the other factors discussed above are also likely to change with age. Again, there is a need to assess what you hope to gain from stock market investment and what factors/constraints should be borne in mind when making the assessment.

CONCLUSION

By spending some preliminary time considering your personal circumstances and characteristics, you will have a fuller understanding of the stock market investment strategy that will suit you best. Your investment in the stock market should be part of your overall approach to personal financial planning. This will require you to make provision for both your short term and longer term financial needs. Now you have a feel for what funds you wish to invest in shares and your attitude to the risks and time considerations of investing, the following chapter will provide more details of the mechanisms for equity investing.

LESSONS TO BE LEARNT

 You should really only invest money in the stock market that you do not need for other commitments.

 It is important to make a clear and comprehensive budget of your income and expenditure, and consider whether you need to redirect some of your spending into savings.

 Planning out your financial targets, how soon you might need to liquidate parts of your investments and what return you require, will enable you to decide where to place your investments.

 It is important to check that you have adequate insurance cover and have made appropriate provision for your retirement.

 You should try and work out your attitude towards the riskiness of various investment strategies.

 There is an equity investment strategy which will suit your time availability.

CHAPTER 15

Stock Market Advice to the Reader

This chapter gives you some general advice on how to undertake your stock market investment. You will need to decide whether to invest directly and manage your own investments, to use the services of an investment manager or perhaps to use a combination of both methods. The chapter introduces unit trusts and investment trusts, which are the main means by which private investors can gain access to the services of professional investment managers. The chapter goes on to discuss how to pick a good fund in which to invest and the advantages and disadvantages of investing using these collective investments. Finally the chapter gives advice on investing directly for yourself.

COLLECTIVE INVESTMENTS

Collective investments work by pooling the money of many investors and using it to buy portfolios of shares or bonds under the direction of a fund manager. The investors gain the benefits of diversification and the expertise of the fund manager. Not surprisingly, there are no free lunches and investors have to pay a variety of charges to participate in these schemes. The two main types of collective investments available in the UK are unit trusts and investment trusts. Despite their similar names and functions, there are a lot of important differences between these two types of trusts. We outline their main features below.

Unit Trusts

NUTSHELL

A unit trust manager invests in a portfolio of shares and/or bonds. The value of the portfolio is then divided into **units**. Each investor's holding is expressed as a number of units.

Unit trusts are established under trust law. The effect of this is that the assets of the unit trust (company shares or bonds) are separated legally from the fund management company. The trust deed of the trust defines the investment objectives of the fund, states the maximum charges allowed and defines the method of calculating the price of units.

Trusts are obliged to hold a diversified portfolio of investments which protects the investor from being subject to the risk of the trust placing all its eggs in one basket. In addition, trusts are only allowed to place a limited proportion of their assets in unlisted securities which is another measure designed to protect unit trust investors from being subject to undue risk.

Unit trusts are called open ended trusts because the number of units available is not fixed. The number of units that can be created by the fund manager is determined by the demand for them.

NUTSHELL

OEICs, or open-ended investment companies, are a relatively new development in collective investment funds. Eventually they may replace unit trusts but the pace of change has been slow so far. OEICs replace the bid offer spread used in unit trusts by a single price with charges listed separately. In addition, OEICs enable umbrella structures to be formed in which a single OEIC can contain a number of sub-funds which can invest in different markets. Investors in the OEIC should be able to switch easily between different sub-funds.

The price of units is determined by the value of the underlying securities in the fund. Thus, in the broadest of terms, if you have invested in a equity based unit trust and the price of shares rises so will the price of the units you hold. Each unit reflects the fortunes of the whole portfolio of investments held by the trust. The price of units are generally quoted in the *Financial Times* and many trusts have their unit prices quoted in a number of other daily newspapers.

There is a huge number of trusts available covering a large range of investment objectives. In April 1998 there were over 1,500 authorised unit trusts in operation.[1] There are groups of trusts which invest in particular geographical areas such as the UK, North America, Europe, Japan, the Far East or Emerging Markets. Some trusts invest across all worldwide markets. Within these groups there are many other subdivisions; some trusts invest only in equities, others only in bonds and some in both. Some trusts aim for capital growth, others aim mainly to provide a good income for their investors. Some trusts specialise in smaller companies, others in large blue chip companies. Some trusts specialise in a particular type of investment situation. For example, 'recovery' trusts buy shares in companies which have been doing badly but which the fund manager believes are going to recover. Yet another subdivision is trusts which invest in particular industries or sectors such as property or commodities. A relatively recent but very fast growing sector of the unit trust market is the group of 'tracker' funds which simply aim to duplicate the fortunes of a particular investment index. In summary, there should be a unit trust available to match almost any investor's taste. The difficult task is deciding which out of the multitude of trusts available are the best investments. This subject is covered further below.

In general, in line with the buoyant equity markets of recent years, unit trusts have been successful investments. The average trust has considerably outperformed an investment in the bank or building society. This overall picture, however, conceals some considerable performance variations between individual trusts. For example, over the five years to 1st March 1998 the best performing unit trust more than tripled investors' money, whereas investors in the worst performing trust would have had only just over a quarter of their original investment left.

Investors in unit trusts have to pay a number of charges. Units trade at two prices - the bid price, which is the price at which the fund managers will buy units, and the offer price, which is the price at which the fund managers will sell units. The difference between the two prices varies from trust to trust but is usually about 6%. Some fund management companies have a lower initial charge but instead charge an exit fee if you sell units fairly early, typically within five years. In addition to the initial charges there will also be a quoted annual fee of usually between 1% and 1.5% of the fund value. As well as the quoted annual fee, investors will have to meet the cost of various other expenses such as custody and audit fees. The size of these additional expenses can be obtained from the fund manager's report. In most cases they are not very significant compared to the quoted fee but for a few, mainly small, trusts they can be prohibitive.

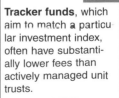

CLOSE-UP

Tracker funds, which aim to match a particular investment index, often have substantially lower fees than actively managed unit trusts.

Investment Trusts

Although their functions are similar, investment trusts are legally quite different from unit trusts. Investment trusts are public limited companies. Thus they are governed by company law, rather than trust law, and are quoted on the London Stock Exchange. Instead of running normal business operations such as retailing or manufacturing, investment trusts have the function of investing in the shares of other companies. Thus investors buying shares in an investment trust are buying a diversified portfolio of assets in much the same way as when they buy units in a unit trust. Investment trusts have somewhat more investment freedom than unit trusts and are able to invest to a greater extent in unlisted investments.

Unlike unit trusts, investment trusts are not open-ended funds but are described as closed-end funds. This means that the number of shares is fixed and does not increase or decrease according to the popularity of the trust. If an investor wants to buy shares in an investment trust he buys them in the stock market in the same way as any other share.

The closed-end status of investment trusts has some important implications. An advantage of a closed-end structure is that the fund manager is not forced to buy or sell assets simply because of changes in the popularity of the trust with investors. This contrasts with the position of a unit trust manager who may, for example, be forced to sell assets (the shares and bonds held by the trust) into a falling market, against their better judgement, because of a large number of unit holders wishing to withdraw from the trust.

Another feature of a closed-end structure is that the price of investment trust shares is determined by supply and demand, not directly by the value of the underlying assets of the trust (the shares and bonds held by the trust) as is the case for unit trusts. The value of the underlying assets held by an investment trust is known as its net asset value (NAV). The NAV per share is calculated by dividing the NAV of the whole trust by the number of ordinary shares in issue. The market price of an investment trust share will not normally be equal to the NAV per share due to the supply and demand considerations mentioned above. In most cases the market price is less than the NAV per share, in which case the trust is said to be trading at a discount to NAV. In this case, buying shares in a trust can be regarded as something of a bargain in that you are buying a portfolio of assets for less than its market value. The problem with this is that although you may have bought the portfolio for a bargain price, there is no guarantee that it will ever be possible to obtain its true value. Most trusts always trade at a discount and in fact the discount may even widen. As a rule of thumb, discounts on trusts tend to narrow when markets are doing well and widen when markets are doing poorly. In general, discounts on trusts have tended to narrow over the last twenty years or so and this has enhanced the return on investment trusts as compared to unit trusts. Another rule of thumb regarding the discounts on particular trusts is that the better the market believes the fund's investment management to be, the lower the discount on the trust. A few trusts which are perceived to be particularly well managed actually trade at a premium to NAV; that, is the market value of shares in the trust is greater than their NAV. In recent years there have been a number of instances where investment trusts which have persistently traded at particularly large discounts have been wound up realising the full value of the underlying assets for the shareholders.

Unlike unit trusts, investment trusts have the freedom to borrow money to buy more assets. The level of a trust's borrowing is known as its gearing. If the trust's investment policy is successful and the assets rise in value at a faster rate than the cost of servicing the loans, gearing can enhance the returns to the shareholders in the trust. Conversely, if the investment policy is not successful, gearing will depress returns to shareholders. The more highly geared an investment trust is, the greater the returns the shareholders can expect but at the expense of increased risk. The gearing of a trust does not have to remain constant over time and some trusts have been successful in managing their gearing to enhance the returns to shareholders. These trusts increase their gearing when they expect markets to do well and reduce it when they are not so confident.

The share prices of investment trusts are shown on the share pages of the *Financial Times*. In addition, the NAV per share and the discount or premium to NAV are shown. There are far fewer investment trusts than unit trusts but

NUTSHELL

The original **split capital** investment trusts issued two classes of shares, one of which collected all the capital growth and the other all the dividend income. These classes were developed to cater for the needs of investors with different objectives and different tax situations. Some trusts have taken this process further and have issued quite a number of classes of shares with different rights. Buying a type of share which is not suitable for your situation can be a very costly mistake. Analysing these trusts can be an enormously complicated task for the potential investor and is not really suitable for the beginner.

there are still several hundred to choose from with a wide variety of investment objectives.

Investment trusts tend to have lower charges than unit trusts. Investment trust shares can be bought in the stock market in the same way as other shares and the costs of doing this are generally substantially less than the front end management charges on unit trusts. For many investment trusts, the total annual charges and expenses are less than 1% p.a. which compares favourably with most unit trusts.

Unit Trusts vs. Investment Trusts

There has been an ongoing debate about whether one type of trust is better than the other. Over the last ten years the average investment trust has outperformed the average unit trust but this may be partly due to a one-off narrowing of investment trust discounts. Investment trusts have the advantages of generally lower costs, more investment flexibility and the ability to gear their returns. Unit trusts are perhaps simpler to understand and are less likely to get into unduly risky situations. Overall, you should remember that finding a good fund manager is much more important than whether your investment is in a unit or investment trust.

CLOSE-UP

PEPs, which are covered in Chapter 14, are often used as a tax free 'wrapper' around a unit or investment trust. PEPs are to be phased out from April 1999 so we have not devoted much space to reviewing their details.

FINDING A GOOD FUND

It is not an easy task to find a good managed investment fund out of the many hundreds available. Probably the worst way to select one is from an investment company's marketing material. Even the most mediocre trusts will have some selectively chosen statistics to show that their past performance has been brilliant. A crafty marketing man will nearly always be able to show some past periods of good performance, no matter how temporary they may have been.

A better way to select a fund is to look at some tables showing the past performance of investment funds as these are at least factual and unbiased. Such tables can be found in a number of investment magazines - for example, *Money Management*. The tables show the returns achieved by funds over various investment periods. You should consider the past performance of each fund in the light of its investment objectives. It is not particularly instructive to directly compare funds investing in very different sectors. For example, a gold fund may have been outstandingly well managed but still produced a poor return compared to a badly managed North American fund if the gold market is very depressed and the US stock market has been booming. Similarly, be wary of going for funds just because they are currently top of the investment tables. A trust may be at the top of the tables because of a single good year when the fund manager was lucky or reckless. It is wise to look for a consistent level of good performance over a reasonably long period. When doing this it is a good idea to look at individual past years rather than long cumulative periods. This is because if a trust has a very good performance in the last year being measured, this will automatically make its cumulative long term figures appear good even if some of the individual years being measured were quite poor.

No matter how careful you are, there are undoubtedly major problems in relying on tables of past performance to select funds. As the advertisements say, 'past performance is no guide to future profits'. There are a number of reasons for this. As we mentioned above, good past performance may have more to do with luck than skill. The best performing funds may be in sectors that are overheated and just about to have a period of underperformance. Sometimes particular fund management approaches seem to lose their effectiveness; for example, fund managers using value based approaches have not done particularly well in the last few years. Successful unit trusts can attract a lot of new money very quickly and the fund manager may not be able to find enough good opportunities to invest this influx of new money with his previous effectiveness. Perhaps most importantly of all, the fund manager may change.

An investment fund will only perform as well as its fund manager and so you should give a lot of weight to this factor. The past performance of a fund is not really relevant if the fund manager has changed. The manager should have a reasonably long track record of success; quite a lot of funds are run by inexperienced managers who are just cutting their teeth. In theory, you should understand and approve of the investment style the manager is going to use. In practice, however, in the UK it is difficult to select a fund primarily on the basis of the fund manager. To even find out who the manager is takes quite a bit of homework, as tables of managers are not generally published. In addition, most managers are very vague about the methods they actually use.

In summary, it is quite a difficult task to choose a good collective investment fund. The unreliability of past performance statistics as a guide to the future and the research needed to try to find a good fund manager means that it is probably as hard to find a good fund as it is to find a good individual share.

IS COLLECTIVE INVESTMENT WORTHWHILE?

We can now consider the advantages and disadvantages of collective investment as compared to direct investment. For people who have very little interest in investment and have no wish to go to the effort of selecting individual shares, collective investment is probably the best way to obtain the benefit of the returns available in the stock market. Collective investment is also a good idea for people with very limited resources who will not be able to buy enough individual shares to obtain reasonable diversification in their portfolio. Collective investment is also the most practical way for the majority of investors to obtain exposure to foreign stock markets. It is not possible for most investors to be expert at selecting shares in overseas stock markets.

Investors going via the collective investment route will gain the expertise of a fund manager. The value of this, however, is very variable depending on the quality of the manager; many fund managers produce very poor results and a keen private investor should not feel at any disadvantage to the majority of fund managers. According to the investment guru, Peter Lynch, the individual buyer should have 'an unbelievable advantage' over the professional.[2] The individual is not subject to undue time pressure and he can hold his investments indefinitely without having to account for them every quarter or every six months. Many professional managers feel that they cannot let the portfolio they manage get too far out of line with that of their peers. If they do badly but so does everyone else, they are unlikely to be sacked. On the other hand if they move away from their competitors and get it wrong, they may well be dismissed. This type of thinking guarantees mediocre performance. Another problem for many professional fund managers is that they manage such large sums of money that they have to invest most of their money in large blue chip companies. Even if they found a fantastic small company investment they would not be able to invest a significant proportion of the assets they manage in the company's shares so the overall effect on their performance would be very small.

Most individual investors deal with many different companies in their everyday lives and they are in a good position to judge which of these might be good investments. For example, the investor may be very impressed with a company he or she deals with at work or with a chain of shops he or she visits. The insights the investor can gain from observing the world can be as valuable as those available to professional fund managers. The investor can also use an investment method which suits his or her own temperament. If an investor makes his or her own decisions, he or she can remove a layer of uncertainty, in that he or she will know that the decisions have been well thought out and that he or she can have faith in them. With collective investment, there is always the worry that the investment manager may lose his or her touch.

A very major disadvantage of the collective investment route is the considerable fees and expenses that are incurred. Over a 25 year investment period, an investor in a typical unit trust would receive a final payout about a third smaller than an investor who achieved a similar investment return but with no investment fees or expenses. Of course, all investment methods will incur some expenses but an individual investor who does not trade very frequently can keep these very low.

INVESTING YOURSELF

The alternative to collective investment is for you to make your own investment decisions. This process can undoubtedly be very rewarding in all senses of the word. This book has reviewed many approaches to finding good equity investments and we have stressed that it is very important not to look at each equity investment in isolation. You should consider how it will fit your overall equity portfolio and your personal circumstances. It is important to make sure you have a suitable level of diversification in your portfolio. Don't lose sight of this and end up with all your eggs in the same basket.

If you are managing your own portfolio, you will need to be aware of the practicalities of dealing in shares. This is by no means a major stumbling block. Modern technology means that share dealing is becoming more accessible and easier all the time. Chapter 16 explains how a state-of-the-art share dealing service works.

INVESTMENT CLUBS

In investment it is always a good thing to talk to other investors and exchange ideas. Professional investors will naturally do this in the course of their employment. It is possible for individual investors to gain the advantages of the insights of like-minded individuals by joining an investment club.

Investment clubs are a way for people to band together to invest in the stock market. Club members pool their money and buy a portfolio of shares. The members decide which shares to invest in. Most clubs will have quite a fund of knowledge through members' differing jobs and interests. Clubs can have between 3 and 20 members[3] and there are around 1,000 such clubs in the UK at the present time.

CONCLUSION

This chapter has outlined the main features of unit and investment trusts. You will now be in a position to assess how these collective investments can help you in your overall investment strategy. Collective investments are potentially useful to most investors as they give convenient access to overseas markets. In addition, they allow investors with limited resources to obtain reasonable diversification. They also enable people with little interest in investment to participate in the equity markets. However, if you have an interest in investment and an understanding of the issues involved, it is likely that selecting your own investments may be a more rewarding way to manage the bulk of your portfolio.

LESSONS TO BE LEARNT

 The two main types of collective investment in the UK are unit trusts and investment trusts.

 The two types of trust have similar functions but are legally quite different.

 Unit trusts are open ended funds and the price of units is determined by the value of the underlying securities in the fund. Investment trusts are closed ended funds and the price of shares is determined by supply and demand.

 There has been a lot of debate about whether unit trusts or investment trusts are better. However, this is a secondary issue compared to the quality of the fund manager.

 It is difficult to find good funds. Past performance is an unreliable guide to the future and it is difficult to obtain sufficient information about fund managers and their methods.

 Collective investment is worthwhile for people with little interest in investment. In addition, it allows investors with limited resources to obtain reasonable diversification. It also allows individual investors to gain exposure to overseas markets.

 Individual investors have considerable advantages over professional investors.

 A major disadvantage of collective investment is the fees and expenses that are incurred.

 When managing your own investments it is important to keep in mind the structure of your whole portfolio.

 Investment clubs are a good way to exchange investment ideas.

CHAPTER 16

The Practicalities of Dealing in Shares

If you have come this far in the book, you are doubtless eager to put what you've learnt into practice. Which, of course, brings us neatly to the practicalities of buying and selling shares. As we saw in Chapter 8, 'Big Bang' fundamentally changed the way the UK stock market operates for the professionals. But, 'Big Bang' has also had significant ramifications for private investors. Notably, competition for business has increased dramatically following the abolition of the high, fixed-rate commissions which were previously in force. What's more, technology developments have also encouraged many new entrants into the marketplace. However, whilst there is now a great deal of choice, this brings its own problems. Just how do you choose the service that best suits your needs? This chapter sets out the key things you need to consider in order to devise your own tailored 'shopping list', as well as covering the core 'nuts and bolts' of share dealing.

CHOOSING A STOCKBROKER

Once you've decided to buy and sell shares, you will need the services of a stockbroker. Although the old image of pin-striped, cigar-smoking high-rollers still lingers in many people's minds, the actuality is quite different.

Today's stockbrokers come in all shapes and sizes - ranging from divisions of high-street banks with national coverage to small, regional firms - and they offer a plethora of services for the private investor.

Let's start by looking at the principal differences between the three main types of services provided by stockbrokers. Broadly speaking, these fall into the categories of **discretionary**, **advisory** and **execution-only**.

 Discretionary brokers are really only suitable for those individuals who have both large amounts of money available to invest up-front (typically £50,000+), and who do not wish to be involved in the decision-making process about which investments to buy and sell. The discretionary broker chooses all the investments for the client's portfolio, usually without prior consultation. By definition, discretionary brokers' charges are the most expensive of the three types.

 Advisory brokers can best be described as a halfway house between discretionary and execution-only services. The private investor can discuss what to buy and sell with his or her broker and any transactions are only carried out with the client's agreement. Many advisory brokers impose a minimum 'portfolio' value for the provision of such services, typically £20,000+.

 Execution-only brokers, most commonly referred to as share dealing services, do not offer any advice on the suitability of individual investments. As their name implies, they simply carry out a customer's instructions to buy or sell. Commission charges are usually lower than either discretionary or advisory brokers, since there are no expensive research analysts to subsidise.

Some firms offer more than one type of service, whilst others specialise in one particular category. However, no matter which type of service or firm you choose, there are several key considerations to bear in mind when making your decision.

What Will You Pay?

Stockbrokers make their living from charging commission on their customers' orders to buy and sell shares. As we've already outlined, these charges can vary enormously depending on the type of service being provided. The structure of such charges also varies considerably. For example, some firms charge commission as a percentage of your order - which could be anything from 0.5% to 1.5% or more. Others impose flat charges, tiered according to the size of the order. In such instances, you may pay, say, £50 for a deal worth between £4,000 and £5,000. However, if there is one simple rule to adhere to, it is this: look beyond the advertised minimum rate - which could be as low as £5! Such 'headline' charges are likely to have restrictions attached - they may apply to very small deals in a limited number of companies. You should always weigh up dealing charges against what your average transaction size is likely to be.

Within this equation, you should also consider whether there are any joining or initial fees to pay. Some brokers will charge you for opening an account. You also need to look out for any additional charges which may be levied for managing or administering your account. This can apply not only to discretionary and advisory services, but also to nominee and sponsored membership accounts - more of which later.

Check The Safety Net

Whichever broker you choose, you need to check that they are both a member of the London Stock Exchange and regulated by The Securities and Futures Authority, the industry watchdog. All regulated brokers participate in the Investors' Compensation Scheme which provides cover up to £48,000 if a firm goes out of business. If you plan to entrust assets (e.g. cash and/or investments) worth more than this, you should consider the standing of the firm. Is it part of a large, reputable group or is it independent? If you are considering dealing with an independent or small company, ask whether there is additional insurance in place.

NUTSHELL

As well as paying commission charges, you have to pay **stamp duty** when you buy shares. This is charged at 0.5% of the value of your purchase.
When you buy **or** sell shares worth more than £10,000, you also have to pay a fixed £1 fee to the Panel on Takeovers and Mergers (known as the PTM levy).

POINTER

You can obtain a list of the **London Stock Exchange's** member firms by calling 0171 797 1372, or from their web site at www. londonstockex.co.uk. Alternatively, the trade association for stock-brokers, **APCIMS**, publishes a list of all its members. You can contact APCIMS on 0171 247 7080 or at www.apcims.org.

CLOSE-UP

The London and Frankfurt exchanges are creating common rules for access to both markets and a single pan-European electronic trading platform.

LOW TECH OR HIGH TECH?

One decision you will have to make once you start dealing in shares, is how you wish to hold your investments. Up until a few years ago, there was only one way - as paper certificates. However, in 1996, a new computerised system for matching sales and purchases was introduced. This system - CREST - was designed to bring the UK into line with other leading international markets, by making reconciliation cheaper, faster and more secure. It means that you can hold shares in electronic form as a computer record - just like your money is held in your bank account - rather than in paper. In principle, private investors now have three choices as to how they hold their investments: in the traditional paper format, or in one of two electronic formats - in a nominee account or through sponsored membership of CREST. Let's look at each of these methods, and their pros and cons, in more detail.

Paper Certificates

Every time you buy shares in a company, the registrar will issue you with a certificate as proof of your legal ownership. When you come to sell the shares, you surrender the certificate back to the company (via your broker). The key points to note are:

! Your name appears on the share register and you automatically receive all communications - such as Annual Report & Accounts and notices of meetings - along with dividends and any shareholder benefits, direct from the company. However, because of this, your name (and address) are publicly available and may be bought for unsolicited mailing purposes.

! You will normally pay higher commission charges for dealing in certificates. This is because of the increased paperwork involved. Some brokers may even insist that you send in your certificate(s) first before you can sell your shares, and others may not allow you to deal in certificated form at all.

Most investors find the paperwork associated with share certificates cumbersome. When you wish to sell your shares, you will have to complete additional transfer documentation, and make sure you return the certificate to your broker within the prescribed timescales. Moreover, when you buy shares in certificated form, you may wait several weeks for your certificate.

 Share certificates are valuable documents and should you lose or mislay them, the company registrar will charge you for a replacement. This can range from a few pounds to considerably more.

Nominee Accounts

A nominee account is a company created for the purpose of holding investments on behalf of investors, and is operated by your broker. Rather than storing mountains of paperwork, investments are maintained as electronic records, facilitating rapid and secure access to the CREST system when necessary.

 Your name does not appear on the share register. The shares are registered in the name of the account operator, although you remain the beneficial owner at all times.

 You do not receive communications, dividends or share perks direct from the company. Most brokers can arrange for you to receive Reports and Accounts and other correspondence, although some make an additional charge for this. Dividends are collected on your behalf and are either sent on to you or else held on account. In the former case, you should always check whether you will receive dividends as and when they are paid, or whether your broker will only forward them at certain intervals. When it comes to perks, most brokers will be able to arrange for any benefits to be retained. However, you should note that a few companies do not allow perks to be passed on to holdings in nominee accounts. Your broker should be able to tell you which companies impose such restrictions.

POINTER

Proshare, an independent body which promotes share ownership, has a voluntary code of practice for nominees. For details of the code, as well the range of other publications and services offered, you can contact ProShare on 0171 600 0984 or at www.proshare.org.uk.

As a general rule, lower commission rates apply to dealing in shares held in a nominee account. But watch out for additional account charges! Many brokers levy administration fees for running your account - ranging from regular management costs to one-off charges for such things as collecting dividends on your behalf.

Since your shares are held with your broker, dealing is made a lot easier and more convenient. There's normally no paperwork to return when you sell your holding, nor do you have to wait for a certificate from the company registrar.

All nominee accounts will provide you with regular statements and valuations of your investments. The frequency, however, can vary from the legal minimum of once a year to quarterly. The most common interval is every six months. Additionally, some accounts provide a 'Consolidated Tax Voucher' at the end of each tax year. This is a useful benefit as it summarises all the dividends received (and tax deducted) on the account during the year and it should make completing the relevant section of your tax return a lot simpler.

Sponsored Membership

There is a second electronic option - sponsored membership of CREST. Here, you can have your own CREST account run by a broker. However, this alternative is not widely available and is mainly restricted to clients of discretionary and advisory firms.

As a sponsored member, you authorise a CREST user (your sponsor) to operate your membership on your behalf. CREST charges the sponsor £20 a year for each sponsored member but you may have to pay your sponsor considerably more than this for administering your account.

As in the case of paper certificates, your name appears on the company register and you therefore have the same direct relationship with the company.

PLACING YOUR ORDER

The London Stock Market trades from Mondays to Fridays, between 9.00 am and 4.30 pm. It is closed on English public holidays. If you call your broker to place an order during these times, you should be quoted the current market price direct from the Exchange.

As we saw in Chapter 8, there are two ways the market produces prices in the UK. The first of these is the 'quote-driven' system, operated by market makers, which covers the vast majority of the 2,000+ shares quoted on the London Stock Exchange. The second is the recently-introduced 'order-book' system - SETS - which is run by the same share wholesalers, although they are known as Retail Service Providers (RSPs) in this context. SETS is presently limited to FTSE 100 shares only, although it is expected that coverage will expand in time.

In practice, it should make no difference to you through which system your order is processed. However, there have been 'teething' problems with SETS which have attracted some publicity. These have centred around the volatility of prices - particularly at the start and end of the day's trading - due to the low volumes of shares being traded at these times. Whilst it is expected that these 'hiccups' will disappear in time, you should still be aware of such possibilities.

CLOSE-UP

Some brokers operate what is called 'delayed execution'. This can mean one of two things. First, your broker may quote an '**indicative**' price. This means your order will be processed without you knowing the exact price. Second, your order may only be dealt at a certain, fixed time of the day and/or week. Again, you will not know at which price your shares were dealt until after the fact.

Agreeing the price

When you place an order during market hours, you normally have two choices. You can instruct your broker to deal '**at best**' - that is, the best market price obtainable at the time. Alternatively, you can set a **limit**. This means you determine the maximum price you are prepared to pay for shares you are buying or the minimum price you will accept for shares you are selling. Not all brokers accept limit instructions. Those that do will usually impose certain conditions. For example, your limit may have to be within certain parameters of the current share price, say 10%, and will usually be valid for a fixed period, typically one trading day. Some brokers levy an additional charge for accepting limit orders.

CLOSE-UP

For example, Halifax Share Dealing accepts limit orders free of charge. If a limit is set Monday to Friday between 8.00 am and 4.00 pm, it is valid for that trading day. Limits set after 4.00 pm or at weekends are valid until the close of trading on the next business day.

These days, many dealing services are also open outside market hours - the Halifax service, for instance, is available 7 days a week. You can still place an order, therefore, even when the market is closed. Again, you can either ask for your instruction to be processed as soon as the market re-opens for business, or set a limit price.

What Happens Next

Once you have placed your instruction, your order will be submitted either electronically or by telephone through to the market. Your broker will then send you a 'contract note' which confirms all the details of your transaction, along with instructions on anything else you may need to do to finalise the deal. You should usually receive this within 48 hours. Always keep your contract notes safe! They are important documents and you may need to refer to them again for tax purposes.

MONEY MATTERS

CLOSE-UP

The UK Market is likely to move to an even shorter settlement time of three days within the next few years, to bring it in line with other international exchanges.

The standard settlement time currently operated by the London Stock Exchange is 5 days. In plain English, all this means is that you have to pay for any shares you have bought, or will receive the money from shares you have sold, no later than **5 business days** from the date of your order. Depending on your broker and the market, it is also sometimes possible to deal for shorter or longer settlement periods.

Depending on your individual stockbroker, there are a number of ways in which you can pay or receive money. As befits the electronic age, the two most popular and convenient methods are by debit card (such as Switch or Visa Delta) or Direct Debit and automatic account credit (BACS). Cheques are sometimes another payment option but most investors find this method unsuitable and unnecessarily cumbersome. Not only is it frequently difficult, given the short time-scales involved, to send a cheque in as payment but also clearing times can mean that money from sale proceeds takes longer to process.

One other option offered by some stockbrokers is a 'cash account', in which investors can deposit money to fund future purchases and also receive money from sales. This method is best suited to those individuals who not only plan to deal on a very frequent basis but can also 'tie up' suitable sums. Making deposits is usually very straightforward but withdrawals often require written, advance notice. Whilst attractive rates of interest may be quoted for such accounts, these are always gross and no tax is deducted at source. The onus for tax declaration rests with the investor.

KEEPING TRACK OF YOUR INVESTMENTS

There are now many ways in which you can keep track of how your shares are performing. These range from live prices direct from the Stock Exchange to closing prices at the end of a trading day.

Newspapers

Most national and major regional newspapers carry prices for the most popular shares. Only the *Financial Times*, however, shows prices for all shares quoted on the London Stock Exchange. For FTSE 100 shares, the price quoted is usually based on the last trade of the day so this could be either the buying or selling price. For all other shares, the closing mid-price is shown which is the halfway point between the buying and selling price at the end of each day's trading. As well as the price, some newspapers also display other information pertinent to the share, such as the highest and lowest price over the last 52 weeks, the gross yield and PE ratio.

Television Text Pages

When the market is open, the three main text providers update the share prices displayed on their financial pages, several times a day. However, it's worth remembering that these prices are 'indicative'. That is, because share prices can move many times during the course of a day, it is extremely unlikely that you will obtain the price displayed on a text page, in the market. The three main providers are BBC 2 Ceefax, Channel 4 Teletext and Sky News Text.

Web Services

It is now possible to obtain share prices from the Web. There are two main types of service available: **instant prices** and **delayed prices**. As their names suggest, instant prices are live from the Stock Exchange, whilst delayed prices are typically updated every 20 minutes. Providers of instant prices invariably charge for their services, although there are usually further features, such as portfolio management software. In addition to one-off joining fees, such services also levy monthly subscriptions according to how much information you want.

For most investors, probably the best option is to use one of the delayed services, since 20 minute intervals should normally be sufficient for even the most ardent price-watcher! What's more, these services are normally available free of charge. Our two favourite sources can be found at:

■ www.iii.co.uk

■ www.moneyworld.co.uk

Both these sites also offer a wealth of information on a wide range of personal finance matters and are well worth a look.

Telephone Services

These days, many leading brokers offer dedicated telephone information lines for share prices. These usually give live prices during market hours and the final or closing mid-prices out of hours. Depending on your broker, such services may be charged at premium or national rates.

SPECIAL CIRCUMSTANCES

Buying and selling shares is easier and more straightforward than ever before. Yet, as in most areas of life, there are times when the smooth course of events deviates from the norm. This next section looks briefly at both your obligations and what you should do if things go wrong.

Your Obligations

All stockbrokers have a duty of care to make you aware of their terms of business. When you place an order to buy or sell shares, you are entering into a legal contract and you must fulfil your part of the bargain.

If you are selling shares, then you must be able to deliver proof of your ownership (e.g. the share certificate) within the prescribed time. Failure to do so can have serious financial ramifications. For example, your broker will have to buy back the shares in the open market. This will mean that you are liable not only for the commission on the original sale, but also the commission and stamp duty on the re-purchase. You will also have to pay for any fluctuations in the share price in the interim period. Many brokers also charge administration costs in such instances. Similarly, if you buy shares but then fail to pay for them, your broker is obliged to sell the shares back to the market. You will then be charged both sets of commission and any difference between the share prices, as well as any administration expenses.

When Things Go Wrong

The Securities and Futures Authority (the SFA) sets down strict rules on how customer complaints must be handled by its regulated firms. If you have cause for complaint, you should contact the Compliance Officer of the company in question. If he or she is unable to resolve your complaint, you can contact the regulator directly. At the time of writing, it is expected that the SFA will shortly re-locate to the offices of the overall governing body, the Financial Services Authority, which can be contacted at:

The Financial Services Authority
25 North Colonnade
Canary Wharf
London E14 5JS

Telephone: 0171 676 1000

LESSONS TO BE LEARNT

 When choosing a stockbroker, don't be seduced by a low headline commission rate! Such rates usually only apply to small, restricted deals and the charges you are likely to pay for your typical transaction may be considerably higher.

 Make sure you understand **all** the charges you will have to pay. Are there any joining fees? Also, with the advent of electronic holdings, you may have to pay account administration or management fees on top of your dealing charges. Read the small print!

 Remember, if you opt to use the services of either a discretionary or advisory stockbroker, the quantity and the quality of the advice you're likely to receive are as critical a decision factor as the charges!

 Make sure you verify that the firm you choose has all the requisite safeguards in place - regulation by The Securities and Futures Authority and membership of the London Stock Exchange are essential.

 If you're opening a nominee account, determine how readily you will have access to such shareholder rights as reports and meetings. In addition, consider how easily can you transfer investments into and out of your account. Some operators may try to 'lock' you into their account by imposing punitive exit charges.

 Are the hours your stockbroker operates convenient for you? Some brokers are only open weekdays during office hours, whilst others provide longer hours of contact, including weekends.

 Will your stockbroker quote you 'live' prices, or will your order be subject to delayed execution? Do you have the option to set price limits and, if so, will there be an extra charge?

CHAPTER 17

Conclusions

This book has attempted to provide a state-of-the-art review of stock market investment for the private investor. In keeping with this overall objective, the conclusions offered here fall into two parts; namely,

■ key lessons to be borne in mind; and

■ specialist readings on stock investment.

KEY LESSONS

Although this book has covered a lot of topics and it has offered many 'lessons to be learnt', we will draw out only broad conclusions here. It should now be apparent that there are no 'quick fixes' or '10 easy steps' to making your fortune from investing on the stock market. Instead, successful stock market investment needs dedication and rigour. In general, we would suggest you bear the following in mind:

! There are a number of approaches to stock market investment, all with different characteristics and time requirements. Be realistic about your time availability, your financial position and your attitude to risk.

! Try out different approaches to see which you feel comfortable with. You will, however, eventually need to adopt an approach and invest sufficient time to make it work. Remember, all of the gurus have been disciplined and patient in applying their particular approach.

! Although success demands discipline and rigour, this does not mean becoming hide-bound. Most of the modern gurus show a degree of flexibility.

! Flexibility comes from a general understanding of trends within the economy and the stock market. Therefore, while you should adopt a particular approach and possibly specialise in a couple of sectors, you should also have a good general knowledge of the social, technological, economic and political forces in operation.

! In other words, no stock investment system will ever replace the need for understanding. Share price movements are the outcome of a complex set of inter-relationships that evolve through time.

This book has been written to give you a good start in understanding what factors, forces and characteristics might be borne in mind when investing in shares. It would be arrogant in the extreme, however, to suggest that the current book is the 'be all and end all' of equity investment writing. There are a number of specialist books that could be usefully read next and it is to these that we now turn.

SPECIALIST INVESTMENT TEXTS

In writing this book we have used many specialist sources and this is not the place to offer a full review. Instead, we have decided to just mention the texts we have enjoyed the most and the ones we believe you will benefit from. Although we have not tried to identify key sources for each of the chapters we have written, the order below follows that of the book.

George G. Blakey, *The Post-War History of the London Stock Market.*[1] This is the definitive guide to the ups and downs of the UK stock market over the last 50 years. It is an enjoyable read and it is a good guide to what drives the movement of the stock market.

Geoffrey Holmes and Alan Sugden, *Interpreting Company Reports and Accounts.*[2] Although there are a number of books on the market concerned with the financial analysis of companies, this is the accepted 'bible' on the subject. Its one shortcoming is that it reads a bit like a manual but given the detail and clarity on offer, this is a price worth paying.

Peter L. Bernstein, *Against the Gods - The Remarkable Story of Risk.*[3] To invest in shares you need to understand what is meant by risk and this is a superb book which describes how notions of risk have changed across the ages. It is beautifully crafted and reads more like a novel about wonderful individuals than a serious work on the exploration of risk.

Peter L. Bernstein, *Capital Ideas - The Improbable Origins of Modern Wall Street.*[4] If you are interested in finding out more about the academic work on stock markets and investment behaviour, this is an exceptional survey of the key results of the past 30 years. While a few academics might moan that some of the treatment of path breaking articles is a bit cursory, you will not find a more accessible and easy to read review than this.

John Train, *The Money Masters* **and** *The New Money Masters.*[5] These are without doubt the best general reviews of investment gurus. Train clearly knows the subject of investment and he is well aquainted with a number of the gurus. He mixes detailed characterisation of the gurus with a rare insight into their various investment techniques. If you want to know more about general approaches to investment, you will be hard pressed to better these books.

Jack D. Schwager, *The New Market Wizards.*[6] If the idea of trading appeals to you as a means of investment, then this book reviews the masters of the game. Although it is

American in outlook (most investment books are), there are many insights to be gained by the UK investor. The book identifies what separates spectacular traders from ordinary players. It is also an entertaining read.

Hillary Davis, *A Million a Minute.*[7] This is also a book about the trading community but it considers the UK and it is slightly more up to date than Schwager. From a series of first hand interviews, she provides good descriptions of the way in which successful traders think and act.

James Morton, *Investing with the Grand Masters* **and Jonathan Davis,** *Money Makers.*[8] These two books have a very similar aim - to understand the techniques and approaches of the UK's top professional investors. While some of the ideas and approaches of fund managers are of interest, it has to be accepted that the lot of the private investor is very different from that of the professional; for a start, the private investor is rarely able to develop the breadth of portfolio of the professional investor, nor is he/she normally willing to bear the same level of risk. None the less, if you have the time, both books offer some insights that might be of use.

Robert G. Hagstrom, Jnr, *The Warren Buffett Way.*[9] While we have tried to describe the key elements of the Buffett approach to investment, space limitations have meant that we have been unable to paint as full a picture as we would have liked. If you want to read more on this master of investment, this is by far the best book available. It is full of detail and rich characterisation and it is an extremely easy read. One of the best single guru books we have read.

Jim Slater, *The Zulu Principle.*[10] It is difficult to be an interested UK investor and not come across the writings and thoughts of Jim Slater. If you feel the need to supplement the many articles on investment by Jim Slater, then this is the best place to start.

Gary Hamel and C.K. Prahalad, *Competing for the Future.*[11] Although these authors do not review the latest thinking on business strategy, their own particular angle on the subject is well worth considering. In general, their approach to strategy has had a profound effect on both academics and industrialists.

Peter Temple, *The Online Investor*.[12] Most of the above books have either reviewed issues of investment or the various approaches of gurus. Few have discussed the implications of advancing computer power and the 'World Wide Web - The Net' for the private investor. This book is superb in this respect. It identifies the information web sites and the on-line software that should be of interest to any private investor. If you intend to invest, then this would be a very worthwhile purchase. It is amazing how just a couple of hours spent searching the web-sites identified in this book will pay dividends. The private investor is now able to access, free of charge, share price data, company accounts/news, analysts' reports, etc. Overall, it is fair to say that recent advances in technology have the potential to massively improve the situation of the private investor; not least, private investors are now able to form virtual communities via the world wide web.

A FINAL THOUGHT

The above has suggested that the ability to belong to an investment community, so long the preserve of the professional investor, is now within the reach of the private investor. The advent of cheap personal computing and the world wide web is redressing the balance between private and professional investors. This is best illustrated by an excerpt from the book by Hillary Davis, *A Million a Minute* on stock market traders. While the excerpt is focused on the US, it suggests what should be available to the private investor in the UK in the near future.

"You're on the internet. Click Finance. Click Merrill Lynch, Dean Witter, Goldman Sachs. Then look at Inside Trading Reports, go to Associated Press Business Wire to check the latest news on companies you are interested in, click Quotes to see where individual stocks are currently trading, then click and read the morning's Financial Times.... Click and order reports from Wall Street's top analysts. Drop into the trading and investing forums to read what thoughts and rumours people are talking about in the market.... Then click on .... cyber-brokers. It provides price quotes, graphs, links to the news wires, analysts' reports and book keeping!"

Essentially, the private investor will no longer be an isolated individual reliant upon a few arm's length sources for share tips. Instead, you will be able to belong to 'virtual communities' with the information, skills and talents to rival that of the professional investor. More importantly, private investor communities will have the in-depth knowledge of individual companies (through participants' everyday working lives) and the motivation to potentially out-strip professional investors. If such communities come together then we will all be celebrating - 'many happy returns'!

REFERENCES

Chapter 1

1 The figures regarding long term investment in the equity and gilts markets used in this chapter have been taken from: *The BZW Equity-Gilt Study*, 42nd edition, BZW Securities Limited, January 1997.

2 Siegel, J. J. (1992), 'The Equity Premium: Stock and Bond Returns Since 1802', *Financial Analysts Journal*, 48, 1, January/February, pp. 28-38.

3 For the German market see Gielen, G. (1994), *Komen Aktienkurse noch Steigen?*, Gabler, Wiesbaden, Germany. For the Japanese market see Hirose, H. and Tso, Y. (1995), 'Japanese Market Returns', unpublished paper, Wharton School, 29th December.

4 Spanier, D. (1980), *The Gambler's Pocket Book*, Mitchell Beazley Publishers, London.

5 Mordin, N. (1992), *Betting For A Living*, Aesculus Press, Oswestry, pp. 77-78.

6 *Financial Times*, 12th November 1994.

7 Schwartz, D. (1995), *The Stock Market Handbook*, 2nd ed., Burleigh Publishing, Stroud, p. 1.

Chapter 2

1 For detail of the development of early capital markets see Neal L. (1990), *The Rise of Financial Capitalism*, Cambridge University Press, Cambridge.

2 Sobel, R. (1982), *Inside Wall Street: Continuity and Change in the Financial District*, Norton and Company, New York.

3 For a fuller analysis of the events and consequences of the 1929 crash, see Galbraith, J.K. (1973), *The Great Crash 1929*, Hamish Hamilton, London; and Thomas, G. and Morgan-Witts, M. (1979), *The Day the Bubble Burst: A Social History of the Wall Street Crash*, Hamish Hamilton, London.

4 The definitive history of the UK stock market from 1945 to 1993 is to be found in Blakey, G.G. (1994), *The Post-War History of the London Stock Market*, Management Books 2000 Ltd., Didcot, Oxon., which is the source for much of the material in this chapter.

5 Blakey, G.G. (1994), *The Post-War History of the London Stock Market*, Management Books 2000 Ltd., Didcot, Oxon., p. 55.

6 For more on how election results impact the market, see Hudson, R., Keasey, K. and Dempsey, M. (1998), 'Share Prices Under Tory and Labour Governments in the UK Since 1945', *Applied Financial Economics*, (forthcoming).

7 For an analysis of the 1987 crash, see Kindleberger, C.P. (1997), *Manias, Panics and Crashes*, John Wiley, New York; Toporowski, J. (1993), *The Economics of Financial Markets and the 1987 Crash*, Elgar, Aldershot; and Miller, M.H. (1991), *Financial Innovations and Market Volatility*, Blackwell, Cambridge, Mass.

Chapter 3

1 Keasey, K. and McGuinness, P. (1995), 'Underpricing in New Equity Listings: A Conceptual Re-Appraisal', *Small Business Economics*, 7, pp. 41-54.

2 Marsh, P. (1979), 'Equity Rights Issues and the Efficiency of the UK Stock Market', *Journal of Finance*, 34, September, pp. 39-62.

3 Miller, M.H. and Modigliani, F. (1961), 'Dividend Policy, Growth and the Valuation of Shares', *Journal of Business*, 34, 4, pp. 411-33.

4 Dimson, E. and Marsh, P. (1986), 'Event Study Methodologies and the Size Effect: the Case of UK Press Recommendations', *Journal of Financial Economics*, 17, 1, pp. 113-42. This is an early example of an ongoing research agenda into this subject by the authors.

5 Jarrell, G.A., Brickley, T.A. and Netter, J.M. (1988), 'The Market for Corporate Control: The Evidence Since 1980', *Journal of Economic Perspectives*, 2, 1, Winter, pp. 49-68.

6 Bradley, M., Desai, A. and Kim, E.H. (1988), 'Synergistic Gains from Corporate Acquisitions and their Division Between the Stockholders of Target and Acquiring Firms', *Journal of Financial Economics*, 17, pp. 3-40.

7 Franks, J.R., Broyles, J.E. and Hecht, M.J. (1997), 'An Industrial Study of the Profitability of Mergers in the UK', *Journal of Finance*, 32, pp. 1513-25.

8 Firth, M. (1979), 'The Profitability of Take-overs and Mergers', *Economic Journal*, 89, pp. 316-28.

9 Jensen, M.C. and Ruback, R. (1983), 'The Market for Corporate Control: The Scientific Evidence', *Journal of Financial Economics*, 11, April, pp. 5-50.

10 Franks, J.R., Harris, R. and Titman, S. (1991), 'The Postmerger Share Price Performance of Acquiring Firms', *Journal of Financial Economics*, 29, pp. 81-96.

11 Keasey, K. and Watson, R. (1991), 'Financial Distress Prediction Models: A Review of their Usefulness', *British Journal of Management*, 2, 2, pp. 89-102.

Chapter 4

1 Black, F. and Scholes, M. (1973), 'The Pricing of Options and Corporate Liabilities', *Journal of Political Economy*, 81, May-June, pp. 637-54.

Chapter 5

1 Moon, P. and Bates, K. (1993) 'CORE Analysis in Strategic Performance Appraisal', *Management Accounting Research*, 4, pp. 139-52.

Chapter 6

1 Kemp, K.W. (1984), *Dice, Data and Decisions*, Ellis Horwood, Chichester, p. 18.

2 Pearson, K. and Lord Rayleigh (1905), 'The Problem of the Random Walk', *Nature*, 72, pp. 294, 318, 342.

3 Bachelier, L. (1900), *Theory of Speculation*. Gauthier-Villars, Paris. Translated by Boness, A.J. (1964) in Cootner, P.A. (Ed.), *The Random Character of Stock Market Prices*, MIT Press, Cambridge, Mass.

4 See Bernstein, P.L. (1992), *Capital Ideas - The Improbable Origins of Modern Wall Street*, The Free Press, New York.

5 Kendall, M. (1953), 'The Analysis of Time Series, Part I: Prices', *Journal of the Royal Statistical Society Series A*, 96, pp. 11-25.

6 Samuelson, P.A. (1965), 'A Proof That Properly Anticipated Prices Fluctuate Randomly', *Industrial Management Review*, 6, Spring, pp. 41-50.

7 See, for example, Fama, E.F. and French, K.R. (1988), 'Dividend Yields and Expected Stock Returns', *Journal of Financial Economics*, 22, October, pp. 3-26; Campbell, J.Y. and Shiller, R.J. (1988), 'Stock Prices, Earnings, and Expected Dividends', *The Journal of Finance*, 43, 3, July, pp. 661-76; Reichenstein, W. and Rich, S.P. (1993), 'The Market Risk Premium and Long-Term Stock Returns', *The Journal of Portfolio Management*, 19, 4, Summer, pp. 63-72.

8 For studies regarding large stocks see Fama, E.F. and French, K.R. (1988), 'Dividend Yields and Expected Stock Returns', *Journal of Financial Economics*, 22, 1, October, pp. 3-26. For studies on small stocks, see Fama, E.F. and French, K.R. (1989), 'Business Conditions and Expected Returns on Stock and Bonds', *Journal of Financial Economics*, 25, 1, November, pp. 23-50.

9 McQueen, G. and Thorley, S. (1991), 'Are Stock Returns Predictable? A Test Using Markov Chains', *The Journal of Finance*, 46, 1, March, pp. 239-63.

10 Hudson, R., Dempsey, M. and Keasey, K. (1996), 'A Note on the Weak Form Efficiency of Capital Markets: The Application of Simple Technical Trading Rules to U.K. Stock Prices - 1935 to 1994', *Journal of Banking and Finance*, 20, pp. 1121-32.

11 Reichenstein W. and Dorsett, D. (1995), *Time Diversification Revisited*, The Research Foundation of the Institute of Chartered Financial Analysts, Charlottesville, Virginia, p. 15.

12 Summers showed that even in a mean reverting market which was, on average, irrationally 30% higher or lower than its true fundamental value, it would be unlikely that tests based on autocorrelation would reject the random walk. See Summers, L.H. (1990), 'Predicting Expected Returns', *Quantifying the Market Risk Premium Phenomenon for Investment Decision Making*. Institute of Chartered Financial Analysts, Charlottesville, Virginia.

13 *The BZW Equity-Gilt Study*, 42nd edition, BZW Securities Limited, January 1997.

14 Two American academics, William Reichenstein and Dovalee Dorsett, have produced similar figures for the US market assuming both a random walk model and a mean reversion model. The results of the two models are fairly similar so we felt there was no need to burden the reader with two sets of figures. For the US figures see Reichenstein W. and Dorsett D. (1995), *Time Diversification Revisited*, The Research Foundation of the Institute of Chartered Financial Analysts, Charlottesville, Virginia.

Chapter 7

1 A very well known book covering some of these episodes is Mackay, C. (1841), *Extraordinary Popular Delusions and the Madness of Crowds*, latest edition 1998, John Wiley, Chichester.

2 Graham, B. and Dodd, D.L. (1934), *Security Analysis*, latest ed 1996, McGraw-Hill, New York, pp. 22-3.

3 Keynes, J.M. (1936), *The General Theory of Employment, Interest and Money*. Macmillan, London, pp. 155-6.

4 This solution was developed by Grossman, S.J. and Stiglitz, J. (1976), 'Information and Competitive Price Systems', *American Economic Review*, May, pp. 246-53.

5 The distinction was first made by Fama, E.F. (1970), 'Efficient Capital Markets: A Review of Theory and Empirical Work', *Journal of Finance*, 25, 2, May, pp. 383-417.

6 Brock, W., Lakonishok, J. and Lebaron, B. (1992), 'Simple Technical Trading Rules and the Stochastic Properties of Stock Returns', *The Journal of Finance*, 47, 5, pp. 1731-64.

7 Hudson, R., Dempsey, M. and Keasey, K. (1996), 'A Note on the Weak Form Efficiency of Capital Markets: The Application of Simple Technical Trading Rules to U.K. Stock Prices - 1935 to 1994', *Journal of Banking and Finance*, 20, pp. 1121-32.

8 DeBondt, W.F.M. and Thaler, R. (1985), 'Does the Stock Market Overreact?' *The Journal of Finance*, 40, 3, July, pp. 793-805; and (1987) 'Further Evidence on Investor Overreaction and Stock Market Seasonality', *The Journal of Finance*, 42, 3, July, pp. 557-81. Paul Zarowin argued that DeBondt and Thaler's findings were caused by the January effect and the Size Effect (which are discussed later in the chapter). See Zarowin, P. (1989), 'Does the Stock Market Overreact to Corporate Earnings Information?', *The Journal of Finance*, 44, 5, December, pp. 1385-99.

9 Foster, G., Olsen, C. and Shevlin, T. (1984), 'Earning Releases, Anomalies, and the Behaviour of Security Returns', *The Accounting Review*, 59, October, pp. 574-603.

10 For stock splits see Bar-Yosef, S. and Brown, L.D. (1977), 'A Re-examination of Stock Splits Using Moving Betas', *The Journal of Finance*, 32, September, pp. 1069-80. For accounting changes see Ball, R. (1972), 'Changes in Accounting Techniques and Stock Prices', *Journal of Accounting Research*, Supplement, 10, pp. 1-38; and Kaplan, R.S. and Roll, R. (1972), 'Investor Evaluation of Accounting Information: Some Empirical Evidence', *Journal of Business*, 45, April, pp. 225-57.

11 See Thaler, R. (1987), 'Seasonal Movements in Security Prices I: The January Effect', *Journal of Economic Perspectives*, 1, 1, pp. 197-201; and (1987), 'Seasonal Movements in Security Prices II: Weekend, Holiday, Turn of the Month, and Intraday Effects', *Journal of Economic Perspectives*, 1, 2, pp. 169-177.

12 Fama, E.F. and French, K.R. (1992), 'The Cross-Section of Expected Stock Returns', *Journal of Finance*, 47, 2, June, pp. 427-65.

13 Haugen, R. (1995), *The New Finance: The Case Against Efficient Markets*, Prentice Hall, Englewood Cliffs, N.J.

14 *Investors Chronicle*, 18th March 1994, pp. 12-13.

15 Seyhun, H.N. (1986), 'Insiders Profits, Costs of Trading and Market Efficiency', *Journal of Financial Economics*, 16, 2, June, pp. 189-212.

16 Jensen, M.C. (1968), 'The Performance of Mutual Funds in the Period 1945-1964', *The Journal of Finance*, 23, May, pp. 389-416.

17 Data from *Money Management*, April 1998. The performance figures have been adjusted so that the fact that the index has no management expenses does not distort the comparison.

18 For an account of this, see Lowenstein, R. (1996), *Buffett: The Making of an American Capitalist*, Orion, London, chapter 17.

19 Berkshire Hathaway Inc., *1988 Annual Report*, p. 18.

20 Markowitz, H.M. (1952), 'Portfolio Selection', *The Journal of Finance*, 7, 1, March, pp. 77-91.

21 Sharpe, W.F. (1963), 'A Simplified Model for Portfolio Analysis', *Management Science*, 9, January, pp. 277-93.

22 Evans, J.L. and Archer, S.H. (1968), 'Diversification and the Reduction of Dispersion: An Empirical Analysis', *The Journal of Finance*, 23, December, pp. 761-7.

23 Black, F. and Scholes, M. (1973), 'The Pricing of Options and Corporate Liabilities', *Journal of Political Economy*, 81, May-June, pp. 637-54.

Chapter 8

1 For more on trading operations in markets, see Davis, H. (1997), *A Million a Minute*, Nicholas Brealey Publishing, London.

2 Davis, H. (1997), *A Million a Minute*, Nicholas Brealey Publishing, London, pp. 179ff.

3 For the inside track on the collapse, see Leeson, N. (1996), *Rogue Trader: How I Brought Down Barings Bank and Shook the Financial World*, Little Brown, Boston; see also Rawnsley, J. (1995), *Going for Broke*, HarperCollins, New York.

4 *Financial Times*, 17th October 1997.

5 For details see *Investors Chronicle*, 9th August 1996, p. 19.

6 Schwartz, D. (1996), 'Head and Shoulders Above the Rest', *The Investors Chronicle*, 21st June, p. 21.

7 Schwartz, D. (1996), 'Separating the Trend from the Noise', *The Investors Chronicle*, 23rd February, p. 21.

8 See, for example, Schwartz, D. (1996), 'The Weakness of Relative Strength', *The Investors Chronicle*, 20th September, p. 21; and also *Investors Chronicle*, 29th November 1996, p. 23.

9 Schwartz, D. (1996), 'Drawing a Line Through Uncharted Waters', *The Investors Chronicle*, 17th May, p. 21.

Chapter 9

1 Hudson, R., Keasey, K. and Dempsey, M. (1998), 'Share Prices Under Tory and Labour Governments in the UK Since 1945', *Applied Financial Economics*, (forthcoming).

Chapter 10

1 See Graham, B. and Dodd, D. (1987), *Security Analysis*, 5th revised ed., McGraw-Hill, New York.

2 For details of the method see Train, J. (1994), *The Money Masters*, HarperCollins, New York, pp. 139-57.

3 O'Shaughnessy, J.P. (1996), *What Works on Wall Street*, McGraw-Hill, New York.

4 Ansoff, H.I. (1965), *Corporate Strategy*, McGraw-Hill, New York.

5 Porter, M.E. (1980), *Competitive Strategy: Techniques for Analysing Industries and Competitors*, Free Press, New York.

6 Porter M.E. (1985), *Competitive Advantage Creating and Sustaining Superior Performance*, Free Press, New York.

7 See Hamel, G. and Prahalad, C.K. (1994), *Competing for the Future*, Harvard Business School Press, Boston, MA.; Hamel, G. and Prahalad C.K. (1989),'Strategic Intent', *Harvard Business Review*, 67, 3, pp. 63-76; and Prahalad, C.K. and Hamel, G. (1990), 'The Core Competence of the Corporation', *Harvard Business Review*, 68, 3, May-June, pp. 79-91.

8 Kaplan, R.S. and Norton, D.P. (1996), *The Balanced Scorecard*, Harvard Business School Press, Boston, MA.; Kaplan, R.S. and Norton, D.P. (1992), 'The Balanced Scorecard - Measures that Drive Performance', *Harvard Business Review*, 70, 1, January-February, pp. 71-9; Kaplan, R.S. and Norton, D.P. (1996), 'Using the Balanced Scorecard as a Strategic Management System', *Harvard Business Review*, January-February, 74, pp. 75-85.

Chapter 11

1 Details of Bolton's approach can be found in Davis, J. (1998), *Money Makers*, Orion Business Books, London, pp. 10ff; and Morton, J. (1997), *Investing with the Grand Masters*, Pitman Publishing, London, pp. 43ff.
2 Davis, J. (1998), *Money Makers*, Orion Business Books, London, p. 34.
3 Davis, J. (1998), *Money Makers*, Orion Business Books, London, p. 150.
4 For details see Schwager, J.D. (1994), *The New Market Wizards*, HarperCollins, New York, pp. 177ff; latest edition (1997), John Wiley, New York.
5 For more information on Linda Bradford Raschke, see Schwager, J.D. (1994), *The New Market Wizards*, HarperCollins, New York, pp. 294ff; latest edition (1997), John Wiley, New York.
6 Schwager, J.D. (1994), *The New Market Wizards*, HarperCollins, New York, p. 300; latest edition (1997), John Wiley, New York.
7 For more on Eckhardt, see Schwager, J.D. (1994), *The New Market Wizards*, HarperCollins, New York pp. 103ff; latest edition (1997), John Wiley, New York.
8 Davis, H. (1997), *A Million a Minute*, Nicholas Brealey Publishing, London, p. 221.
9 For an interesting review of Shaw's approach, see Davis, H. (1997), *A Million a Minute*, Nicholas Brealey Publishing, London, pp. 215ff.
10 For more on Internet trading, read Temple, P. (1997), *The Online Investor*, John Wiley, Chichester; Davis, H. (1997), *A Million a Minute*, Nicholas Brealey Publishing, London, pp. 244ff; and Brown, D.L. and Bentley, K. (1995), *Cyber Investing*, John Wiley, New York.

Chapter 12

1 For more information about Templeton, see Train, J. (1994), *The Money Masters*, HarperCollins, New York, chapter 7.
2 For more information on Taube, see Morton, J. (1997), *Investing with the Grand Masters*, Pitman Publishing, London, chapter 13; and Davis, J. (1998), *Money Makers*, Orion Business Books, London, chapter 4.
3 For more information about Soros, see Train, J. (1994), *The New Money Masters*, HarperCollins, New York, chapter 4. Soros has also written two books: Soros, G. (1994), *The Alchemy of Finance: Reading the Mind of the Market*, John Wiley, New York; and Soros, G. with Wien, B. and Koenan, K. (1995), *Soros on Soros: Staying Ahead of the Curve*, John Wiley, New York.
4 For more information on Rogers, see Train, J. (1994), *The New Money Masters*, HarperCollins, New York, chapter 1. Rogers has also written a book on investment: Rogers, J. (1995), *Investment Biker : Around the World with Jim Rogers*, John Wiley, Chichester.
5 For more information about Wilson, see Train, J. (1994), *The Money Masters*, HarperCollins, New York, chapter 9.
6 For more information on Wanger, see Train, J. (1994), *The New Money Masters*, HarperCollins, New York, chapter 8.
7 Slater's thoughts on market timing are explained in detail in Slater, J. (1992), *The Zulu Principle*, Orion, London, chapter 18.

Chapter 13

1 See Graham, B. and Dodd, D. (1987), *Security Analysis*, 5th revised ed., McGraw-Hill, New York; and Graham, B. (1997), *The Intelligent Investor*, 3rd revised ed., latest edition, HarperCollins, New York.

2 Profile of Jayesh Manek, *Investors Chronicle*, 21st November, 1997, pp. 16-17.

3 Goldsmith, W. and Clutterbuck, D. (1997), *The Winning Streak: A Study of Top Performing Firms*, Orion Business Books, London.

4 For more detail see, Lynch, P. with Rothchild, J. (1989), *One Up on Wall Street*, Simon and Schuster, New York; and Lynch, P. with Rothchild, J. (1993), *Beating the Street*, Simon and Schuster, New York.

Chapter 14

1 The basic templates for Figures 14.1 and 14.2 are sourced from Tondeur, K. (1996), *Your Money and Your Life*, Triangle Books, London.

2 In Figure 14.1, your expenditure is split between your methods of payments. Spending by direct debit or standing order, is recorded first. Some payments may be made monthly, some quarterly and some annually. Your irregular spending for each month can be budgeted on the basis of the month in which the expenditure falls and the method used to make the payment. Spending by cash, cheque, giro, debit card or electronic cash, occurs in the month of the purchase. For payment by credit card or store card, the cost is added to your outstanding debt (e.g. to balance 'A'). The debt is reduced in the month by your chosen level of credit card payment (e.g. by payment 'O').

3 For a simple approach to planning your finances for equity investing, see Cohen, B. (1997), *The Armchair Investor*, Orion Business Books, London, pp. 9-15.

4 See *Investors Chronicle*, 6th February 1998.

Chapter 15

1 See, for example, *Money Management*, April 1998, p. 124.

2 Train, J. (1994), *The New Money Masters*, HarperCollins, New York, p. 210.

3 If there are more than 20 members the club has to form a limited company.

Chapter 17

1 Blakey, G.G. (1994), *The Post-War History of the London Stock Market*, Management Books 2000 Ltd., Didcot, Oxon.

2 Holmes, G. and Sugden, A. (1997), *Interpreting Company Reports and Accounts*, 6th revised ed., Prentice-Hall, London.

3 Bernstein, P. L. (1996), *Against the Gods - The Remarkable Story of Risk*, John Wiley, New York.

4 Bernstein, P. L. (1992), *Capital Ideas - The Improbable Origins of Modern Wall Street*, The Free Press, New York.

5 Train, J. (1994), *The Money Masters*, HarperCollins, New York; and Train, J. (1994), *The New Money Masters*, HarperCollins, New York.

6 Schwager, J.D. (1997), *The New Market Wizards*, John Wiley, New York.

7 Davis, H. (1997), *A Million a Minute*, Nicholas Brealey Publishing, London.

8 Morton, J. (1997), *Investing with the Grand Masters*, Pitman Publishing, London; and Davis, J. (1998), *Money Makers*, Orion Business Books, London.

9 Hagstrom, R.G., Jnr (1995), *The Warren Buffett Way*, John Wiley, New York.

10 Slater, J. (1992), *The Zulu Principle*, Orion, London; see also Slater, J. (1996), *Beyond the Zulu Principle*, Orion, London.

11 Hamel, G. and Prahalad, C.K. (1994), *Competing for the Future*, Harvard Business School Press, Boston, MA.

12 Temple, P. (1997), *The Online Investor*, John Wiley, Chichester.

GLOSSARY

ACT: Advance Corporation Tax paid by companies on shareholders' dividends.

AGM: a company's Annual General Meeting held once a year to approve the report and accounts and the final dividend, and vote on any proposed motions (such as the re-election of directors).

AIM: the Alternative Investment Market. Launched by the Stock Exchange in 1995 as a market for smaller companies. AIM sets lower standards of entry than the Stock Exchange Official List (main market). Shares traded on AIM pose higher risks than fully listed ones but may offer investors certain tax advantages.

Aftermarket: a collective term for both exchange and over-the-counter markets, in which stocks are bought and sold after they are first issued. Also known as the secondary market.

Bargain: the stock market term for a share sale or purchase.

Bulldog: a UK domestic security - especially a bond - which is owned by an overseas investor.

Bullet: a bond with a single redemption date. It goes straight from issue to maturity with no possibility of either the issuer or investor redeeming it early.

Capital gain: the profit you make between the buying and selling price of shares.

Capital growth: the rise in the value of your initial investment.

Charting: capturing the patterns of the overall market or an individual share price on a line, bar or other type of graph.

Chinese walls: regulations which are supposed to prevent conflicts of interest arising in integrated securities firms.

Commission: the fee charged by a stockbroker for carrying out a customer's instruction to buy or sell shares.

Consideration: the money value of a transaction (number of shares multiplied by the price) before adding or deducting commission, stamp duty, etc.

Cum: Latin for 'with'. Used to denote rights and entitlements that come with a share at the time it is bought. For example, 'cum dividend' or 'cum rights'. The opposite of 'ex'.

Discount: when the market price of a newly issued share is lower than its issue price. The opposite of 'premium'.

EGM: Extraordinary General Meeting. Any meeting of a company's shareholders other than its AGM.

Ex: the opposite of 'cum'. Used to indicate that the buyer is not entitled to participate in whatever forthcoming event is specified. For example, 'ex dividend' or 'ex rights'.

Final dividend: the dividend paid by a company at the end of the financial year.

Flotation: when a company's shares are sold to investors and quoted on the stock market for the very first time.

Gross: before tax has been deducted. The opposite of 'net'.

Hedging: protecting against or limiting losses on an existing shareholding or portfolio by establishing an opposite position in the same or equivalent stock(s).

Insider dealing: the purchase or sale of shares by someone who possesses 'inside' information about the company. This is information on the company's performance or prospects which has not yet been made available to the market as a whole, and which, if available, might affect the share price. In the UK, such deals are a criminal offence.

Interim dividend: a dividend declared part way through a company's financial year, authorised solely by the directors.

Liquid: used to describe a market where there are many buyers and sellers, and consequently it is easy to deal. Investors who hold cash are said to 'be liquid' and those who have sold their holdings have 'gone liquid'.

Margin trading: when an investor buys (or sells short) shares by depositing part of their market value and borrowing the balance from a stockbroker. Although common in the US, not widely available in the UK.

Market size: the number of shares in which a market maker is prepared to deal, either as a buyer or seller, at the current, displayed prices.

Merger: the joining of two companies, under either friendly or hostile terms.

Net: after tax has been deducted. The opposite of 'gross'.

Nominal value: the value ascribed to a share when it is first authorised and issued by a company. It bears no relationship to a share's market value. Also known as 'par value'.

Partly paid: shares may be issued partly-paid, meaning that the full value of the investment will be paid in several instalments, only the first of which is required at issue. Such issues are therefore 'geared'.

Penny shares: traditionally any shares trading at a low price - typically less than 20 pence. The term is now defined by the regulators as the shares of any company valued at less than £100 million and trading on a bid/offer spread of 10% or more. Penny shares are considered more speculative investments.

Preliminary figures: a company's full-year results, declared as a prelude to the publication of the annual report and accounts.

Premium: if the market price of a new share is higher than its issue price. The opposite of discount.

Primary market: in which a company first offers to sell shares to investors, with the proceeds from the sale going to the organisation.

Prospective: relating to the next set of results. Prospective earnings are those expected for the year in which a company is currently trading. A prospective PE ratio may be more meaningful than an historic one where the market is expecting a significant growth or fall in earnings.

Proxy: a form by which a shareholder votes in absentia. Proxies can also be used to transfer voting authority to another party.

Quote: if a company has a quote (or 'is quoted'), its shares can be bought and sold on the stock market.

Record date: the deadline, determined by a company's board of directors, by when an investor must be recorded as an owner of shares in order to qualify for a forthcoming dividend or share distribution.

Registrar: an organisation or an individual that takes responsibility for maintaining a company's share register.

RIE: Recognised Investment Exchange. An exchange which meets the legal requirements for recognition, e.g. the London Stock Exchange and Tradepoint.

SEAQ: Stock Exchange Automated Quotations - the quote-driven, screen-based system through which market makers display their prices for buying and selling shares.

Samurai: a domestic Japanese security held by a non-resident.

Scrip issue: the free issue of new shares to existing holders in proportion to their existing holdings. Used typically to bring down a weighty share price and make the shares more tradeable. Also referred to as a 'bonus issue' or a 'capitalisation issue'.

Settlement: once a deal has been made, the settlement process transfers stock from seller to buyer and arranges the corresponding movement of money between buyer and seller.

Shell: A moribund company whose main value resides in its listing on a stock exchange. Commonly taken over by entrepreneurs who inject their own business interests into the company and use the stockmarket quote to raise equity finance via a series of rights issues or takeover bids. Previous examples include WPP and Pizza Express.

Stag: an investor who applies for a new issue in the hope of being able to sell the shares at a profit as soon as dealing starts.

Stock Exchange Official List: the main market. Companies on the Official List have been vetted by the Stock Exchange Quotations Department and are subject to all the listing rules in the Stock Exchange Yellow Book.

Stop loss: a limit placed by an investor on the amount he or she is prepared to lose on an investment.

Thin market: arises when there are few buyers or sellers for a security. Typically gives rise to increased price volatility. Also called an illiquid market.

Touch: the closest bid/offer spread available between competing market makers in a particular share. If one market maker is quoting 55 to 60 pence while another is quoting 57 to 62 pence, the touch is 57 to 60 pence.

Transfer: the form signed by the seller of a share authorising the company to remove his/her name from the register and substitute that of the buyer.

Underwriter: an institutional investor who effectively insures a new issue (or rights issue) by agreeing to buy all shares which are not sold to other investors.

Volatility: the relative amount or percentage by which a share's price rises and falls during a period of time.

Volume: the total number of shares traded (bought and sold) in a given period of time.

White knight: a company or an individual which rescues another company which is in financial difficulty, especially one which saves a company from an unwelcome take-over bid.

Yankee: an American domestic security held by a non-US resident.

INDEX